GENDER IN

Series editors:
Lynn Abrams, Cordelia Beattie, Pam Sharpe and Penny Summerfield

The expansion of research into the history of women and gender since the 1970s has changed the face of history. Using the insights of feminist theory and of historians of women, gender historians have explored the configuration in the past of gender identities and relations between the sexes. They have also investigated the history of sexuality and family relations, and analysed ideas and ideals of masculinity and femininity. Yet gender history has not abandoned the original, inspirational project of women's history: to recover and reveal the lived experience of women in the past and the present.

The series Gender in History provides a forum for these developments. Its historical coverage extends from the medieval to the modern periods, and its geographical scope encompasses not only Europe and North America but all corners of the globe. The series aims to investigate the social and cultural constructions of gender in historical sources, as well as the gendering of historical discourse itself. It embraces both detailed case studies of specific regions or periods, and broader treatments of major themes. Gender in History titles are designed to meet the needs of both scholars and students working in this dynamic area of historical research.

Queen and country

MANCHESTER 1824
Manchester University Press

ALSO AVAILABLE
IN THE SERIES

Myth and materiality in a woman's world: Shetland 1800–2000 Lynn Abrams

Destined for a life of service: Defining African-Jamaican womanhood, 1865-1938 Henrice Altink

Gender and housing in Soviet Russia: private life in a public space Lynne Attwood

Love, intimacy and power: marital relationships in Scotland, 1650–1850 Katie Barclay

History, patriarchy and the challenge of feminism (with University of Pennsylvania Press)
Judith Bennett

Modern women on trial: sexual transgression in the age of the flapper Lucy Bland

Gender and medical knowledge in early modern history Susan Broomhall

'The truest form of patriotism': pacifist feminism in Britain, 1870–1902 Heloise Brown

Artisans of the body in early modern Italy: identities, families and masculinities Sandra Cavallo

Women of the right spirit: paid organisers of the Women's Social and Political Union (WSPU) 1904–18 Krista Cowman

Modern motherhood: women and family in England, c. 1945-2000 Angela Davis

Masculinities in politics and war: gendering modern history
Stefan Dudink, Karen Hagemann and John Tosh (eds)

Victorians and the Virgin Mary: religion and gender in England 1830–1885
Carol Engelhardt Herringer

Living in sin: cohabiting as husband and wife in nineteenth-century England Ginger S. Frost

Jewish women in Europe in the Middle Ages: a quiet revolution Simha Goldin

Murder and morality in Victorian Britain: the story of Madeleine Smith
Eleanor Gordon and Gwyneth Nair

The military leadership of Matilda of Canossa, 1046–1115 David J. Hay

The shadow of marriage: singleness in England, 1914–60 Katherine Holden

Women police: gender, welfare and surveillance in the twentieth century Louise Jackson

Noblewomen, aristocracy and power in the twelfth-century Anglo-Norman realm Susan Johns

The business of everyday life: gender, practice and social politics in England, c.1600–1900
Beverly Lemire

Women and the shaping of British Methodism: persistent preachers, 1807–1907 Jennifer Lloyd

The independent man: citizenship and gender politics in Georgian England Matthew McCormack

Women, travel and identity: journeys by rail and sea, 1870-1940 Emma Robinson-Tomsett

Infidel feminism: secularism, religion and women's emancipation, England 1830-1914 Laura Schwartz

The feminine public sphere: middle-class women and civic life in Scotland, c.1870–1914 Megan Smitley

Being boys: working-class masculinities and leisure Melanie Tebbutt

Elizabeth Wolstenholme Elmy and the Victorian feminist movement: the biography of an insurgent woman Maureen Wright

QUEEN AND COUNTRY
SAME-SEX DESIRE IN THE BRITISH ARMED FORCES, 1939–45

Emma Vickers

Manchester University Press

Copyright © Emma Vickers 2013

The right of Emma Vickers to be identified as the author of this work has been asserted by her in accordance with the Copyright, Designs and Patents Act 1988.

Published by Manchester University Press
Altrincham Street, Manchester M1 7JA, UK
www.manchesteruniversitypress.co.uk

British Library Cataloguing-in-Publication Data is available

Library of Congress Cataloging-in-Publication Data is available

ISBN 978 1 7849 9118 0 paperback

First published by Manchester University Press in hardback 2013

This paperback edition first published 2015

The publisher has no responsibility for the persistence or accuracy of URLs for any external or third-party internet websites referred to in this book, and does not guarantee that any content on such websites is, or will remain, accurate or appropriate.

Printed by Lightning Source

For Corinna, Steve, Sarah, Fran, Kellie and my students at Lancaster and Reading.

Contents

LIST OF FIGURES	*page* ix
LIST OF TABLES	x
FOREWORD	xi
ACKNOWLEDGEMENTS	xiii
ABBREVIATIONS	xv

	Introduction	1
1	Inclusion	24
2	Keeping up appearances	50
3	Playing away	75
4	Make do and mend: military law and same-sex desire	104
	Conclusion	151
	Epilogue	162

BIOGRAPHIES OF INTERVIEWEES	165
BIBLIOGRAPHY	167
INDEX	195

List of figures

1. 'Some seafaring gentlemen may be particular'. Caption: 'Good looks are to be taken into consideration in the choosing of recruits for the American Navy. Our cartoonist thinks that "Sailors don't care" will be an out-of-date saying before long.' © The British Library Board. All Rights Reserved.   31
2. 'Our beautiful women athletes'. Caption: 'We are told that women athletes are now of the graceful feminine type. / We presume the manly ones keep to drawing rooms.' © Mirrorpix, Solo Syndication.   32
3. Radclyffe Hall and Una Troubridge, 1927. © Fox Photos/Hulton Archive/Getty Images.   35
4. Ronald Niebour's satirical take on medical testing. Caption: 'That will be about all – now goodbye and good luck to you.' © Mirrorpix, Solo Syndication.   38
5. Sailors of HMS *Duke of York* relax in a canvas bath, date unknown. © Imperial War Museum.   54
6. Hula-Hula 'girls' rehearsing their Christmas act on board a destroyer depot ship, Scapa Flow, 18 December 1942. © Imperial War Museum.   96

List of tables

1	Comprehensive summary of court-martial convictions (British other ranks, home and overseas), 1 September 1939 – 31 August 1945.	109
2	Breakdowns of court-martial cases and convictions for indecent behaviour in the Army, RAF and Royal Navy, 1 September 1939 – 30 August 1945.	110
3	Queer offences registered in the Judge Advocate General's charge books for the Army, 1939–45.	114
4	Homosexual offences known to the police and proceedings taken in England and Wales, 1939–1945.	116

Foreword

From the early 1980s, at the time of the annual Remembrance Day and VE Day ceremonies, I organised the laying of pink triangle wreaths at the Cenotaph in London to commemorate the LGBT victims of Nazism and LGBT service personnel who died fighting fascism. Within hours, these wreaths would disappear, removed by the police or the British Legion who claimed they were offensive and insulting to the war dead. In 1985, on the fortieth anniversary of VE Day, a wreath was once again laid at the base of the Cenotaph. This time, it was not removed. We had won the first of many battles to secure the recognition that LGBT military personnel sought and deserved.

During the 1990s, the LGBT direct action group OutRage! built on this success and organised a series of Queer Remembrance Day ceremonies immediately following the official commemorations. These included a formation of pink flag bearers, muffled drums, and a large pink triangle "Never Forget" sign and wreath. To our surprise, not only did the police allow our annual processions to the Cenotaph but we also received warm applause from the public.

One of our most honoured supporters and participants was Dudley Cave, a gay army veteran who had served in the Far East during the Second World War. He was captured by the Japanese and survived working on the Burma-Thailand "Death Railway".

Cave became an outspoken critic of the Ministry of Defence. His message to the MoD was simple: acknowledge that queer men and women risked their lives between 1939 and 1945 to protect a country that officially did not allow them to serve and that criminalised their right to love. He strongly supported the OutRage! campaign to end the ban on LGBT people serving in the military.

Statistically speaking, it is very likely that up to 500,000 LGBT people served in the UK armed forces during the Second World War; yet they returned to a country to face widespread prejudice, ostracism, blackmail, discrimination and the risk of arrest and imprisonment.

Eventually, in 1999, the European Court of Human Rights declared the military gay ban unlawful discrimination, which required the UK government to amend the regulations to permit LGB people to serve.

Since then, the armed forces has expanded and redefined its stance on sexual and gender diversity. The Ministry of Defence has yet to apologise for its mistreatment of LGBT personnel before 1999 but it is now held to account by a code of conduct and actively defends the right of its LGBT members to serve openly.

This has been publicly affirmed by Hannah Winterbourne and Alya Holdom, two trans* members of the Army and the RAF respectively. They represent one of the biggest challenges now faced by the military; namely the integration and acceptance of individuals who identify as trans*. In this sense, and in spite of huge progress, the battle is not yet fully won. We cannot be complacent and must ensure that the Ministry of Defence affirms and supports all minority and vulnerable personnel.

Queen and country is a fascinating, commendable book. It reminds us of the pre-history of the battle for LGBT rights and acceptance within the armed forces. As well as giving a voice to the lives and experiences of LGBT personnel in the Second World War, it documents official disapproval and the often outrageous attempts to suppress same-sex desire among members of the armed services. Lest we forget.

Peter Tatchell

Acknowledgements

Together, Lancaster University and the ESRC funded this research. I am exceptionally grateful for their support. Age Concern and Anchor Homes deserve my thanks too, particularly Linda Shepherd and Brenda McPherson who went above and beyond in publicising my work within their respective organisations. My thanks also go to Dagmar Herzog for offering me the chance to publish for the first time and for patiently and enthusiastically overseeing the re-drafting process, and to Sarah Waters for discussing the sources that she used for *The Nightwatch* and more importantly, responding with kindness and enthusiasm. Lastly, I owe a great deal to Nick Patrick and the team at *Making History* who set the ball rolling in the best possible direction.

Queen and Country is richer because of the willingness of my colleagues to engage in dialogues with me on subjects as diverse as Radclyffe Hall, sexual geographies and military law. In this respect, I owe a great deal in particular to Matt Houlbrook, who has been consistently sympathetic and encouraging. However, if there is one person who has helped, cajoled, encouraged and taken the piss more than any other it is Felix Schulz. He never wavered and always listened, a crucial skill at three o'clock in the morning when the novelty of contributing to the sum of human knowledge has worn thin.

My friends and family also deserve credit for living with my obsession, allowing me to live on their floors during my frequent trips to London and for understanding the peaks and troughs of academic life. Laura has fulfilled her role as best friend admirably, even in the face of persistent moaning, tiredness and personal crises. Liana has also been wonderful, not least for hosting my numerous visits to London with good grace and genuine enthusiasm and for prising out my sociability after long and dusty days at The National Archives. I also owe a great deal to Fran and to Sarah, who, at various stages of this book, have kept me sane with their love and encouragement.

There are two people who deserve more credit than anyone for *Queen and Country* and they are Stephen Constantine and Corinna Peniston-Bird. I am grateful to them for their training, their enthusiasm and their care. This book is for them, and for my magnificent respondents who welcomed me into their homes and shared their stories with me. Your voices are finally being heard.

Chapter three includes sections of a paper from *Feminist Review* (2010), reproduced with the permission of Palgrave Macmillan. Similarly,

ACKNOWLEDGEMENTS

I have used sections from an article in the *Journal of Lesbian Studies* (2009), reproduced here with the permission of Taylor and Francis. I would like to thank the trustees of the Imperial War Museum for allowing access to the collections, and to each of the copyright holders. While every effort has been made to trace all the copyright holders, the author and the Imperial War Museum would be grateful for any information that might help to trace the families of L. Goossens, W. A. Hill, R. H. Lloyd-Jones, E. McNelie and J. Wallace.

August 2012

Abbreviations

ADM	Admiralty
AIR	Air Ministry
AMP	Air Member for Personal
ATS	Auxiliary Territorial Service
BBC	British Broadcasting Corporation
BBC PWA	British Broadcasting Corporation People's War Archive
BLSA	British Library Sound Archive
BOSA	Brighton Our Story Archive
CAB	Cabinet
CRIM	Records of the Central Criminal Court
DEFE	Records of the Ministry of Defence
DPP	Director of Public Prosecutions
DPR	Director of Public Relations
DPS	Director of Prosecution Services
EMS	Emergency Medical Service
ENSA	Entertainments National Service Association
GCHQ	Government Communications Headquarters
HMSO	His/Her Majesty's Stationary Office
HO	Home Office
IWM DD	Imperial War Museum Department of Documents
IWM DP	Imperial War Museum Department of Photographs
IWM SA	Imperial War Museum Sound Archive
JAG	Judge Advocate General
LAB	Ministry of Labour
LGBT	Lesbian/Gay/Bisexual/Transgender
LMA	London Metropolitan Archives
MEPO	Metropolitan Police
MH	Ministry of Health
MO	Mass Observation
MOD	Ministry of Defence
PMC	Public Morality Council
POW	Prisoner of War
PS	London Metropolitan Magistrates Court
PTU	Primary Training Unit
RAF	Royal Air Force
RAMC	Royal Army Medical Corps
RN	Royal Navy
SNLR	Services No Longer Required

ABBREVIATIONS

SWWEC	Second World War Experience Centre
TNA	The National Archives
TOW	Tower Bridge Magistrates' Court
WAAF	Women's Auxiliary Air Force
WO	War Office
WRAF	Women's Royal Air Force
WRNS	Women's Royal Naval Service

Introduction

1967 marked a watershed in English law. Twenty-two years after the end of the Second World War, the Sexual Offences Act decriminalized same-sex acts between men in England and Wales.[1] Before the introduction of the new legislation, the hero of Alamein, Field Marshal Bernard Montgomery, urged the House of Lords not to sanction it.

> Our task is to build a bulwark which will defy the evil influences seeking to undermine the very foundations of our national character. I know it is said this is allowed in France and some other countries. We are not French, we are not from other nations, we are British – thank God.[2]

While Montgomery could not slow the momentum of change to civilian law nor shake off the rumours that he himself desired other men, his concerns were at least shared by policymakers within the armed forces.[3] Military chiefs and the Wolfenden Committee agreed that decriminalising homosexual acts in the forces would affect discipline and threaten the safety of low-ranking servicemen.[4] As a result, they remained punishable by military law even though they ceased to be illegal between consenting civilian men over the age of twenty-one.

By the middle of the 1990s, human rights campaigns spearheaded by *Stonewall*, *OutRage!* and *Rank Outsiders* were increasing their pressure on the government to overturn the ban.[5] Within Parliament, debate raged. In 1995, Harry Cohen, Labour MP for Leyton, argued for the inclusion of queer personnel in the armed forces by referring back to the Second World War:

> This year is the 50th anniversary of the end of the last war. The Minister [Roger Freeman] should remember that then the country was happy for many people of homosexual orientation to fight and to lay down their lives for it. Their orientation was not held against them by the

country then, so why is the Minister adopting such a backward attitude now?[6]

Some of the most poignant arguments for inclusion came not from campaigners and politicians but from heterosexual veterans of the Second World War writing to the national press. Their letters helped to inform the debate, revealing not only the existence of men and women who desired members of the same sex, but their unquestionable value to the armed forces. As one veteran recalled, 'In 1943 I had a Divisional Officer, a captain of Marines, who was overtly gay. He was also a heavily decorated hero. He was the first of many gay servicemen and women I met during four years in the Navy and later the R.A.F. I did not see or hear of any trouble [or] loss of discipline.'[7]

In a letter to *The Independent*, another veteran highlighted the irrelevance of sexuality to service.

> I never detected that any of my colleagues in the skilled and demanding work then being carried out by GCHQ were homosexuals, nor would it have occurred to us that it could make the slightest difference to our acceptability or usefulness. But if the authorities had suddenly decided in the middle of the Second World War to expel all homosexuals from the armed forces - now that really would have been damaging. If Britain could win the war without expelling homosexuals from the armed forces, then I should have thought the British armed services could survive, and indeed flourish, in peacetime without worrying about the homosexuals in their ranks.[8]

The general public also appeared to support the lifting of the ban. In May 1997, two television chat-show phone-ins showed that 75 per cent and 80 per cent respectively of those calling in believed that the ban on gays and lesbians serving in the military should be lifted.[9] Two years later, a national opinion poll commissioned by Stonewall revealed that seven out of ten Britons believed that gays and lesbians should be allowed to serve.[10] In the face of this rising tide of support, the Ministry of Defence continued its unflinching adherence to its policy, even though its foundations were beginning to look increasingly vulnerable. On one memorable occasion, a serving member of the armed forces who was sitting in the audience of *Question Time* tried to explain his objection to serving with an 'out' colleague and eventually concluded, amid much audience hilarity, that he was scared by the thought of sharing a shower.[11]

Out on the streets of the capital, the activities of Peter Tatchell and *OutRage!* were beginning to have a significant effect on the visibility of the issue in the public domain. On 2 November 1997 Tatchell organised a 'Queer Remembrance Day' which was followed up by similar days in 1998 and 1999. Tatchell's main mouthpiece was the queer Army veteran Dudley Cave, a former prisoner of war and a staunch critic of the Ministry of Defence. For twenty years before his death, Cave campaigned against the Royal British Legion's refusal to acknowledge that queer men and women served and died protecting Britain's interests and lambasted their unwillingness to accept the involvement of LGBT organisations in Remembrance Day. In 1997 Cave marched at the head of a 'Queer Remembrance Day' parade. Following Cave's lead, campaigners followed the last group of veterans marching past the Cenotaph. They carried pink flags, and laid pink triangles at the base of the memorial in a protest against the refusal of the armed forces to allow queer personnel to serve and their failure to acknowledge that thousands had served during the Second World War. The British Legion publicly denounced the ceremony as 'distasteful'.[12] By 1999, the protest had burgeoned into a significant day of protest after *OutRage!* was approached by the partner of a queer serviceman who had recently died. He claimed that the British Legion prevented him from joining the widows and widowers on the parade past the Cenotaph because same-sex partners were not recognised. This response should have come as no surprise. In the early 1980s, the Legion's Assistant Secretary, Group Captain D. J. Mountford, had condemned moves to promote the acceptance of queer men and women as an attempt to 'weaken our society', and declared that such individuals had no right to complain about being ostracised by Legion members.[13]

Despite the attempts of Tatchell and the evident momentum generated in the public domain, the ban on gays and lesbians serving in the armed forces was retained until 2000 due to three fundamental concerns: the potentially disruptive influence of 'homosexual practices' on military discipline, the desire to prevent the abuse of authority by those in charge of junior personnel, and the security risk implied by the presence of queer personnel, specifically the threat of blackmail.[14] Not even the memory of apparent inclusivity in Britain's 'finest hour', nor the visible presence of queer veterans on the streets, could influence policymakers to change.

Returning to Tatchell's campaign to lift the ban, the cornerstone of his argument rested on the estimation that some 250,000 queer men served in the British armed forces during the Second World War, an assessment which he based on findings from the 1990–91 National Survey of Sexual Attitudes and Lifestyles. Six per cent of the survey's respondents declared that they had experienced sexual contact with a member of the same sex.[15] Tatchell's figure did not incorporate women, nor did it consider those who experienced same-sex love or intimacy but defined themselves as heterosexual. In 1999, *OutRage!* doubled Tatchell's figure to 500,000 to include lesbians as well as bisexual men and women.[16] This later figure still excluded those who preferred not to label their sexuality so rigidly.

In reality, the numbers were likely to have been much higher. During the Second World War, 6,508,000 men and women served in the armed forces.[17] It is possible that as many as 392,480 of the 6,508,000 might have identified themselves as queer, an assessment taken from a 2005 study which estimated that 3.6m of the adult population possessed a queer identity. This is over one in seventeen, based on a total population of just under 60 million.[18] I however, am more intrigued by the figures that were not considered by *OutRage!*, that is, those men and women who experienced some form of same-sex intimacy but did not define their sexuality by it. Based on a 1949 study compiled by Mass Observation, which discovered that one in five people out of a sample of 450 had experienced some form of intimacy with members of the same sex, it might follow that some 1,300,000 personnel could fall into this category. While these figures are obviously speculative, at the very least they suggest that a significant proportion defined their sexuality by their desire for members of the same sex or had experienced some form of same-sex intimacy.[19]

It is the task of *Queen and Country* to explore these desires and their intersection with military discipline in the context of the Second World War. In some senses this book is an unapologetic act of historical retrieval, written in order to create a discursive space for a group of veterans who have until now been silent. Their story has often been presupposed but rarely articulated. Suppositions have ranged from the assumption that the illegality of same-sex activity meant that men and women who desired members of the same sex could not possibly have served in the armed forces during the Second World War, to inaccurate summaries of indecency convictions which portray the institution as punitive and reactionary. My aim in writing *Queen and Country* is not only to interrogate these myths but also to explore the complex interaction between same-sex desire and the State. In this sense the following four chapters offer more than simply a record of the armed forces and its attempts to regulate the activities of its personnel; they illuminate how men and women lived, loved and survived in institutions which, at least publicly, were unequivocally hostile towards same-sex activity within their ranks. *Queen and Country* also tells a story of selective remembrance and the politics of memory, exploring specifically why same-sex desire continues to be absent from the historical record of the war. In examining this absence, and the more intimate minutiae of cohesion, homosociability and desire, *Queen and Country* pushes far beyond traditional military history in order to cast new light on one of the most widely discussed conflicts of the twentieth century.

Why the Second World War?

Despite the perennial interest in the Second World War, a study of same-sex desire in the British armed forces has never materialised. In Canada, the United States and Australia, Paul Jackson, Alan Bérubé and Garry Wotherspoon have all written excellent studies of their respective countries.[20] In Britain, however, not even seasoned historians of sexuality have grappled with the topic. Apart from Matt Houlbrook's work on homosex in the Brigade of Guards between 1900 and 1960, queer history has largely ignored the militarised body, choosing instead to focus on male experiences of urban space and on sexological discourse as a means to explore how sexual practices and identities have been experienced, defined and understood.[21]

Perhaps not unsurprisingly, in the field of military history, the issue of same-sex desire has also been conspicuously absent. At best, it has appeared only in passing in more general histories of men at war. In *Acts of War: The Behaviour of Men in Battle*, Richard Holmes dismisses same-sex desire in one page, concluding that 'There is much more to love in wartime than the scramble for sex'.[22] Similarly, David French's latest monograph, *Military Identities: The Regimental System, the British Army and the British People 1870–2000*, dedicates little more than a page to the issue.[23]

In the realm of social history, and in spite of a vigorous dialogue on the issue of citizenship and national identity during the war, there has been no discussion of citizenship and same-sex desire between 1939 and 1945.[24] Sonya Rose's work, *Which People's War?*, which otherwise comprehensively debunks the mythical status of the Second World War, comes closest to suggesting the need for such a focus.[25] Indeed, her discussion of good-time girls and their 'anti-citizen' status offers up a number of unanswered questions. For instance, did the wartime discourse of cooperation open up the imaginative possibilities for toleration, acceptance or looking away, or merely heighten a sense of opposition against 'the other?' How did the presence of same-sex desire affect notions of citizenship and national identity during the war? And finally, in the post-war period, why has the queer experience of war been largely omitted from the historical record and popular memory? *Queen and Country* will address these issues and in doing so suggest ways in which the study of the 'people's war' might be revised and extended.

In the absence of a serious and sustained treatment of same-sex desire between 1939 and 1945, a handful of popular studies by authors including Alkarim Jivani, Emily Hamer, Cate Haste, Paul Fussell and John Costello have filled the gap.[26] All of these works deal relatively succinctly with queer involvement in the Second World War, either, as in the case of Jivani, as part of larger histories on queer men and women in twentieth-century Britain, or, as in the case of Paul Fussell, as part of a larger work on behaviours during the Second World War. They are studies which tend to possess sketchy empirical foundations, something which produces a galling trend towards abstraction and generalisation. Paul Fussell has unwittingly produced one of the best examples of this ill-informed treatment. The only comment that he makes on the issue of same-sex expression (or in his words, 'that sort of thing') is that it was 'so rare as to engender no special notice or comment. If we do hear now and then of such "minority" sexual compensations, they seem largely limited to POW camps'.[27] Fussell's unwillingness to elucidate on the nuances of the phrase 'that sort of thing' and his unsubstantiated claim that same-sex activity was confined to prisoner of war camps articulate two of many misapprehensions which have become received knowledge. This project began in the spirit of wanting to question the simplistic coherence of these monochromatic narratives and out of a desire to add a new level of empirical depth and analytical focus to the issue of same-sex desire in the British services between 1939 and 1945.

This revisionist agenda is underpinned by a deep curiosity about the inner sanctum of the armed forces and the opportunities and restrictions engendered by the Second World War. Examining sexuality through the lens of the war provides an unparalleled opportunity to explore the intricacies of human desire in a time of national emergency and moreover, subjective and institutional understandings and responses to that desire. Despite the illegality of same-sex acts between men (or, in the case of women, moral distaste of them), the military institution did not resolutely oppose bonds between men and between women, bonds which included emotional intimacy and sexual contact.

Fighting a different war

Aside from my inherent curiosity about the existence of same-sex desire in the British armed forces between 1939 and 1945, *Queen and Country* also emerged out of a wish to explore why the contributions of those who desired members of their own sex had so far been neglected and why, in the period following the end of the Second World War, their presence was almost entirely written out of the historical record and contemporary memory. Indeed, despite clear evidence that the Second World War fostered a 'for the duration' toleration and in some cases, acceptance, a handful of veterans denied this side of the story and were quick to condemn my research. The story of their objection, and the search for those who were willing to speak out, is worth telling at length, not least because it sheds light on the continued sanctity of the Second World War in British mythology.

The paucity of existing oral history recordings meant that I began my own search for respondents early on in the life of the project. Originally, I hoped to make a generic appeal for servicemen and women to come forward and discuss their experiences of love, sex and romance. This would have resulted in a wider pool of respondents, but I would have spent precious time attempting to sift out the memories of those who merely referred in passing to same-sex activity. To avoid this, I directed all of my appeals to self-identified queer veterans of the war and to their friends, relatives and colleagues. All of these appeals, whether intended for the local press or a publication aimed specifically at queer men and women, were virtually identical. As I would later discover, however, they cast a very specific net around a demographic that was not always eager to define the perimeters of its desire.

Over the course of a year I targeted 440 local newspapers, 22 of which featured my appeal on their letters page. I also approached various publications aimed at the LGBT community including the *Pink Paper*, *Diva* and *Gay Times*. Only *Gay Times* published my appeal, which resulted in five interviewees. Appeals to *Navy News* and *The RAF Newsletter* were unsuccessful, and *The People's Friend* declined to print my appeal without offering an explanation for their decision apart from that, as one representative put it, they 'preferred not to'.[28] The journal of the Royal Army Medical Corps and the *Psychiatric Bulletin* (which is produced for current and retired psychiatrists) both published my appeal but I received no response from the readers of either. However, correspondence with OurStory Scotland, an LGBT history archive, led to one contact, a veteran of the New Zealand Army with whom I conducted a pilot interview. I also placed an appeal in the newsletter of the LGBT archive Brighton OurStory. Other smaller avenues included a nationally known pub for older gay men in London's West End and a dating forum for older men which declined to publicise my research on the grounds of confidentiality. I also posted messages on the internet forums *At Ease* and *Proud to Serve*, both of which target self-identified queer men currently within or retired from the armed forces, and on the BBC History War and Conflict Forum. None of these appeals led to any contacts.

Over the course of my second year of research, I increased the intensity of my search and began extensive mailings to different agencies and organisations. I sent a copy of my appeal to every veterans' organisation in the UK, which number over 100, and I also worked with Age Concern, which maintains a programme of resources, publications and events for its LGBT clients. With the help of its National Development and Policy Officer, a copy of my appeal was sent to an extensive national network of local and regional organisations that work with the older LGBT population. I also collaborated with Age Concern Gloucestershire and an appeal was included in their newsletter.

No responses were forthcoming from these appeals, so I piloted a slightly different approach, and contacted a sample of care homes for the elderly, 156 in total, many of which are affiliated to the armed forces. In addition Anchor Homes, which maintains one of the biggest networks of care homes and sheltered accommodation in the country, agreed to publicise my research. This culminated in an appeal being included in the Winter 2005 edition of *Anchor News*, a newsletter which is circulated to an average of 26,000 residents four times a year. I received no responses to either invitation, something which led me to question how easy it might have been for residents to respond to such appeals.

Frustratingly, my efforts to find interviewees through national appeals on the radio were also unsuccessful. Following a request to Radio 4, I was contacted by Nick Patrick, the producer of *Making History*. We produced a ten-minute feature on my research which was aired in November 2005 and involved two of my interviewees. I also worked with the producer Jo Coombes in the research and production of 'Cleaning out the camp', a programme which examined the policies of the armed forces towards same-sex activity from the end of the Second World War up to the present day. This was aired in June 2007.[29] At a more local level, I was interviewed, at my own request, by BBC Radio Manchester for their weekly news and discussion programme *Gay Talk*. An e-mailed request to BBC Radio Derby also resulted in an appeal being made on the air in 2006.

The response from these radio appeals was minimal, and while this was disappointing, it was not surprising given that I was targeting an ageing generation who had lived a great deal of their lives under a veil of

INTRODUCTION

secrecy and repression. It is also highly likely that contemporary labels simply did not accurately reflect the diversity of sexual identities and practices. This might certainly have been the case with Phyl, a retired nurse who had served in the Queen Alexandra's Royal Nursing Corps during the war. Chris Pawsey, a family friend of Phyl, had heard my appeal for respondents on the radio programme *Making History* and had contacted me to say that I should interview Phyl. He 'felt sure that Phyl was a lesbian', but had never asked her. Then a frail ninety-four-year-old, Phyl had never formally declared her sexuality but had always lived with women, sharing a home in Sussex with her companion Kaye before moving into a care home.

After e-mailing Pawsey again to discuss my concerns, we decided that he would talk to Phyl about my research and see how she responded. Following much consideration, he also made the decision to ask her outright if she desired women. Recalling their conversation, Pawsey told me that Phyl had informed him that she had always enjoyed the company of both sexes and had never had a physical relationship with another woman, although she mischievously added that she was 'prepared to give it a go' for me. In the end, I chose not to interview Phyl. Imposing a label on her seemed, at best, an inappropriate and contemporaneous imposition by a desperate academic. Given that my quest in pursuing the project was to write the wartime contributions of men and women who desired members of the same sex back into the historical record, accepting this uncertainty was exceptionally difficult. There are, however, some enigmas which should be allowed to slip under our anthropological urge to classify. Phyl is one of them. Her spirit pervades this book, offering a constant reminder that, wherever possible, we must avoid easy, reductionist assumptions about sexual identity and behaviour.

The most significant publicity that the project received was both unexpected and accidental. In 2005, my request for veterans of the Second World War to share their memories reached the head of the Monte Cassino veterans association, John Clarke. He was so incensed that he reported the story to a journalist at *The Sun*.[30]

> In our day homosexuality was a crime - and I don't know of any gay men I saw service with. She wanted me to contact members of my association. After I spoke to one or two of them they went berserk ... wouldn't the money be better spent elsewhere? They would be better off finding someone to do a write up about the trauma of combat.[31]

Clarke also constructed same-sex desire as un-British: that is, inconceivable in the British armed forces yet commonplace in other fighting forces. (In a letter to me Clarke claimed to have discovered dead German soldiers wearing make-up.[32]) However, the real root of his argument was not the foreign menace of same-sex desire but its illegality which, in his mind, meant that they could not possibly have been recruited into any of the services.

Three days after the article was published in *The Sun*, the *Sunday Sport* offered its comment. The article, written by the paper's publisher David Sullivan, the self-proclaimed 'voice of common sense', called my research 'an exercise in political correctness which will, no doubt, offend many people of a generation who have a very different attitude to homosexuality than exists today'.[33]

This gap between the 'hidden' narratives of my queer interviewees and the 'non-existent' narratives of veterans like Clarke has been reiterated continuously by those who have opposed my research. For instance, one veteran framed his objections around the sacredness of the Allied campaign. By highlighting of the existence of queer personnel in the armed forces, he believed that I was denigrating that sacredness and fabricating the past.

> I recommend you study what true history you can find and do not think of inventing false stories. There were virtually none for you to find because we treated such nonsense at best as a stupid joke or at worst as not worth wasting time on.[34]

By far the most offensive letter was written by a male correspondent who alleged that I was a 'corrupted tart' and a 'PC milky liberal'. He compared the threat of same-sex desire to that of global warming and asserted that 'we never even thought of homosexuals in our day. (Or poofters as we would have called them!)'[35] Given the frequency and polemical vigour of these objections, it is hardly surprising that only ten respondents volunteered to tell me their stories. Indeed, it is highly likely that fear of condemnation and moral distaste inhibited a significant number of veterans from coming forward as potential interviewees and by extension, presenting themselves as participants in the 'people's war'.

These responses offer clear evidence of the threat posed by the queer soldier to the conventional memory of the war and also to concepts of British military masculinity and homosociability. This latter term describes the preference of men and women to work and socialise with members of their own sex. As one of the central tenets of the armed forces, homosociability has what Garry Wotherspoon terms a 'close homosocial proximity' to expressions of seme-sex desire.[36] This relationship will be explored in more detail in chapter two, but it is worth noting here just how disruptive some judge same-sex desire to be to the sacred bonds that men, in particular, form with one another while on active service. Indeed, many of the letters that I received from veterans tuned into this disjuncture, citing the incompatibility of same-sex desire and military masculinity, and the perceived threat of the predatory, penetrative sexuality of active queer men to the supposedly vulnerable heterosexual soldier. There is, however more at work here than simply fear and ignorance. The Second World War is still popularly perceived as the 'people's war', a conflict which mobilised vast swathes of the populace who in turn, abandoned their differences in the name of winning the war. It was a conflict in which, unlike subsequent campaigns, the delineation between good and bad was entirely clear. By extension then, some veterans who objected so vigorously to my research did so because they did not want the sacredness of their war to be dirtied by a naïve PhD student who had not shared in that collective experience.

What might be termed 'the hierarchy of commemoration' has also played a significant role in influencing the reaction of some veterans. As the Second World War moves from memory to history, those who feel forgotten seek validation and public acknowledgement. When one group calls for recognition, others follow, setting their contribution against that of other veterans. Perhaps the most telling examples of this process is the granting of badges to both the Bevin Boys and the Land Army in 2007, gestures which followed the unveiling of Britain's only memorial to the women of the Second World War in 2005.

Many surviving veterans are acutely aware of their cultural value and visibility in this hierarchy. They are also quick to object if a group that is deemed to possess lesser value is granted public recognition before them. John Clarke, for instance, felt particularly aggrieved that I was acknowledging queer veterans before the 'forgotten' soldiers of Monte Cassino. In the case of the former, their contributions are undermined in the mind of veterans like Clarke because of the presumed incompatibility between same-sex desire and a perception of military service which demarcates the contributions of queer men and women as inferior to those of their heterosexual counterparts.

What all of these responses neglect is the long-established relationship between the armed forces and same-sex desire. From the classical world up to the present day, same-sex desire has loomed large within fighting forces.[37] The wilful denial of this history, particularly in relation to the Second World War, reflects a historical amnesia, imposed by those who associate same-sex expression with military ineffectiveness.

One of the many tasks of *Queen and Country* is to explore this relationship.

Sources

As most historians of sexuality have discovered, the problem with recovering queer history, especially from 'official' sources, is that in some respects it does not wish to be discovered. Institutional paper trails on same-sex activity have disappeared or been disposed of. What does survive is usually sketchy and often euphemistic. In records lodged in The National Archives for instance, same-sex desire is shrouded in a vast array of search terms including 'indecency', 'misfit' and 'unnatural'.

In terms of the Second World War, there is very little official documentation that discusses same-sex activity. Therefore, while 'official' records, when they exist, help to determine the texture of *Queen and Country*, they are counterbalanced by the subjectivities of my interviewees and other autobiographical works. Such a wide-ranging, multi-layered approach reflects both the ethos of this research and the constrictions placed upon my research by the limitations of the archival record.

The fragmentary nature of the institutional story demanded a patient and rigorous methodology. Some of these fragments consisted of brief passing references or paragraphs in post-war policy documents, while others constituted larger policy directives on the issue of same-sex desire in the services. The London Metropolitan Archives and The National Archives hold the most material, including the papers of Letitia Fairfield, a senior doctor with the Army and the author of the previously undiscovered ATS memo, 'A special problem'.[38] In The National Archives, I became engaged in a lengthy process of requesting that particular files that were closed to the public should be opened. The review process could take up to a month and I was only successful in three cases, the contents of which were all significantly censored before I received them.[39]

The information that emerged from my archival research documented the disciplinary issues inherent in the presence of same-sex activity and how the services responded to it. This information was augmented by contemporary manuals of military law and medical and psychiatric texts which helped to clarify how the medical community conceptualised same-sex desire in the 1940s.[40] I have also engaged with primary material from The National Archives which documents the work of the medical boards during both world wars, in order to assess the extent to which certain definitions were employed to identify men and women who desired members of the same sex at their medical inspections. The London Metropolitan Archives holds an extensive collection of Letitia Fairfield's papers, and the records of the Public Morality Council which attempted to deter immorality by patrolling the streets and reporting their findings to the police. The Wellcome Library was also a useful archival resource, given that it holds the papers of a number of eminent wartime psychologists and psychiatrists, including John Bowlby. In addition to these records I also discovered three advisory publications published during the war which discuss the perceived peculiarities of wartime sexual behaviour; G. L. Russell's *Sex Problems in Wartime* (1940), George Ryley Scott's *Sex Problems and Dangers in War-Time: A Book of Practical Advice for Men and Women on the Fighting and Home Fronts* (1940) and *The Red Light: Intimate Hygiene for Men and Women* by Rennie MacAndrew (1941).[41] Parliamentary debates, official medical histories and official reports such as the *Report on the Committee on Amenities and Welfare Conditions in the Three Women's Services* which investigated rumours of immorality in the women's auxiliary services, supplemented this material and also revealed the extent of the authorities' concern with heterosexual activity.[42]

Aside from archival material, autobiographical and semi-autobiographical works have helped to contextualise the lived experience of same-sex attraction and identity during the war. Benge's *Confessions of a Lapsed Librarian* is an autobiographical collection of essays which discuss the author's service in the Army during the Second World War and his later careers as a writer and a librarian. He describes his service life and the queer men that he worked with in refreshingly candid terms and positions them as 'good fellows', a term which he uses to demarcate those who he considered to be valuable members of his unit. Joan Wyndham's wartime diary *Love is Blue* is also useful for its brief references to queer personnel in the WAAF.[43]

In addition to this published material, the oral testimony that I managed to collect helped considerably to offset the 'official' institutional story of how individuals experienced same-sex desire in the services. Over the course of four years between 2004 and 2007, I interviewed ten men aged from their mid-eighties to their early nineties in semi-structured sessions that each lasted between one and four hours. Their wartime careers ranged from cooks and flight engineers to meteorologists, and they served as far afield as Africa, Egypt and India. They all served out the war until the cessation of hostilities and brief biographies of each man can be found in the appendix.

For many of my interviewees, their decision to tell their stories was motivated by a need to render themselves visible, thereby exposing the hypocrisy of the armed forces following the end of the war. Others sough to justify their presence in the services, perhaps to counter dominant cultural constructions of queer men as weak and cowardly. This particular stereotype is reflected in the most dominant post-war construction of same-sex desire in the services, the television series *It Ain't Half Hot Mum*. Written by the creators of *Dad's Army*, Jimmy Perry and David Croft, and first aired in 1974, the series focused on the exploits of a Royal Artillery Concert Party based in India. One of the sitcom's central characters was the hyper-masculine, battle-hardened Battery Sergeant Major Williams, played by Windsor Davies, who referred to his underlings, the performers, as a 'bunch of pooftahs'. Here lay the comedic value of the series. Perry was able to draw out the tension between the statuesque archetype of military masculinity played by Davies and the less than manly performers under his command. Not surprisingly, the series did little to create a positive public image of same-sex desire.[44]

An extension of my interviewees' tendency to counter dominant cultural stereotypes was their use of a narrative which sought to root the presence of same-sex desire in military history.[45] Before the start of our interview for instance, Richard Briar reeled off a list of military figures including Alexander the Great, Achilles and Julius Caesar, all of whom he identified as possessing a queer identity. Driven by a desire to justify and understand his identity, Briar's excavation of military history for suitable models of same-sex desire dominated our exchanges, not only to counter narratives that positioned same-sex activity in the military as disruptive but also as a means of anchoring his own sexual identity in a transhistorical framework. His interview was also driven by another agenda; the need to explain the particular dynamics of the relationships that he experienced with heterosexual men. His rationalisation for these affairs, which centred on the concept of the passive queer man as a 'receptacle', resonated with contemporary understandings of sexual activity between men and boys in ancient Greece. What Briar was therefore seeking was a framework of legitimation which he could use to conceptualise his wartime experiences.

Another common feature of the interview sessions was the telling of frank and explicit sexual stories. While this could have been the result of my careful attempts to establish a trusting relationship with my interviewees, it is also possible that my respondents were reacting to the contemporary culture of sexual openness and using it to articulate their memories of a time when sex and sexuality were private matters.

Simon Szreter and Kate Fisher also discovered this interplay between contemporary sexual culture and personal recollection in their most recent work, *Sex before the Sexual Revolution*, which uses oral history to explore the mechanics and meanings of love and sex between 1918 and 1963. As they observed:

> ... the changes in public discourses around sex provided respondents with both a reason and an ability to talk about sex. We did not primarily find oral history interviewees willing to discuss their private lives because their own attitudes to sex had changed and become less private, but because strong feelings on the differences between contemporary society and the lives they had lived induced them to talk.[46]

Interestingly, all of my respondents expressed their distaste for the sexual openness which drives the modern-day queer community. For instance, Richard Briar lamented the openness of some queer men in his home city. The surreptitious sexuality so quietly exuded by men in the 1940s has been replaced by a sexuality that, in Richard's opinion, is brash and pervasive.

While my interviewees often made comparisons between the 1940s and lamented the openness of contemporary queer life, they also found it difficult to dissent from contemporary constructions of same-sex desire. Five of my interviewees responded to the advertisement in *Gay Times*. *Gay Times* is at the forefront of the modern queer scene, a scene which is arguably defined by sexual activity. In telling me their stories of wartime sexual activity, my interviewees utilised the most prevalent narrative within queer culture, namely sex. The power of this narrative became most evident when I interviewed Dennis Campbell.[47] His final words to me were: 'You didn't ask me why I'm not in a relationship!' He felt compelled to explain that despite his sexual success during the war, he'd never found the right partner and had always enjoyed his own company. This parting shot was clearly Dennis's way of achieving a sense of psychic comfort. He did not wish to portray himself as an 'abnormal' queer man, and he could not dissent fully from popular discourses which emphasise the importance of openness, coupling and regular sexual activity.

Terminology

Queen and Country takes a contextual, time-specific approach to the study of same-sex desire in the British armed forces. Such an approach is now considered to be *de rigueur* for the historian of sexuality. As Jonathan Ned Katz succinctly expresses it in *Love Stories*, intimacies between men and between women need to be located in 'the erotic and emotional institutions of their own times'.[48] It is an approach which seeks to illuminate not only the historical specificity of desire but also the ways in which institutions have sought to define and categorise desire in order to understand and control it. In the context of the Second World War, it would simply be too reductionist to pin a modern queer identity on men and women who lived and loved through the 1930s and 1940s. To do so would not only legitimate the imposition of a modern-day lens (which favours one of two binary categories of sexual identity) on a multiplicity of acts and identities but would also presuppose a level of sexual and emotional consciousness and reflection which many did not possess. Of course, the historian of sexuality is caught in a double bind. In order to understand, categorise and fathom meaning, we must establish an organisational paradigm. This does not mean however, abandoning the notion of fluidity. Indeed, it is only by examining the fissures, tensions and contradictions of human behaviour (and how that behaviour has been categorised) that we might come to understand how and why they have been ignored.

With this in mind, I use John Howard's term 'homosex' throughout the book to describe a broad spectrum of sexual intimacy and activity between men and between women.[49] It is a term which makes no assumption about the sexual identity of its participants and it emphasises the individual significance of a sexual act rather than its wider cultural interpretation. In the context of service life, the term 'homosex' allows us to conceptualise the intersection between same-sex desire and what might be termed 'normative' sexuality and the range of interactions that occurred. It also provides us with an important interpretive mainstay, a means of understanding behaviour which refuses to fit neatly into contemporary categories of desire. For instance, the men (and to a lesser extent, women) whose identities were not queer but who experienced 'homosex' in the services, and who, for numerous reasons, declined to discuss it or write about it have, not unexpectedly, evaded my questioning gaze. It was therefore left to self-identified queer men and women who experienced 'homosex' with their comrades to fill in the silences. Sometimes, stories were vocalised by my respondents, many of whom discussed conducting sexual relationships with men who possessed a strong sense of their heterosexuality. On other occasions, stories emerged from the transcripts of court proceedings, from documentary evidence and from the diaries and reminiscences of those who witnessed the activities of their comrades. As fragmentary and ephemeral as these second-hand stories appear, they offer an unparalleled opportunity to understand activity which defies the intelligibility of traditional paradigms. Without the conceptual framework offered by Howard, they are interactions which would be almost impossible to interpret. In addition to homosex, I also use the term 'queer' to denote those who defined their identities by their attraction to members of the same sex. Despite its contemporary links to the gay rights movement, it was also one of many labels that formed part of my interviewees' vocabulary in the 1940s.

In addition to homosex, there is a further theoretical concept which has influenced the analytical shape of *Queen and Country* and that is 'passing'. First developed by Elaine Ginsberg in her monograph *Passing and the Fictions of Identity*, the term is used to explore how African Americans sought to be perceived as white and how their adoption of an alternative identity helped to facilitate social blending.[50] In the context of personnel on active service during the Second World War, passing provides an exceptionally important means of understanding how a large proportion of personnel who desired members of the same sex survived in the services. As I go on to explore in chapter two, personnel passed or dissented, their performances switched on and off to match the intricacies of particular social contexts. Such impersonations helped to facilitate social blending in situations where outright disclosure might have jeopardised an individual and their place within a group.

As *Queen and Country* will go on to elucidate, between 1939 and 1945, sexual acts between men were illegal in both civilian and military contexts. In the military, same-sex activity fell under section 18 of the Army Act. In statute law, the illegality of same-sex acts was solidified by the Labouchère amendment to the Criminal Law Amendment Act of 1885, which rendered all same-sex activity between men as an offence owing to the creation of the offence of gross indecency. However, while this appeared to be a monumental change in the law it actually reinforced existing statutes that went back to the rule of Henry VIII and increased the range of offences that could be prosecuted.[51] Same-sex acts between women were not illegal in civilian law or in the women's services, but they were deemed to be highly detrimental to discipline and cohesion.

While the law existed as the ever-present regulator, *Queen and Country* will show that in the context of homosex in the armed forces during the Second World War, it was less than consistently applied. The question therefore becomes when, why and how were those legal frameworks put into operation? The institution did not oppose bonds between men and between women. On the contrary, homosociability was one of the fundamental tenets of the services. When opposition was voiced, it was largely because extensions of that foundational relationship were deemed to have become detrimental to the cohesion, morale and functionality of a unit. Overwhelmingly, then, the implementation of military law in relation to same-sex activity was determined not by moral distaste but by pragmatism.

There is another theme which is explicitly linked to the notion of passing and performance in the armed forces, and that is 'playing away'. It refers not only to men and women on leave in Britain's towns and cities but also moments of transgression and subversion experienced by personnel while on active service and in periods of leisure. Much has been written about the role of the city in providing a backdrop for sexual expression and homosocial experimentation.[52] *Queen and Country* expands this work by exploring how the various spaces appropriated and utilised by the armed forces shaped same-sex subculture and influenced the performance of the individual. For the most part, however, men and women on active service were confined to their immediate location, unable to visit towns and cities unless they were granted leave. This forced many to discover and forge their own sites of expression and sociability in the barrack huts, shower blocks and 'secret corners' that constituted their lived environment during the conflict. Unlike the city, in which surveillance was rather more concentrated and prosecution was more likely, the complexities of group membership and the exigencies of the war meant that it was often more convenient for colleagues and officers to turn a blind eye to same-sex activity that occurred within the confines of the unit.

The structure ahead

Chapter one, 'Getting in', examines the medical, legal and cultural understandings of same-sex activity and identity in the late nineteenth and early twentieth centuries in order to understand how and to what extent the medical boards that operated between 1939 and 1945 identified and excluded bodies that were deemed to desire members of the same sex. Chapter two, 'Keeping up appearances', focuses on the life of service personnel; how they lived, loved and survived within the armed forces. Among other themes, this chapter examines the importance of homosociability and the mechanics of passing. Chapter three, 'Playing away', explores the experiences of personnel during moments when the veil could be lifted, whether on leave, on stage, away from authority, in foreign climes or simply away from the strictures of familial authority. Chapter four, 'Make do and mend', interrogates how men and women deemed to desire members of the same sex were conceptualised and treated by the armed forces. It uses court-martial records, court transcripts, official papers and personal testimony to map out how those caught out by the system were understood and treated. By the end of *Queen and Country*, we will have a clearer picture of how self-identified queer personnel and those who engaged in homosex experienced the Second World War when on duty, at play and when experiencing the sharp end of military law. We will have also interrogated the place and power of the 'people's war' in the memories of those who, in spite of their desires and the illegality of their sexual expression, fought for the freedom of Britain and its allies.

Notes

1 Scotland did not decriminalise consensual sex between men until 1980.
2 '94-49 vote for change in homosexual law', *The Times* (25 May 1965).
3 See also S. Hall, 'Letters show Monty as "repressed gay"', *Guardian Online* (26 February 2001), www.guardian.co.uk/Archive/Article/0,4273,4142165,00.html, accessed 2 January 2007, and N. Hamilton, *The Full Monty: Montgomery of Alamein, 1887–1942*, 1 (London: Allen Lane, 2002). Although Montgomery's alleged queerness has never been discussed in any depth, there is some evidence to suggest that he might have been attracted to other men. His biographer Nigel Hamilton expressed the view that Montgomery repressed his sexuality and excelled as a commander of men because of his deep love for them. John Alcock, a queer man who joined the Army Catering Corps in 1945, concluded from Montgomery's alterations to the Army's rules that 'that's just what a queer would do, alter things.': John Alcock interviewed by Paul Marshall, 1985, Hall-Carpenter Oral History Project, British Library, Sound Archive (hereafter BLSA), catalogue reference: C456/003 tape 1, side 1 © British Library. Further anecdotal evidence comes from a letter written by the partner of John Beardmore. John was queer and served as a sub-lieutenant in the Royal Navy. His partner, Steve, worked as a sergeant for the Army Headquarters of the Second Army alongside his queer brigadier. In a letter from Steve to John which was written in the summer of 1944, Steve described how 'my brig. [brigadier] calls me Steve in front of Monty [Montgomery] who blushes and clearly hates my guts but says nothing. I have my suspicions about him anyway too. After all, it takes one to know one.' Transcript of interview with John Beardmore, 3bmtv, *Conduct Unbecoming*, Channel 4, 1996, pp. 8–9.
4 Home Office, *Report of the Committee on Homosexual Offences and Prostitution* (London: HMSO, 1957), p. 53.
5 *Stonewall* was founded in 1989. It was originally conceived as a professional lobbying group. In recent years its activities have expanded into research and legal test cases. *OutRage!* is a non-violent direct action group famous for its controversial public campaigns. *Rank Outsiders* (later renamed AFLaGA) was founded in 1992 to contest the expulsion of queer personnel.
6 *Hansard Parliamentary Debates*, House of Commons, 4 May 1995, vol. 259, col. 458. In 1996, Freeman was the Minister of State for Defence Procurement.

7   A. Whitehead, letter to *The Guardian*, Weekend (23 March 1996).
8   A. Vans, letter to *The Independent* (3 February 1993).
9   E. Hall, 'Middle England comes out; Colonel Blimp is on the defensive but the rest of Britain doesn't mind gays in the forces', *The Independent* (21 May 1995).
10 'Gays win military legal battle', *BBC News Online* (27 September 1999), http://news.bbc.co.uk/1/hi/uk/458625.stm, accessed 4 February 2011.
11 Hall, 'Middle England comes out', *The Independent* (21 May 1995).
12 'Gay leaders defend Cenotaph ceremony', *BBC News Online* (2 November 1997), http://news.bbc.co.uk/1/hi/uk/20258.stm, accessed 19 August 2007.
13 Obituary for Dudley Scott Cave at the Knitting Circle, www.knittingcircle.org.uk/dudleycave.html, accessed 19 August 2007.
14 Ministry of Defence, *Report of the Homosexuality Policy Assessment Team* (London: Ministry of Defence, 1996), pp. 226–42.
15 P. Tatchell, 'When the Army welcomed gays', www.petertatchell.net/military/when_the_army.htm, accessed 18 April 2005. 18,876 people aged between 16 and 59 were questioned for the survey. See the UK Data Archive, survey SN3434 at www.data-archive.ac.uk/findingdata/snDescription.asp?sn=3434&key=Sexual, accessed 3 January 2007. The 1990 study was followed up in 2000 by the *National Survey of Sexual Attitudes and Lifestyles II* which conducted 12,110 interviews with men and women aged between 16 and 44. See the UK Data Archive, survey SN5223 at www.data-archive.ac.uk/findingdata/snDescription.asp?sn=5223&key=Sexual, accessed 3 January 2007.
16 See 'UK Remembrance Day honour', *BBC News Online* (14 December 1999) http://news.bbc.co.uk/1/hi/uk/519408.stm, accessed 1 May 2006.
17 W. F. Mellor (ed.), *History of the Second World War: United Kingdom Medical Series – Casualties and Medical Statistics* (London: HMSO, 1972), p. 829.
18 D. Campbell, '3.6m people in Britain are gay – official', *the Observer* (11 December 2005), p. 13.
19 Mass Observation Archive Topic Collection, Sexual Behaviour 1939–50, box 4, Sexual Behaviour, Report on Sex (1949).
20 A. Bérubé, *Coming Out under Fire* (New York: Free Press, 1990), P. Jackson, *One of the Boys* (Montreal and Kingston: McGill-Queen's University Press, 2004), G. Wotherspoon, 'Comrades-in-arms: World War II and male homosexuality in Australia', in J. Damousi and M. Lake (eds), *Gender and War: Australians at War in the Twentieth Century* (Cambridge: Cambridge University Press, 1995).
21 M. Houlbrook, 'Soldier heroes and rent boys: homosex, masculinities and Britishness in the Brigade of Guards: c.1900–1960', *Journal of British Studies*, 42:3 (2003), pp. 351–88. For work on urban space and same-sex desire see M. Houlbrook, *Queer London: Perils and Pleasures in the Sexual Metropolis, 1918–57* (Chicago and London: University of Chicago Press, 2005), M. Cook, *London and the Culture of Homosexuality, 1885–1914* (Cambridge: Cambridge University Press, 2003), and S. Brady, *Masculinity and Male Homosexuality in Britain 1861–1913* (London: Palgrave, 2005). In terms of sexology, see for example, H. G. Cocks, *Nameless Offences: Homosexual Desire in the Nineteenth Century* (London: I. B. Tauris, 2003), and C. Waters, 'Havelock Ellis, Sigmund Freud and the State: discourses of homosexual identity in interwar Britain', in L. Bland and L. Doan (eds), *Sexology in Culture* (Chicago: University of Chicago Press, 1998).

22 R. Holmes, *Acts of War: The Behaviour of Men in Battle* (London: Phoenix, 2004), p. 108.
23 D. French, *Military Identities: The Regimental System, the British Army and the British People 1870-2000* (Oxford: Oxford University Press, 2005).
24 See R. Weight and A. Beach (eds), *The Right to Belong: Citizenship and National Identity in Britain, 1930-1960* (London: I. B. Tauris, 1998), A. Lant, *Blackout: Reinventing Women for British Wartime Cinema* (Princeton: Princeton University Press, 1991), C. Gledhill and G. Swanson (eds), *Nationalising Femininity: Culture, Sexuality and Cinema in World War Two Britain* (Manchester: Manchester University Press, 1996), and G. L. Mosse, 'Nationalism and respectability: normal and abnormal sexuality in the nineteenth century', *Journal of Contemporary History*, 17:2 (1982), pp. 221-46, and *Nationalism and Sexuality: Middle Class Morality and Sexual Norms in Modern Europe* (New York: Fertig, 1985).
25 S. O. Rose, *Which People's War? National Identity and Citizenship in Britain 1939-1945* (Oxford: Oxford University Press, 2003), p. 106. On the issue of sexual citizenship during the war see also Gillian Swanson's latest monograph, *Drunk with the Glitter: Space, Consumption and Sexual Instability in Modern Urban Culture* (London: Routledge, 2007) pp. 13-31.
26 See A. Jivani, *It's Not Unusual* (London: Michael O'Mara, 1997), E. Hamer, *Britannia's Glory: A History of Twentieth-Century Lesbians* (London: Cassell, 1996), C. Haste, *Rules of Desire* (London: Chatto, 1992), P. Fussell, *Wartime: Understanding and Behaviour in the Second World War* (Oxford and New York: Oxford University Press, 1989), and J. Costello, *Love, Sex and War: Changing Values, 1939-1954* (London: Collins, 1985). More recently, *A Gay History of Britain* dedicates two and a half pages to the Second World War. See M. Cook, R. Mills, R. Trumbach and H. G. Cocks (eds), *A Gay History of Britain: Love and Sex between Men since the Middle Ages* (Oxford: Greenwood, 2007) pp. 148-50.
27 Fussell, *Wartime*, p. 109.
28 E-mail from C. Heap to Emma Vickers, 11 August 2005.
29 BBC Radio 4, *Making History*, 'Gays and lesbians in the British forces during World War Two', 29 November 2005 BBC Radio 4, 'Cleaning out the camp', 21 and 28 June 2007.
30 G. Patrick, 'Were you only gay in Army? Heroes slam quiz insult', *The Sun* (13 October 2005).
31 E. Scott, 'Gay soldiers study sparks war of words', *South Manchester Reporter* (20 October 2005).
32 Letter from J. Clarke, 10 October 2005.
33 D. Sullivan, 'Lesbo honest. This is a waste of time!', *Sunday Sport* (16 October 2005). More recently the ESRC awarded Dr Roisin Ryan-Flood of Essex University £82,000 to research the migration of Irish gays and lesbians to London. The decision sparked similar derision from the Tax Payers' Alliance who questioned the value of the study. See M. Reynolds, 'Your £82,000 bill for "study" of Irish gays', *Daily Express* (28 March 2008), p. 31.
34 E-mail from S. H. to Emma Vickers, 31 August 2005.
35 Letter from R. M. to Emma Vickers, 6 February 2006.
36 Wotherspoon, 'Comrades-in-arms', p. 208.

37 See B. R. Burg (ed.) *Gay Warriors: A Documentary History from the Ancient World to the Present* (New York: New York University Press, 2002), Houlbrook, 'Soldier heroes and rent boys', pp. 351-88, Cocks, *Nameless Offences*, pp. 139-44, A. N. Gilbert, 'Buggery and the British Navy, 1700-1861', *Journal of Social History*, 10:1 (1976), pp. 72-98, and A. D. Harvey, 'Homosexuality and the British Army during the First World War', *Journal of the Society for Army Historical Research*, 79 (2001), pp. 313-19.

38 See Fairfield's obituary in the *British Medical Journal* (11 February 1978), pp. 372-3.

39 The following files were opened at my request: The National Archives (hereafter TNA), MEPO 2/8859, Activities of homosexuals, soldiers and civilians: co-operation between the Army and the police 1931-50, TNA, MH 102/187, Wellesley Nautical School: copy of Chief Inspector's report concerning an investigation into indecent behaviour among the boys, 1939, and TNA, AIR 2/13859, WRAF: procedure in the treatment of immorality, 1945-68. Before I was able to view this last file, a journalist from *The Guardian* reported on its contents. See A. Travis, 'How the Air Force kept secret watch to track down lesbians', *The Guardian* (22 August 2005). The process of redaction usually occurs before the records are transferred to the archive. However, files are sometimes redacted by staff. See http://www.nationalarchives.gov.uk/documents/information-management/foi_guide.pdf, p. 17.

40 S. Freud, *Three Essays on Sexuality* (London: Pelican, 1977), H. Ellis, *Studies in the Psychology of Sex*, vol. 1 (London: F. A. Davis and Co., trans. 7th edn, 1892), E. Carpenter, *The Intermediate Sex* (London: Allen and Unwin, 9th edn, 1952), W. Norwood East and W. H. de Hubert, *Report on the Psychological Treatment of Crime* (London: HMSO, 1939). See also W. Norwood East, *Medical Aspects of Crime* (London: J. and A. Churchill, 1936).

41 G. L. Russell, *Sex Problems in Wartime* (London: Christian Movement Press, 1940), G. Ryley Scott, *Sex Problems in War-Time: A Book of Practical Advice for Men and Women on the Fighting and Home Fronts* (London: T. Werner Laurie, 1940), R. MacAndrew, *The Red Light: Intimate Hygiene for Men and Women* (London: Wales Publishing, 1941).

42 *The Markham Report: Report of the Committee on Amenities and Welfare Conditions in the Three Women's Services* (London: HMSO, 1942), A. Salusbury MacNalty and W. F. Mellor, *Medical Services in War* (London: HMSO, 1968), F. A. E. Crew (ed.), *History of the Second World War: The Army Medical Services, Administration II* (London: HMSO, 1955), War Office, *The Soldier's Welfare - Notes for Officers* (London: HMSO, n.d.).

43 R. C. Benge, *Confessions of A Lapsed Librarian* (London: Scarecrow Press, 1984), J. Wyndham, *Love is Blue* (London: Flamingo, 1987).

44 A similar tack was pursued by Peter Nichols in his 1977 novel and play *Privates on Parade* which documents the journey of the central character, Stephen Flowers, and his induction into a world of gay innuendo and drag with the Song and Dance Unit of South East Asia. It was also filmed: *Privates on Parade* (dir. Michael Blakemore, HandMade Films, 1982).

45 See Burg (ed.), *Gay Warriors*.

46 See C. Szreter and K. Fisher, *Sex before the Sexual Revolution: Intimate Life in England 1918-1963* (Cambridge: Cambridge University Press, 2010), p. 13.

47 Dennis Campbell, interviewed by Emma Vickers, 22 November 2005.

48 N. Katz, *Love Stories* (Chicago: University of Chicago Press, 2001), p. 9.
49 J. Howard, *Men like That: A Southern Queer History* (Chicago: University of Chicago Press, 1999), p. 18. Nan Alamillia Boyd has discussed Howard's methodology in 'Who is the subject? Queer theory meets oral history', *Journal of the History of Sexuality*, 17:2 (2008), pp. 177–89.
50 E. K. Ginsberg (ed.), *Passing and the Fictions of Identity* (Durham NC: Duke University Press, 1996), pp. 2–3.
51 See Cocks, *Nameless Offences*, p. 17, and A. McLaren, *The Trials of Masculinity* (Chicago: University of Chicago Press, 1997), pp. 218–19.
52 See for instance Houlbrook, *Queer London*, H. Bech, *When Men Meet: Homosexuality and Modernity* (Chicago: University of Chicago Press, 1997), M. Turner, *Backward Glances: Cruising the Queer Streets of New York and London* (New York: Reaktion, 2003), D. Higgs, *Queer Sites* (London: Routledge, 1999), D. Bell and G. Valentine (eds), *Mapping Desire* (London: Routledge, 1995).

1

Inclusion

When Jimmy Jacques was twenty, he was summoned to a recruitment centre on Walworth Road in south-east London to undergo a medical inspection.[1] It was 1940, and Britain was attempting to conscript as many functional bodies into the armed forces as possible. In church halls and inspection centres across the country, a vast assortment of physiques queued and stripped in the name of national emergency. Over the course of the Second World War, some 7,100,409 men and women were quantified and classified by medical boards organised by the Ministry of Labour.[2] These examinations were a chaotic synthesis of military necessity, fervent patriotism and a preoccupation with physical health. Jacques, who was then working as a projectionist at a cinema in Hounslow, was like any other recruit, apart from one imperceptible difference. He was, and is, queer. He passed into the armed forces unnoticed and served out the war in the Army until 1946, when he was demobbed.[3]

It would be easy to presume that the illegality of homosex between servicemen (and the moral distaste that characterised attitudes towards same-sex activity between women) would provide a clear mandate for the armed forces to exclude queer bodies at the first possible opportunity. Once recruited and on active service, the identification and exclusion of trained personnel became significantly harder and, crucially, harder to justify. This chapter explores whether the medical boards possessed the diagnostic ammunition to identify and exclude those who were deemed to desire members of the same sex and the extent to which the armed forces directed them to do so. It begins with a discussion of medical testing during the First World War, thereby laying the ground for a discussion of testing between 1939 and 1945, both as it was implemented by the medical boards and how it was experienced by personnel.

Same-sex desire and the medical boards, 1870–1918

Britain's embarrassing performance in the Boer War (1899–1902) and its revelations about physically weak and 'degenerate' Britons tuned into already prevalent fears about poverty and the population boom within the lower classes. As Heggie and Bargielowska have both highlighted, however, it was Britain's inadequacy in the war rather than oft-cited rates of rejection that influenced the government to reappraise the physical health of its potential combatants. Following the end of the war and in light of damaging evidence that questioned the efficacy of the victorious British Army, strengthening the male physique became a priority.[4] This fixation was particularly evident within the public school system. In the latter half of the nineteenth century, exercise had already been introduced into public schooling to divert the potentially destructive energies of young adolescent boys. Team games and other physical activities were also thought to improve morality and character, a belief which was heavily derived from the philosophy of muscular Christianity. According to the head of Rugby School, Thomas Arnold, exercise would imbue young men with 'the body of a Greek and the soul of a Christian knight'.[5] It was a gendered, middle-class philosophy based on the image of Jesus as a spiritual leader and a strong, athletic carpenter.

Aside from the public school system, state schools were also forced to place a greater emphasis on physical training in the wake of the war. In 1902, for instance, the Board of Education in consultation with the War Office issued a *Model Course of Physical Training* which consisted largely of military drill.[6] According to *The Times*, such 'elementary training' would 'lay the foundations of a military spirit in the nation'. Without this spirit, warned the author, 'recruiting will never be on a healthy basis'.[7]

Not unsurprisingly, young women educated in elementary schools during this period experienced a much tamer curriculum which focused on domestic science. Whereas young boys were trained to be fit and disciplined, young girls were expected to excel in their own, gendered education in preparation for their future roles as wives and mothers. These widely divergent paths were deeply rooted in the social and political framework of British society and were prescriptive enough to render any divergence from them as an abnormality.

As we might expect, there had to be countertypes to these gendered ideals, and the period between 1870 and 1914 marks a deeply important phase in their construction. According to George Mosse, it was a time when 'the enemies of modern, normative masculinity seemed everywhere on the attack: women were attempting to break out of their traditional role; "unmanly men" and "unwomanly" women ... were becoming ... more visible'.[8] Mosse also identifies an increasing public and scientific preoccupation with sexuality and its categorisation and control. Partly as a result of the work of the Austrian sexologist Richard von Krafft-Ebing, the 'sexual deviant' became a distinct countertype, a countertype which would continue to hold the attention of sexologists well into the middle of the twentieth century.[9] It was an era of classification, when 'sexologists codified perversion and devised criteria to demarcate the normal from the pathological'.[10] However, for all of its classification and codification, sexology sat on the peripheries of popular medicine until well after the end of the Second World War. Until then, the criminological model, which classified same-sex attraction as an unnatural vice, reigned supreme in the minds of all but a few progressive doctors and psychiatrists.[11]

There is little evidence to suggest that sexology had a discernible impact on the classification of bodies between 1914 and 1918. By extension, there is no proof that the doctors employed on the medical boards possessed the skills to identify and label the queer recruit, especially since they were primed to look for physical rather than moral degeneracy. The outbreak of the First World War, and the national emergency that ensued, drowned out debates surrounding effeminacy, decadence and same-sex desire, debates that had been instigated by the public trials and prosecution of Oscar Wilde in 1895.[12] Although there were certainly undesirable physical forms which were graded accordingly by the medical boards, these gradings were not made with reference to effeminacy or presumed same-sex desire. Only those men who displayed serious and permanent physical disabilities were excluded. While some sexological thinkers were beginning to conceptualise same-sex desire as an innate, fixed condition, the most prevalent attitude in 1914 was that it was a crime which derived from a moral failing. What the war provided was the ideal therapeutic opportunity to cure these men and remould their bodies and minds into more desirable specimens of British manhood.

As Mosse argues, the First World War 'made man as warrior the centre of its search for a national character'.[13] The search for national 'warriors' was, however, less a search and more of a cursory glance. Between August 1914 and December 1915, 2,466,719 men volunteered for the forces.[14] Conscription was enforced in January 1916 and continued until the end of the war. During this period, a further 2,504,183 men entered the armed forces.[15] Throughout the period of voluntarism, men were classified as either 'fit' or 'unfit' for military service and doctors were paid one shilling for every man they passed and nothing for those they rejected. This monetary incentive combined with strong feelings of patriotism, pressures of time, vast numbers of men and the urgent need for soldiers resulted in a system that was nothing less than chaotic. Examinations frequently took place at speed in cold, noisy and overcrowded buildings. Between November 1917 and November 1918, the boards carried out over 250,000 examinations. Each board was forced to inspect sixty men a day (a quota that was frequently overshot) in two-and-a-half-hour sessions, so that each man was assessed in about five minutes. The boards were staffed by 2,500 doctors, meaning that each practitioner was responsible for about 1,000 decisions each.[16]

Apart from the problem of volume, the boards were also said to be making, according to Winter, 'disastrous, and, in some instances, fatal misdiagnoses of recruits who should not have been accepted for military service'.[17] Such misdiagnoses were 'disastrous' not only for the Army and the individual concerned but also for the government and its system of disability pensions. For instance, it was common for men suffering from severe disabilities to be placed in higher grades on the premise that military service would remedy their defects. The assumption was that if a man was fit enough for work, he was fit enough for the Army.[18] Men were also classified not by their fitness at the time of examination but on their predicted fitness after they had been 'straightened out' after three or four months in uniform.[19] In fact, the medical boards and the armed services worked on the basis that a man could be physically and mentally moulded into an effective combatant. Accordingly, the Army's overwhelming priority was to select men who, at the most basic level, displayed a physique that could be fashioned into an archetypical specimen of British manhood through a regime of marching, drilling, field exercise and Army rations.

However, this fashioning process was a utilitarian compromise. The Army did not aim to create warriors out of civilians; rather it hoped to improve and standardise the bodies that came before its boards in order to render them as useful as possible. In most cases, it succeeded. Robert Roberts makes reference to servicemen on leave from the Army who returned to Salford during the First World War. The men's newly fashioned bodies, described as 'heavier, taller, confident, clean and straight', astounded the local residents.[20] Such physical remoulding could only occur on bodies which were malleable and free from severe disability. What is more, it was a process that relied upon a particular countertype which could offer a contrast to the type of man that one could become, namely the weak, pale and effeminate candidate who could be straightened out by a no-nonsense diet and a sharp injection of military discipline. It was a countertype that dominated perceptions of masculinity in the interwar period and had a significant influence on notions of the ideal recruit during the mobilisation of bodies between 1939 and 1945.

Health and same-sex desire, 1918–39

After the First World War, the health of the nation was once again placed under the spotlight. Reporting on the medical boards and their inspections of the 2,500,000 men called up between 1917 and 1918, the government claimed that the health of the nation was severely in decline. It was clear that civilian health required serious investment. In 1918, Lloyd George spoke of nation-building and the importance of improved health to the future of the British race. His rallying cry – 'you cannot maintain an A-1 Empire with a C-3 population' – played on the classification system used by the medical boards and the obligation of all fit British men to protect their territorial gains.[21]

In the light of these revelations about the health of the British populace, the interwar period witnessed a resurgent interest in public health which mirrored the concerns of policymakers directly after the Boer War. As a result, the government invested heavily in a number of basic provisions; nutrition, housing and sanitation all improved dramatically between 1918 and 1939, for instance, and there was a year-on-year decline in rates of mortality and morbidity.[22]

Aside from physical health, the interwar period also saw a fledgling interest in mental health and particularly that of combatant men. This was largely due to the rising magnitude of what was known inadequately as 'shell shock'. In the wake of the war, the government set up the Southborough Committee to investigate the issue and how it might be dealt with. In 1922 the committee concluded that in the event of a future conflict, candidates should be screened for 'at least an average degree of mental and nervous health and stability'.[23] This recommendation stemmed largely from the horrific effects of shell shock and the use of the death penalty for those found guilty of 'cowardice', which, it was said, could have been avoided in some cases if candidates had been screened more thoroughly.[24]

After the First World War, psychiatric vetting also had a financial element. In March 1939, official records stated that 40,000 people were receiving pensions for war-induced mental disorders and a further 80,000 had received final awards.[25] In the autumn of 1938, and in an attempt to deal with cases of neurosis and avoid a repeat of the massive post-war pensions bill, the Minister of Pensions, Sir Herwald Ramsbotham, drew together a committee of neurologists and service representatives. The main expert was Dr Francis Prideaux, the Ministry of Pension's psychiatric adviser. Following the line of the 1922 Shell Shock Committee (referred to as the Southborough Committee after its chair, Lord Southborough), Prideaux argued that there was a difference between genuine victims of war-induced neurosis and predisposed, congenital and thus 'undeserving' neurotics whose mental stability was questionable before they were recruited into the armed forces.[26] According to Prideaux, many of the latter were given pensions and awards after the Great War, largely due to public pressure and a shortage during the war of trained medical staff to accurately diagnose neurosis.[27] It was even argued that neurosis was not caused by trauma and would only occur if the patient could gain some advantage from becoming neurotic, such as a pension for instance.[28]

In consultation with six other doctors, Prideaux recommended that, in dealing with cases of neurosis in a future war, no pensions should be paid for war neurosis and no man should be discharged from the fighting services for neurosis during the war.[29] Crucially, the committee also recommended the establishment of a comprehensive system of preventative medicine in the form of a psychiatric examination for each recruit. However, as Captain L'Etang later pointed out, 'Even the witnesses before the Southborough Committee never succeeded in stating exactly how mental instability in a recruit could be measured, assessed or defined. Psychiatrists did eliminate a large number of men, but they based their diagnosis of unsuitability on many of the points that the witnesses before the Committee stated were unreliable.'[30] Moreover, despite the recommendations of the Southborough Committee, physical health remained the benchmark and there were no coordinated attempts to screen new recruits for mental stability until 1942, when a Directorate of Psychiatry was established at the War Office. This delay, in addition to the principle that no man should be discharged from the forces after being diagnosed as neurotic, restricted the effectiveness of the British Army.[31]

In all of these discussions about mental health and the need to assess it in the event of a future war, there was no place for same-sex desire and certainly no link between it and mental collapse. Freud's notion of 'arrested development' was certainly starting to gain currency, but there is little evidence to suggest that his wider theories on homosexuality as an identifiable mental illness had much prevalence in medical circles, nor that they or any other techniques were being used to map same-sex desire. However, Chris Waters marks out the 1930s as a decade when optimism about the value of psychiatric treatment for homosexuality was increasing, based on the notion that same-sex attraction was a medical rather than a moral problem and that there was no automatic link between appearance and same-sex desire.[32] Alongside this was a growing understanding, expressed most clearly by William Norwood East and W. H. de B. Hubert in their influential *Report on the Psychological Treatment of Crime*, that same-sex desire could be either environmental or innate. Those that fell into this latter category were deemed to be the least suitable for psychiatric intervention.[33]

Outside medical circles, the interwar period witnessed a significant increase in the circulation of information about same-sex attraction, a knowledge that was fashioned in the most part by sexual advice literature and distilled in the public domain by the predominant mouthpiece – the popular press. It was a consciousness that was shaped by the most visible flag bearers of same-sex desire, namely the effeminate man and the masculine woman. As evident markers of sexual and gender transgression, they provided heterosexual society with clear embodiments of difference.

Despite these cultural indicators, public discussion was veiled under a pervasive stigma of silence. In the press, the issue was rarely discussed in open terms, apart from what Frank Bolton described as stories documenting 'indecent acts' between 'choir boys and priests and scouts and scout masters' in the popular press.[34] This culture of evasion and silence is expressed most clearly by Arthur Ferrier's cartoon, 'Some seafaring gentlemen may be particular', which appeared in the *Sunday Pictorial* in 1929.

To the contemporary observer, Ferrier's rendering of the American sailors as effeminate, effete and superficial suggests same-sex desire but does not overtly name it other than by the suggestive term 'particular'. In a similar way, Haselden's depiction of 'manly' athletes from 1926 does not make an explicit connection between masculine performance and queer desire. While both depictions pander to popular labels and stereotypes, they evade any overt reference to same-sex desire. What is more, away from these popular constructions, queer identity was in a process of transition and diversification. By 1939, queer men were actively moving away from their popular association with working-class queans. Deplored by discreet, largely middle-class queers, the presence of these effeminate men began to decline, replaced by those who were keen to emulate the private sexuality exalted by middle England. Discretion and self-control had become the norm. Queer men began policing their appearance, and those of their associates, and were quick to deplore the effeminacy and openness of men whose unbridled sexuality damaged

INCLUSION

Figure 1 'Some seafaring gentlemen may be particular.' Caption: 'Good looks are to be taken into consideration in the choosing of recruits for the American Navy. Our cartoonist thinks that "Sailors don't care" will be an out-of-date saying before long.'[35]

Figure 2 'Our beautiful women athletes.' Caption: 'We are told that women athletes are now of the graceful feminine type. / We presume the manly ones keep to drawing rooms.'[36]

their anonymity. Houlbrook describes this transition from 'overt' to 'covert' as being rooted in the need to avoid 'the loss of status associated with being a quean ... the growing marginalisation of visible gender transgression within queer urban life' and 'the increasing public prominence of "modern" medical etiologies of sexual difference'. As he goes on to explain:

> In the 1950s ... newspapers began to frame their exposés of queer urban life within the binary opposition between 'homo' and 'heterosexual'. Rather than a womanlike character, the 'homosexual's' difference was located in his choice of a male partner. At the same time ... more compelling conceptions of same-sex desire became current. In this context, many men still understood themselves as queans ... but they were a declining majority.[37]

In this sense, same-sex desire and identity were beginning to be understood not by visible gender inversion or effeminacy but by choice of sexual partner. Moreover, while popular renderings of same-sex desire may have remained stagnant, among men and women who desired members of their own sex, identities were diversifying in ways that went far beyond popular imaginings.

One example of this stagnation comes from a series of so-called 'pansy cases' during the 1930s. The most notorious of these was the Holland Park raid of 1932, in which sixty people, the majority of whom were men in female drag, were arrested.[38] Plain-clothes policemen had surveyed men dancing together and kissing, activity which secured convictions for twenty-seven revellers who were prosecuted for keeping a disorderly house and conspiring to corrupt public morals. They were sentenced to between three and twenty months in prison.[39] It was the response of the press that offers the most conclusive evidence that effeminacy and gender inversion were still being associated with sexual transgression. The *Daily Mail* depicted 'hysterical young men ... weeping, crying out and fainting in a crowded dock'.[40] The *News of the World* similarly described one defendant who collapsed and was picked up by a 'muscular warden' who 'flung him across his shoulders like a child'.[41] As Houlbrook points out, the men were infantilised and depicted as weak, emotional and unmanly, in contrast to the strength and muscularity of the warden.

Although the evidence is far from unequivocal, it nonetheless suggests that queer identities were shifting just as the association between effeminacy and same-sex desire was beginning to solidify in the public domain. This process was the result of a combination of factors, specifically a glut of new prosecutions, the subsequent press attention and the development of medico-scientific theories. At the same time, it was an association that was far from universal. Norman Haire's 1934 *Encyclopaedia of Sexual Knowledge* betrays a more nuanced understanding of same-sex desire: '[Effeminacy] does not by any means apply to all inverts ... there exist homosexuals with a manly appearance and even an essentially masculine character. But the effeminate type is much more striking and is therefore regarded as typical'.[42] Marie Stopes was less open to the notion of variation. Writing in *Enduring Passion*, Stopes perpetuated the dichotomous labelling of the queer by referring to 'men with an excess of the "feminine" qualities and "masculine" women'.[43]

Just as popular imagination mapped same-sex desire onto the male body through effeminacy, queer women were conceptualised through the lens of masculinity. Despite the fact that by the 1930s the lesbian community as a whole was beginning to diversify its sartorial style, the masculine-identified woman was still the predominant model. As Laura Doan has discussed in great detail, this had much to do with the release, in 1927, of the now instantly recognisable portrait of Radclyffe Hall and Una Troubridge. Hall's appearance in court a year later, when she dressed in masculine clothing to defend *The Well of Loneliness*, helped to solidify her association with same-sex desire. Indeed, her trial marked something of a sartorial watershed in the public identification of the lesbian.

> Some of the styles and accoutrements we now associate unquestionably with lesbianism did not signal unequivocally something about sexuality until the cultural dissemination of Hall's photographic portrait set the masculine woman – as a category of sexuality – apart from her fashionable friends.[44]

Before 1928 women in masculine garb had constituted a familiar and understood facet of public life. From the adventurous women who passed as soldiers and sailors to the music-hall tradition epitomised by the male impersonator Vesta Tilley, cross-dressing women had formed part and parcel of popular culture.[45] After the First World War, the fluidity of class and gender boundaries allowed women to experiment with masquerading as a discourse and cross-dressing became *de rigueur* for the fashionable woman about town. As Quentin Crisp observed:

> The short skirts, bobbed hair, and flat chests that were in fashion were in fact symbols of immaturity ... the word 'boyish' was used to describe the girls of that era. This epithet they accepted graciously. They knew that they looked nothing like boys. They also realized that it was meant to be a compliment. Manliness was all the rage.[46]

By the late 1920s, masculine-style fashion had fallen out of favour, pushed out somewhat forcibly by Radclyffe Hall's trial and its tangi-

Figure 3 Radclyffe Hall (standing) and Una Troubridge, 1927.[47]

ble impact on the visibility of the lesbian. Her aggressively polemical defence of her identity, combined with her masculine appearance in court and her relatively well-known relationship with Una Troubridge, triangulated into a discernable lesbian identity.[48]

Hall's appearance at court and that of her 'femme' lover Troubridge crystallised definitions of the mannish gender invert and the feminine partner. Seemingly then, the lesbian had suddenly become visible. The journalist and lesbian Evelyn Irons was profoundly dismayed by the publicity invoked by the case, not least because it heightened the public's sensitivity to the implications of women wearing masculine apparel. 'In those days it was drawing too much attention to what had been going on for a long time. We didn't want to be disturbed. The minute it came out, if you wore a collar and tie "Oh you're Radclyffe Hall, Miss!" And it wasn't at all happy. The whole thing just became a crusade in which you had to take a stand.'[49]

While it would be unwise to dispute the power of Radclyffe Hall in solidifying the first public manifestation of the lesbian, definitional ambiguities still abounded. The case of Colonel Leslie Ivor Victor Gauntlett Bligh Barker is but one example of this ambiguity. Barker was a female-to-male cross-dresser who was tried for a number of misdemeanours in 1929. Barker had married a woman in a civil marriage ceremony and lived and worked as a man under the guise of providing for his son.[50] His crimes included theft and perjury although much of the press attention focused on Barker's masterful impersonation of a man and the circumstances surrounding his marriage to Elfrida Haward. Haward maintained that she did not know the colonel was a woman 'until [she] read about it in the newspapers'.[51] Barker had convinced his wife that he had sustained an abdominal injury during the First World War that prevented him from having normal sexual relations. Both the law courts and the press struggled to frame Barker's sexuality within a discourse of sexual deviancy and chose largely to view it as an ingenious masquerade, prompted by Barker's need to provide for his son and enter spheres of employment which were not open to women.[52]

Barker's case demonstrates that female cross-dressers and masculine garb were not definitively linked to sexual deviancy. Indeed, to assume that this might have been the case elides important nuances between lesbianism, transgender identity and any number of reasons why a woman might don masculine clothing. What is clear is that while lesbianism may have formed a distinct part of public discourse, there was no coherent public consensus about lesbian identity until at least the middle of the twentieth century. Indeed, as Oram points out, any manifestly clear association between masculine garb and same-sex desire between women did not emerge until the late 1940s.[53]

While we might therefore talk about an increasing circulation of information pertaining to same-sex desire it is difficult to establish just how widely and coherently same-sex desire was understood. While the links between visible gender inversion and queerness were becoming less ambiguous, this absence, of an audible discourse of queerness, means that it would be unrealistic to claim that knowledge was pervasive and widespread.[54] This is certainly borne out in the activities and attitudes of the medical boards that reformed to appraise the bodies of potential combatants on the eve of the Second World War. Once again, the boards were grappling with the need to push as many fit recruits into service as possible. This, along with the prevalent criminological model of same-sex desire as a crime that was committed rather than an identity that was possessed, rendered it something of an irrelevancy.

Same-sex desire and the medical boards, 1939–45

During the two world wars, medical testing was a complicated logistical operation that altered very little during the interwar period. Each recruit continued to be examined for their height, distinguishing features and general condition including sight, reflexes and hearing. The assumption that military service would remedy defects and improve physiques also continued. In 1938 the Committee of Imperial Defence Manpower Sub-Committee, which issued the code of instructions for the medical boards, stated that 'it [is] unfair to a recruit if a civilian Medical Board should categorise him as "For sedentary duties only" when he [is] the type whose physique would rapidly improve by training'.[55]

Before the Second World War, the National Service (Armed Forces) Act of 1939 had made men between the ages of 18 and 41 liable to conscription. In December 1941, the National Service (No. 2) Act extended conscription to cover men aged between 18 and 51, and unmarried women between the ages of 20 and 30. In 1942, the age limit was extended to include 19-year-old women.[56] These demands were accompanied by frequent revisions in the criteria of selection; standards were continually modified and interpreted with increasing subcategories and increasing degrees of leniency.[57] By 1945, there were approximately ninety-two subcategories.[58] As we might expect, these alterations 'confuse[d] the examiners and lower[ed] their effectiveness'.[59]

From 1940, the Medical Boards used the capital letters A to C to describe recruits who were fit for general Army duties at home and/or abroad. Categories A and B designated a man as fit for overseas service and category C men were fit for home service only. In addition, men in category D were temporarily unfit and men classed in category E were deemed to be permanently unfit for service.[60]

For the women's services, the Ministry of Labour and National Service Medical Boards took over the examination process in May 1941. In the WAAF and the ATS, this ensured that medical testing effectively matched that within the Army and the RAF for men apart from specific questions about menstruation.[61] The WRNS only accepted women of a Grade A physical standard and, based on the premise that a healthy body mirrored a healthy mind, they did not conduct intelligence tests. In all three of the women's services, there is no evidence to suggest that queer women were being identified and excluded at intake based on masculine characteristics or sartorial style. Indeed it would seem that it was pregnancy rather than lesbianism which concerned the authorities the most.

In the male services, inspections of the body during the Second World War still relied, almost without exception, on the categories that had defined acceptable and unacceptable physiques in the First World War. Each medical board consisted of between three and five doctors who were expected to examine thirty men in two and a half hours.

As the average age of the men increased, the number examined was reduced to twenty-five and later, in May 1942, to twenty-two, to allow the boards to assess the 'nervous stability of each man'.[62] The entire process had to take place in five minutes (six and a half minutes maximum) and was predominantly concerned with outward signs of physical health including weight, height and hearing.

Speed was imperative, as was the recruitment of as many good or improvable bodies as possible. As in the First World War, patriotism on the part of the inspectors also played a part in the work of the boards. Indeed the psychologist J. R. Rees believed that the medical boards possessed the attitude that 'no-one must be allowed to get away with it'.[63]

Figure 4 Ronald Niebour's satirical take on medical testing. Caption: 'That will be about all – now goodbye and good luck to you'.[64]

This is confirmed by Ben Shephard in *A War of Nerves*. Shephard states that many of the doctors on the civilian medical boards were 'elderly, patriotically-minded GPs' who were able to weed out those who displayed obvious signs of dullness or mental defect, but consistent with the 'healthy body, healthy mind' rhetoric, were not averse to passing suspected 'shirkers' and slow recruits who were physically fit or those whose condition might be expected to improve.[65] In this way, only those candidates who displayed extreme cases of disability and dullness were excluded by the medical boards.

Just as the boards negotiated the system, so did those who underwent the tests. It was entirely possible, and common, for men to defy the system of classification by choosing between medical boards or by taking advantage of different interpretations of the rules either to get in or to stay out. Charles Chabbot, for example, passed his medical for the RAF in 1939 despite the absence of one kidney. After he had lied about his missing organ, the doctor saw his scar and passed him regardless.[66] Bribery was also alleged to be a problem; it was claimed that men who sought to avoid service could bribe the medical board before their inspection or pay a medical practitioner to produce a false certificate of exemption or discharge for as little as half a crown.[67] Alternately, an unfit stand-in could be arranged. These episodes undermined the legitimacy of the medical boards even further and led the MP for Westhoughton, Rhys Davies, to question whether the boards were 'functioning properly'.[68] Davies was certain that discharges on medical grounds were far more numerous in the Second World War than they had been between 1914–18 and, moreover, that countless men were being passed as fit and then being immediately discharged.

This inefficiency should come as no surprise, given that the boards were once again attempting to process large numbers of men and women in a painfully short space of time. As during the First World War, gradings were made on the premise that military service would improve the physiques of those less than A1 and that physical health was indicative of mental health. Accordingly, the government believed that the vast majority of Britain's shirkers and feeble-minded men could be remoulded. Questions of effeminacy and degeneracy seemed to play no real part in the considerations of the boards. Such factors were seemingly lost in the face of necessity, the primacy of physical health and an absence of intelligible popular and scientific diagnostic typologies. In the event that queer men and women were identified by the boards, it is likely that most were passed into the services, not least because the boards could only identify archetypal versions of queerness and men who displayed these characteristics were exactly those who would benefit from the no-nonsense diet, discipline and exercise regime that was meted out by the services. Indeed given that queerness was largely conceptualised as a moral failing and a vice, it was not unreasonable of the Army in particular to think that it could 'straighten out' such individuals. Overwhelmingly, however, same-sex desire was a crime that was committed rather as an identity that was possessed. Cutting queer men and women off at the pass was both pre-emptive and virtually impossible.

Reversing the gaze: queer experiences of the medical boards

Away from policy documents and government debates, there is little anecdotal evidence to suggest that sexuality figured in the minds of the doctors employed on the medical boards. In fact, none of the men who were interviewed for *Queen and Country* remembered being questioned about their sexual orientation. Albert Robinson was a grocer's assistant in 1939 and felt that he was unwillingly 'dragged' into the Army. He viewed his medical inspection as an unavoidable part of the mobilisation process.

> I think it was pretty quick. They just, you know, touched you down here and [measured] your height and all this business ... you had to strip ... cough, for hernias and er, [they listened to] your back with the scope thing and that was it ... I suppose you sort of felt embarrassed in a way that you'd got to strip off to, you know, but then it's necessary, isn't it?[69]

It was Albert's embarrassment at being required to strip in front of the medical board, rather than any fear that his sexuality might be discovered, that dominated his recollections of the event. Jimmy Jacques, on the other hand, was rather less embarrassed than Albert. During our interview, Jacques proudly announced his particulars as they were recorded by the doctors who examined him; 'five foot ten, 117 and three quarter pounds, my chest size was 32 and a half inches, I had a fresh complexion ... blue eyes and brown hair'.[70] Jimmy may have been reluctant to join the Army but there was certainly a great deal of pride in having an A1 body. Conversely, Jacques' sexuality was the one thing that the doctors did not attempt to classify.

> ... they didn't even ask, not in my particular case: they didn't ask you if you were queer. You see, it was against the law. You must remember this ... I mean, there were lots of people that were queer in the Army, and in the Navy and in the Air Force as you can imagine and you just kept everything hushed up ... I just acted as you would normally ... with people until you found out who was and who wasn't.[71]

Jimmy's 'normal' performance alludes to a style of self-presentation which was both everyday and 'normal' in the sense that it was aligned both to heteronormative standards of behaviour and the discretion which had become the norm in the interwar period. It was a performance that was no doubt replicated countless times by queer men at medical boards across the country. Francis Kennedy was an aircraft fitter before he was conscripted into the Royal Engineers in 1943. Like many of his generation, Francis was vehemently pacifist and desperate not to be accepted. His attempts to convince the medical board that he had had a heart condition failed and he was passed fit for Army duties. Francis felt that the examiners 'were really only concerned about whether you were fit for soldierly duties … at no time was I ever asked that question [are you a homosexual?] … you just behaved normally'.[72] This was also the case for Richard Briar, who registered for military service when he was eighteen. Barely out of full-time education and 'extremely healthy', he passed his initial medical test 'with flying colours' without any mention of his sexuality.[73]

For all of my respondents, the physical inspection was a rite of a passage rather than a moment where their bodies might betray their sexual preference for other men. Jimmy's A1 body, as yet unmaimed by the demands of the Royal Artillery, was a source of great pride to the young Londoner. Francis was similarly unperturbed by the process. Just like every other recruit, these men were bound not only by moral compulsion (or, in the case of conscription, legal compulsion) but they undoubtedly felt a wide range of emotions; patriotism, excitement, reluctance and genuine fear. Some recruits also felt the stirrings of desire, and experienced a welcome introduction to the potential temptations of service life. Dennis Campbell, then a handsome eighteen-year-old volunteer, remembered his medical test for the RAF in Edinburgh in 1943 not only because of his ticklish feet (and the subsequent kick that the doctor who was examining his reflexes received) but because he was chatted up by a fellow recruit from Doncaster. Dennis shared a drink with the man in the bar of the North British Hotel, after which the pair spent the night together.[74]

Apart from the experiences of my straight-acting interviewees, the reaction of the medical boards to those who performed their queerness overtly through visible gender inversion provides us with further evidence of their inclusionary attitude. Before the war, Terry Gardener had carved out a successful career as a drag artiste and was understandably keen to avoid service, so that he could continue his lucrative career in show business. His friends advised him that he could guarantee his exemption if he behaved as outrageously as possible in front of the medical board. Unfortunately for Terry, and in spite of a deliberate display of effeminacy, he was passed and sent into the Navy as a cook.[75] This seems to suggest that particular medical boards or individual practitioners either did not regard effeminacy as indicative of a queer identity, or that it was not a reason to justify exclusion.[76]

It is also not unreasonable to suggest that the medical boards might have been forewarned about men who might try and avoid military service through displays of effeminacy. Indeed, one recognised tactic of avoiding service was feigning epilepsy; in 1940, Jack Robotka and his brother Samuel unsuccessfully tried to evade service by claiming to suffer from the condition.[77] When it came to overt displays of queerness however, it is unlikely that there was a specific directive which sanctioned the exemption of men and women. Instead, judgements were highly subjective, and driven by the notion that individuals could be straightened out and that 'shirkers' should not be allowed to evade their obligations.[78]

There is only one known example of a recruit being rejected because of an overtly queer performance and that is Quentin Crisp. A self-fashioned bohemian, his audacious self-presentation ran against the fashion for dignified discretion.[79] Despite his determination not to fit in, in April 1940, Crisp heeded legal compulsion. As an able-bodied, technically unemployed man, he dutifully turned up to his appointment with a medical board in Kingston upon Thames, south-west London.

> My appearance was at half-mast. I wore no make-up and my hair was hardly more than hooligan length … [although] still crimson from having been persistently hennaed for seven years and, although my eyebrows were no longer in Indian file, it was obvious that they had been habitually plucked. These and other manifestations disturbed the board deeply. Even while I was merely having my eyes tested, I was told, 'You've dyed your hair. This is a sign of sexual perversion. Do you know what those words mean?' I replied that I did and that I was a homosexual. Within a minute, the entire governing body had gone into a spasm of consternation behind a hessian screen. After a while, a great effort was made by everyone to regain composure and I was passed onto another doctor. He asked me why I dyed my hair … From my hair, interest passed to my anus with which the doctors tampered for some time. Their private dreams of what the lives of homosexuals were like must have been very lurid … one of them asked me if I thought I could walk four miles. I, who had stalked the street for hours, was secretly piqued by this … no amount of humility would now avail. A young man appeared, holding at arm's length … a sheaf of papers which he tore up with a flourish. 'You'll never be wanted', he said and thrust at me a smaller piece of paper. This described me as being incapable of being graded … because I suffered from sexual perversion.[80]

The key component of Crisp's account is that he was rejected after a doctor identified his dyed hair as a 'sign of sexual perversion', a discovery which led to Crisp's open acknowledgement of his sexuality.[81] While this verbal confirmation appeared to surprise the panel, his rejection may be linked to the location of his inspection. Historically, openly effeminate queans had formed a visible part of London's fabric since the late nineteenth century.[82] It is therefore likely that the GPs who worked on boards in London and in the surrounding areas were rather more attuned to queer typologies than their colleagues working outside the capital.

Having demonstrated the absence, even by 1939, of a coherent schema for mapping same-sex on to the body, it is perhaps not surprisingly that from a psychiatric perspective, the story is almost exactly the same. The medical boards that operated between 1939 and 1945 were almost exclusively preoccupied with the identification of men and women susceptible to mental breakdown, and those whom they considered to be 'dull'. While efforts were being made, albeit imperfectly, to identify and exclude those who were mentally unstable and unsuitable for military service, same-sex desire was never explicitly mentioned in any of the literature that refers to psychiatric testing during the conflict. The only evidence of psychiatric intervention is anecdotal. 'Neil', interviewed by Hugh David for *On Queer Street*, was determined to get into the forces. At his medical, he was seen by a psychiatrist who asked him whether he was queer. 'I just looked shocked and said, "No!"'[83] There is no evidence from official archival sources to suggest that this line of questioning was pursued with any consistency by psychiatrists or doctors, either as a measured response to an outward sign of queerness or as part of a formalised scheme of questioning. In this sense, any attempts to exclude queer men and women at their medicals would most likely have been snap judgements, based on hunches or prejudices about 'misfits' or those who were considered to be 'odd' or irredeemably unsuitable. Moreover, while the civilian medical boards were issued with a memo on diagnosing psychotics, it is unlikely that same-sex desire was classified as a psychotic disorder.[84] Some doctors may even have subscribed to the view that queer men were attracted to the armed forces and made effective soldiers. In 1915 for instance Ernest Jones highlighted the role of sexual desire in prompting men to enlist, citing their attraction to 'fascinating ... horrors' and 'the homosexual desire to be in close relation with masses of men'.[85] Charles Berg followed a similar line in an article written in 1942 in which he briefly conjectured whether the act of war represented the expression of unconscious fantasies and an emotional 'homosexual substitution'.[86] The most detailed exploration of the issue came from R. E. Money-Kyrle. In 1937 the psychiatrist delivered a paper to the Oxford Anthropological Society which highlighted the effects of 'unconscious homosexuality' on soldiering, specifically for 'unconscious inverts', that is men who denied their attraction to other men despite it being obvious to the observer. Of these some internalised their aggression and were able to display a self-sacrificial devotion to their fellow men, while others, who externalised their aggression, were useful soldiers because they could be moulded into effective killers.[87] While it is unlikely that these musings were considered by the medical boards, their radical suggestion, that queer men stood at the pinnacle of martial suitability, questioned what would become an almost axiomatic relationship between queerness and national service.

Conclusion

Following the end of the First World War, the government attempted to rationalise the process of medical testing in order to prevent a repeat of the huge post-war pensions bill. However, the exigencies of the Second World War, and in particular the pace at which the recruitment process was forced through, yet again facilitated the entrance of thousands of physically and mentally defective recruits into the services. All three elements of the entrance test were unsystematic and unreliable. In this sense, if it was possible for physically impaired men to be classed as A1 despite evidence to the contrary, and for 'dullards' to enter the forces in numbers, it was clearly possible for men and women who desired members of the same sex to negotiate their own recruitment. In terms of their testing and subsequent recruitment, it is unlikely that many men and women were rejected, except in manifestly obvious cases, and even then, exclusion was unsystematic. Even those who displayed deliberate gender inversion were often accepted, suggestive of a lack of consensus, staff ignorance or uninterest, a certain degree of leniency and a determination not to let shirkers escape their obligations.

By the 1940s, queer identity had evolved into a diverse set of presentations and styles. However, popular markers of same-sex attraction were limited to two specific typologies; the effeminate quean and the masculine woman. Even if the medical boards had identified these candidates, it is highly unlikely that they would have been prevented from entering the armed forces. When faced with those who performed outside these typologies, the medical boards were powerless to identify and exclude them. Nor might they have chosen to, given the desperate need for manpower. Overwhelmingly, the boards and the War Office were forced to address the recruitment of mass bodies – and their multiple manifestations and expressions – with pragmatism.

In terms of my interviewees, the performances that they delivered were extensions of their own discreet behaviour which in part, stemmed from the gradual decline of overt sexual presentation. Thus, when Jimmy Jacques stated that he 'acted as you [would] normally', he was implying that his performance was normal based on his own standards of behaviour and the discretion that had become the norm.[88] Like countless other men and women who volunteered or responded to the government's legal compulsion, Jacques joined the Army to fight for his country. There is little evidence to suggest that an overt display of sexuality would have presented a challenge to that service.

Notes

1 Jimmy Jacques, interviewed by Emma Vickers, 21 July 2005.
2 A. Salusbury MacNalty, *The Civilian Health and Medical Services*, 1, *The Ministry of Health Services; Other Civilian Health Services and Medical Services* (London: HMSO, 1953), p. 358.
3 Jimmy Jacques, interviewed by Emma Vickers, 21 July 2005.
4 See V. Heggie, 'Lies, damn lies, and Manchester's recruiting statistics: degeneration as an "urban legend" in Victorian and Edwardian Britain', *Journal of the History of Medicine and Allied Sciences* 63 (2008) pp. 178–216, and Z. Bargielowska, *Managing the Body: Beauty, Health and Fitness in Britain, 1880–1939* (Oxford: Oxford University Press, 2010), pp. 62–104. See also R. Soloway, 'Counting the degenerates: the statistics of race degeneration in Edwardian England', *Journal of Contemporary History*, 17:1 (1982), pp. 137–64.
5 Thomas Arnold, the head of Rugby School, quoted in G. J. DeGroot, *Blighty: British Society in the Era of the Great War* (London: Longman, 1996), p. 32.
6 Bargielowska, *Managing the Body*, p. 87.
7 'The problem of the Army', *The Times* (24 February 1903), p. 6.
8 G. L. Mosse, *The Image of Man* (Oxford: Oxford University Press, 1996), p. 78.
9 Mosse, *The Image of Man*, pp. 83, 86–106.
10 C. Waters, 'Sexology', in H. G. Cocks and M. Houlbrook (eds), *The Modern History of Sexuality* (London: Palgrave, 2006), p. 45.
11 See D. Rapp, 'The early discovery of Freud by the British general public', *Social History of Medicine*, 3:2 (1990), pp. 217–43, and Waters, 'Havelock Ellis, Sigmund Freud and the State'.
12 Alan Sinfield argues that the publicity which surrounded Wilde's case constructed the writer as a visible countertype and helped to forge an association between effeminacy, flamboyancy and homosexuality. 'At that point the entire, vaguely disconcerting nexus of effeminacy, leisure, idleness, immorality, luxury, insouciance, decadence

and aestheticism, which Wilde was perceived variously as instantiating, was transformed into a brilliantly precise image': A. Sinfield, *The Wilde Century: Effeminacy, Oscar Wilde and the Queer Moment* (London: Cassell, 1994), p. 3. However, as precise as this image may have been, it nevertheless lacked a sense of cultural coherence. Indeed the clarion call of queerness so often attributed to Wilde failed to resonate loudly and widely in the public domain in the same way that later cases in the 1930s, such as the Holland Park raid of 1932, for instance, did.

13 Mosse, *The Image of Man*, p. 110.
14 DeGroot, *Blighty*, p. 43.
15 I. R. Bet-el, *Conscripts: Lost Legions of the Great War* (Stroud Sutton, 1999), p. 2.
16 J. M. Winter, 'Military fitness and civilian health in Britain during the First World War', *Journal of Contemporary History*, 15:2 (1980), p. 222.
17 Winter, 'Military fitness and civilian health', p. 218.
18 Under the 1917 Review of Exemptions Act, thousands more men from the farms, factories and mines were examined and reclassified for a second time in order to restock the Army. Hansard Parliamentary Debates, House of Commons, vol. 92, cols 1485, 5 April 1917.
19 Winter, 'Military fitness and civilian health', p. 218.
20 R. Roberts, *The Classic Slum: Salford Life in the First Quarter of the Century* (Harmondsworth: Penguin, 1973), p. 189.
21 Lloyd George, quoted in 'The war and after', *The Times* (13 September 1919), p. 7.
22 J. Stevenson, *British Society 1914–45* (London: Allen Lane, 1984), pp. 203–4. See also S. Constantine, *Social Conditions in Britain 1918–1939* (London: Methuen, 1983).
23 Salusbury MacNalty and Mellor (eds), *Medical Services in War*, p. 18. See also *Report of the War Office Committee of Enquiry into 'Shell Shock'* (London: HMSO, 1922).
24 D. French, 'Discipline and the death penalty in the British Army in the war against Germany during the First World War', *Journal of Contemporary History*, 33:4 (1998), pp. 531–45.
25 R. H. Ahrenfeldt, *Psychiatry in the British Army in the Second World War* (London: Routledge and Kegan Paul, 1958), p. 10.
26 B. Shephard, '"Pitiless psychology": the role of prevention in British military psychiatry in the Second World War', *History of Psychiatry*, 10:40 (1999), p. 520.
27 Shephard, '"Pitiless psychology"', p. 503.
28 Shephard, '"Pitiless psychology"', p. 510.
29 TNA, LAB 6/144, Scheme for eliminating recruits with latent disabilities from being examined by medical boards 1939–53, 'Neuroses in wartime', 15 December 1939.
30 H. J. C. J. L'Etang, 'A criticism of military psychiatry in the Second World War', part 3, *Journal of the Royal Army Medical Corps*, 97 (1951), p. 320.
31 Shephard, '"Pitiless psychology"', p. 510.
32 C. Waters in Cocks and Houlbrook (eds.) *The Modern History of Sexuality*, p. 173, and McLaren, *The Trials of Masculinity*, p. 220.
33 East and de Hubert, *Report on the Psychological Treatment of Crime*, pp. 21, 84–7.
34 Frank Bolton, interviewed by Emma Vickers, 19 June 2006. See also A. Bingham, *Family Newspapers? Sex, Private Life, and the British Popular Press 1918–1978* (Oxford: Oxford University Press, 2009), pp. 173–80.

35 A. Ferrier, 'Some seafaring gentlemen may be particular', *Sunday Pictorial* (17 February 1929), p. 11. © British Library Board.
36 W. K. Haselden, 'Our beautiful women athletes', *Daily Mirror* (9 June 1926). © British Library Board.
37 Houlbrook, *Queer London*, p. 164. See also R. Hornsey, *The Spiv and the Architect: Unruly Life in Postwar London* (Minneapolis: Minnesota University Press, 2010) pp. 7–10.
38 M. Houlbrook, '"Lady Austin's camp boys": constituting the queer subject in 1930s London', *Gender and History*, 14:1 (2002), p. 31.
39 Houlbrook, '"Lady Austin's camp boys"', p. 31.
40 Houlbrook, '"Lady Austin's camp boys"', p. 50.
41 Houlbrook, '"Lady Austin's camp boys"', p. 50.
42 N. Haire, *Encyclopaedia of Sexual Knowledge* (London: London Encyclopaedic Press, 1934), p. 391.
43 M. Stopes, *Enduring Passion* (New York: Blue Ribbon, 1931 [original London: Hogarth Press, 1923]), p. 38.
44 L. Doan, *Fashioning Sapphism: The Origins of a Modern English Lesbian Culture* (New York: Columbia University Press, 2001), p. 14.
45 J. Vernon, 'For some queer reason: the trials and tribulations of Colonel Barker's masquerade in interwar Britain', *Signs: The Journal of Women in Culture and Society*, 26:1 (2000), p. 47, A. Oram and A. Turnbull (eds), *The Lesbian History Sourcebook: Love and Sex between Women in Britain 1780–1970* (London: Routledge, 2001), pp. 11–49, A. Oram, *Her Husband Was a Woman! Women's Gender-Crossing in Modern British Popular Culture* (London: Routledge, 2007), and J. Wheelwright, *Amazons and Military Maids: Women Who Dressed as Men in the Pursuit of Life, Liberty and Happiness* (London: Pandora, 1989).
46 Q. Crisp, *The Naked Civil Servant* (London: Fontana, 1977), p. 27.
47 Radclyffe Hall and Una Troubridge, 1927. © Getty/Hutton.
48 See D. Cohler, *Citizen, Invert, Queer: Lesbianism and War in Early Twentieth-Century Britain* (London: Minnesota University Press, 2010).
49 *It's Not Unusual*, Wall to Wall Productions, BBC 2, 1997, episode 1.
50 Since gender is socially constructed and performative, it is appropriate to refer to Barker as 'he' rather than 'she'.
51 'Colonel Barker in the dock at the Old Bailey', *Daily Herald* (25 April 1929). See also Wheelwright, *Amazons and Military Maids*, pp. 1–6.
52 Vernon, 'For some queer reason', pp. 37–62.
53 Oram, *Her Husband Was a Woman!*, p. 155.
54 Anecdotal evidence seems to corroborate this. One member of the ATS was said to have written on a postcard to her mother asking her: 'What are lesbians? We've got two of them here.' Her mother's reply is a telling example of the pervasive invisibility of lesbianism in the public domain. She wrote back with the words: 'I've asked Daddy and he has explained it to me. We will discuss it with you next time you come home.' (IWM DD 01/19/1, E. McNelie, p. 2).
55 TNA, CAB 57/16, Code of instructions for civilian medical boards, 1937–38, Committee of Imperial Defence, Manpower Sub-Committee, Medical Code Sub-Committee, Minutes of the Thirteenth Meeting of the Sub-Committee, 10 March 1938, p. 2.

56 *Hansard Parliamentary Debates*, House of Commons, vol. 376, cols 1027–30, 2 December 1941.
57 C. M. Peniston-Bird, 'Classifying the body in the Second World War: British men in and out of uniform', *Body and Society*, 9:4 (2003), p. 35.
58 Peniston-Bird, 'Classifying the body in the Second World War', p. 35.
59 E. Ginzburg, quoted in Salusbury MacNalty and Mellor, *Medical Services in War*, p. 183.
60 Salusbury MacNalty, *The Civilian Health and Medical Services*, p. 348.
61 Air Ministry, *The Women's Auxiliary Air Force* (London: The Air Ministry, 1953), p. 38.
62 Salusbury MacNalty, *The Civilian Health and Medical Services*, p. 351.
63 J. R. Rees, quoted in Ahrenfeldt, *Psychiatry in the British Army*, p. 32. This was also the case in America. An anonymous doctor wrote to *The Lancet* in 1941 rebuking the 'misguided patriots among examining doctors who can't see why "a bad hat should get away with it"'. See 'Mental Fitness of U.S Recruits', *The Lancet*, 1941:2, pp. 103–4.
64 R. Niebour, 'That will be about all – now goodbye and good luck to you.' *Daily Mail* (26 May 1941). © Solo Syndication.
65 B. Shephard, *A War of Nerves: Soldiers and Psychiatrists 1914–1994* (London: Pimlico, 2002), p. 187.
66 IWM Sound Archive (hereafter IWM SA), 8/14, C. Chabbot.
67 *Hansard Parliamentary Debates*, House of Commons, vol. 376, cols 1235, 4 December 1941, and vol. 385, cols 1558–60, 9 December 1942. See also Juliet Gardiner, *Wartime: Britain 1939–1945* (London: Review, 2005), pp. 592–3.
68 *Hansard Parliamentary Debates*, House of Commons, vol. 377, cols 1369, 10 February 1942.
69 Albert Robinson, interviewed by Emma Vickers, 5 October 2005.
70 Jimmy Jacques, interviewed by Emma Vickers, 21 July 2005.
71 Jimmy Jacques, interviewed by Emma Vickers, 21 July 2005.
72 Francis Kennedy, interviewed by Emma Vickers, 5 December 2005.
73 Richard Briar, interviewed by Emma Vickers, 9 November 2005.
74 Dennis Campbell, interviewed by Emma Vickers, 22 November 2005.
75 Jivani, *It's Not Unusual*, p. 62.
76 In the RAF, ground trades such as accounting, catering and secretarial work were assumed to attract a higher proportion of queer men. Indeed, the Air Ministry investigated both RAF Lytham and RAF Cranwell in the 1950s for evidence of same-sex activity. Officials focused their investigations on the ground trades and, in particular, nursing orderlies. TNA, AIR 2/10673, RAF and WRAF, homosexual offences and abnormal sexual tendencies 1950–68, minutes from A/D.G.M.So, 2 August 1955.
77 See TNA, MEPO 3/1147, Private Jack Robotka alias Robotkin: alleged epileptic: with brother Samuel conspiring to evade military service or secure discharge on medical grounds, 1940.
78 For an example of the way in which homosexuality was invoked as an avoidance tactic in America, see S. Terkel, *'The Good War': An Oral History of World War Two* (London: Hamilton, 1985), p. 167.
79 Jimmy Jacques remembered crossing the road whenever he saw Crisp approach-

ing. Jimmy Jacques, interviewed by Emma Vickers, 21 July 2005. See also 'John' in J. Weeks and K. Porter (eds), *Between the Acts: Lives of Homosexual Men, 1885–1967* (London: Rivers Oram, 1998), p. 176.

80   Crisp, *The Naked Civil Servant*, pp. 115–6. See also A. Barrow, *Quentin and Phillip* (London: Macmillan, 2002), p. 135.
81   Sex differentiation has been linked to hair length for at least a century. Field Marshal Lord Wolseley famously proclaimed that 'longish hair ... is the glory of a woman but the shame of a man'. See N. F. Dixon, *On the Psychology of Military Incompetence* (London: Futura, 1976), p. 208.
82   Personal testimony suggests that queans were widely accepted in the East End. See John's account in Weeks and Porter (eds), *Between the Acts*, p. 176. Frank Brown, who served in the RAF, also believed this to be the case and recalled one occasion when his father wolf-whistled at a quean as he passed them on the street.
83   Interview with 'Neil' in H. David, *On Queer Street: A Social History of British Homosexuality 1895–1995* (London: Harper Collins, 1997), p. 142.
84   The only document which might contain some reference to queer men was circulated to the Ministry of National Labour and National Service and produced by the Medical Advisory Committee. The document is called 'Memorandum for Civilian Medical Boards on the Detection of Psychopaths'. Despite an extensive search, I have been unable to find it.
85   E. Jones, 'War and individual psychology', in *Sociological Review*, 8:3 (1915), p. 177.
86   C. Berg, 'Clinical notes on the analysis of war neurosis', *British Journal of Medical Psychology*, 19:2 (1942), p. 185.
87   R. E. Money-Kyrle, 'The development of war: a psychological approach', *British Journal of Medical Psychology*, 16:3 (1937), p. 235.
88   Jimmy Jacques, interviewed by Emma Vickers, 21 July 2005. See also Houlbrook, *Queer London*, pp. 162–6, and Hornsey, *The Spiv and the Architect*, pp. 7–10.

2

Keeping up appearances

In 1944, John Brierly, then a twenty-two-year-old engineer from Sheffield, joined the Royal Signal Corps. Most of John's peers had joined the armed forces in their late teens but a period of reserved service in the armaments industry temporarily put paid to John's desire to do the same. In 1944, John's father allowed him to choose between the continued safety of his reserved occupation or a period of service in the Army. John chose the latter. His story begins at Catterick, a busy training camp where he quickly discovered that his survival as a queer man was dependent on fitting in with his peers. While they were busy pasting pictures of scantily clad women on the inside of their lockers, John's preference for cars and men could not be telegraphed quite so overtly. By way of a compromise, he found a picture of a car that he liked with a woman draped over the bonnet. It was a ruse that he would maintain until his demobilisation in 1947.[1]

John's quest to fit in is a familiar story. In training units across the country, men and women who desired members of the same sex invoked a whole range of passing strategies and disguised their desires in the name of group cohesion. This chapter will explore the mechanics of this masking or passing, asking specifically how personnel lived, loved and survived in an institution that was deeply heteronormative. It is a story not only of regulation but also of ingenuity, opportunity and endurance.

From civvies to service personnel: Primary Training Units

Once inside the inner sanctum of the armed forces, recruits were hurled into an alien world characterised by absolute control. Military efficiency depended on reducing the individuality of each recruit, instilling obedience to military authority and ensuring that each recruit formed part of a bonded team. This process is most evident in the Primary Training Units

(PTUs) where men and women received their initial instruction. It was at their PTUs that recruits were forced to fit into military routine and regulation, a process which demanded varying degrees of physical and emotional adjustment. The first adjustment involved substituting the ties of family, Church and community, the conventional bastions of social order, with a new, hybrid form of family created by and within the confines of the military establishment.[2] At the head of each wartime family was the officer. Their obligation was to lead their recruits and maintain the twin bastions of morale and discipline.

Training usually lasted for around six weeks, during which time recruits were indoctrinated into their service and their unit through a crash course in military etiquette and regulation. It was a structured, monitored existence founded on complete and absolute adherence to military commands and regulations. Before the outbreak of war, Jimmy Jacques had worked as a projectionist for the British Picture Corporation. He was conscripted into the Army and joined the 82nd Field Regiment Royal Artillery. As he commented, 'You're in the Army … All your own personality … is finished. All you have to do is what they say you have to do and that's all there is to it.'[3] Every facet of life was monitored, including bedtimes, exercise, ablutions, meals and periods of leisure. There was no place for individualism, privacy or prudery. The intensity and initial strangeness of this new, heavily regulated life was difficult for many to cope with. John Booker was conscripted into the Army and served in the Royal Signals as a translator, eventually becoming a captain. When he was asked to describe his feelings on hearing that he was to serve in the Army, Booker recalled feeling 'absolute dread, horror. I was scared stiff. [It was] a completely alien, macho, brutal life that I had no experience of'.[4] Names became secondary to service numbers and bodies were inoculated, kitted out and rid of all individuality. In the weeks that followed, recruits were taught how to wash, dress, make their beds and tidy their living quarters, clean and polish, perform menial labour, march and parade, exercise and behave appropriately towards NCOs and commissioned officers. Training was deliberately designed to toughen up new recruits and test their nerves. Len Waller began his Army training in 1940, a process seemingly devoid of humanity. 'Every day we were marched and yelled at up and down the barrack square. We were cursed, humiliated, degraded and worked until we were fit to drop. At the end of each day's training we were allowed to relax by sitting astride our beds polishing and burnishing a bewildering array of equipment.'[5]

To survive, new recruits had to acclimatise quickly, which meant getting used to new living conditions and heeding the rules, however inane they appeared to be. John Brierly served in the Royal Signals as a telecommunications mechanic. He described his PTU camp at Catterick as 'damp and dark. We were put into huts that had been condemned in the First World War. They had minimum sanitation and no heating and there was lots of military bullshit'.[6] Banality was the staple diet of the lower-ranking soldier and servicewoman. Each and every order had to be obeyed, including what Brierly and the rest of the services understood as 'bullshit'; the polishing, sweeping, folding, parading and drilling that characterised life at training camp.[7]

Such apparently mindless tasks were meant to teach the recruits how to follow orders instinctively and maintain morale through personal smartness. However, they were initially widely resented. In the eyes of other ranks, they had no higher purpose than satisfying the petty demands of overzealous officers.[8] Unclean bedclothes, eating utensils or uniforms were chargeable offences, as were missing kit, and dull buttons and toecaps. During initial training, recruits could expect inspections on a daily basis. These were undoubtedly a group effort; one person's dirty sheets could result in the entire barrack hut being punished. In such endeavours friends could usually be relied upon to help to replace lost kit, burnish a set of buttons, or remove a stain.[9]

Survival was undoubtedly a group effort; no sooner had new recruits arrived than they began the process of buddying up. The relationships that were subsequently formed played an exceptionally important function in assuaging anxiety, grief and doubt and facilitating group cohesion and morale. In this bonding process, patriotism and the willingness to make sacrifices for the good of the nation were usually secondary considerations. What mattered, and what encouraged men and women to work and fight on a daily basis, was family; not simply biological family but also 'service kin'. These relationships were absolutely fundamental to the achievement of cohesion and the maintenance of morale. Recruits inevitably came to rely upon each other, a reliance which was often much deeper than any relationship formed in peacetime, because hardships were shared and the war imbued life with a transient, almost ephemeral quality. On a day-to-day basis, there was no guarantee that friends would be seen again. Death was not the only separator; postings, commissions and training courses were more frequent and could fracture the stability of a unit.[10]

In the absence of family units, men and women bonded together in same-sex groupings or 'families' which were cemented by comradeship and characterised by a deep sense of loyalty, trust and commitment. As Joanna Bourke states, 'Love for one's comrades was widely regarded as the strongest incentive for murderous aggression against a foe identified as threatening that relationship.'[11] One of the most evocative descriptions of this relationship is offered by George MacDonald Frazer, a soldier who fought in Burma during the last years of the Second World War.

> It was the section that mattered to the private soldier. It was his military family; those seven or eight other men were his constant companions, walking, sleeping, standing guard, eating, digging, patrolling, marching, and fighting. And he got to know them better, perhaps, than anyone in his whole life except his wife, parents and children. He counted on them, and they on him.[12]

In the women's services too, friendships between women were actively encouraged as 'an essential part of a well-balanced and happy life'.[13] These reciprocal, altruistic relationships motivated men and women to carry out their duties. They also made service life and in particular the rigours of active service 'more tolerable'.[14] In some instances, bonds between recruits did not merely make life tolerable but actually helped to preserve and sustain it. Take for instance the 'buddy' or 'oppo' system in the Navy (which will also be discussed later on) whereby new recruits would be allocated to two colleagues, specifically a more senior colleague for guidance and a recruit similar in age. A less formal system of 'buddying up' operated in the Army, the RAF and the women services. Each person's buddy was responsible for ensuring the health, well-being and survival of their opposite number. In short, they provided an emotional connection, thereby facilitating a sense of loyalty in what was otherwise an impersonal, monolithic force.

Life was also sustained, both in a physical and a psychological sense, by everyday routines such as washing, cooking and eating. It was usual for recruits to wash alongside each other, take baths together and sometimes sleep together. (See Figure 5.) These activities provided residual traces of a ritual domesticity which had typified 'normality' before the war and helped to cement group identity and cohesion and maintain health and morale.[15]

Len Waller for instance, described how he and eleven of his friends slept together in the middle of their billet, 'huddling and cuddling together' to keep out the cold.[16] Similarly, R. H. Lloyd-Jones described two men in his barrack hut who shared the same bed. 'Nobody commented on this or made any criticism … they were both of a pleasant type and their behaviour was perfectly proper.'[17] In this instance, the men's fondness for sharing the same bed was accepted because it fell within the parameters of

Figure 5 Sailors of HMS *Duke of York* relax in a canvas bath, date unknown.[18]

a homosocial friendship. This gave them a licence to engage in what was viewed as little more than an extension of camaraderie.

Intimacies like these are discussed by Santanu Das in the context of the First World War trench literature. In order to understand the range of homosocial interaction that occurred during the Great War, Das calls for 'a different and less distinctly sexualized array of emotional intensities and bodily sensations, a continuum of non-genital tactile tenderness that goes beyond strict gender divisions, sexual binaries, or identity politics'.[19] It is exactly this kind of approach which is necessary if we are to understand the complex interactions that occurred between men and between women during the Second World War. It is an approach which avoids the sexualisation of same-sex interaction but can also accept the presence of sexual intent.

In this sense, attempting to understand this spectrum of homosocial expression is not a simple task. As we have seen, intimacy and homosociability were fundamental canons of the institution. In fact, non-sexual same-sex intimacies formed part of the very fabric of service life. Between men, ritualistic patterns of affection and recognition such as patting, punching and fighting served an important function within the services. Likewise, less aggressive forms of affection between women such as hugging and hand-holding were overwhelmingly accepted.

An inherently fascinating feature of the armed forces, then, is the close proximity between homosociability and same-sex desire.[20] Frank Bolton, a former meteorologist in the RAF, remembered wrestling with a comrade who would often become aroused.[21] He went on to describe his feelings about serving in an all-male environment. 'Let's face it. You're queer and you're surrounded by men. I was living in a man's world and I was queer and you can't ask for much more than that'.[22] Bolton flourished in the all-male environment of the RAF precisely because it allowed him to determine the boundaries of his own desire. This was also the case for Sarah Allen who described the onset of war as a 'Godsend' because it meant that she could escape her home and a stifling network of boyfriends in whom she had very little interest. While serving in the ATS, Allen discovered that her unit contained a small contingent of queer women. While serving alongside these women, Allen would experience her first physical relationship with a woman.[23]

The war therefore had a profound effect on the lives of those who desired members of the same sex. It facilitated migration from home and provided a previously unavailable opportunity for social mixing with other like-minded people. John Alcock recalled that the first twenty-four hours of his life in the Army were 'terrible'. On meeting his first queer friend, however, life became 'plain sailing. We'd go to pubs together and … camp it up'.[24] Likewise Vick Robson joined the WAAF when she was nineteen. After serving at Long Benton, a barrage balloon station, she decided to train as an electrician and was sent to Ullsworth. 'I got in with some girls stationed there, and they said "Are you like us?" So it started off again and I thought "Oh, I'm back on Cloud Nine again."'[25]

In addition to social mixing, the war also allowed a generation of young men and women the chance to explore their desires in an environment that was wholly dependent on physical intimacy and close, interpersonal relationships. Richard Briar, a lance corporal in the Ordnance Field Park, was already conscious of his attraction to other men before he entered the Army, but he maintained that his service in the Army was an education both sexually and socially because he was able to mix with a greater range of men and experience a higher frequency of sexual activity than he would have done in his pre-war life. Likewise, the services offered something of a boon to queer women. As Emily Hamer points out, lesbians were attracted to the idea of uniformed service because it sanctioned 'lack of femininity, encouraged them not to marry and allowed them to live in a women-only environment'.[26] Although it is impossible to quantify just how many queer women entered into the services, they were certainly not an insignificant presence. One heterosexual veteran, Edith Newman, who served as an ammunition officer in the Army, recalled feeling 'horrified' at the 'enormous amount' of lesbianism that she encountered during her service in the ATS.[27]

For many then, the war represented a moment of freedom; familial constraint was temporarily ruptured and the ephemeral, transient nature of service life prompted experimentation, self-discovery and opportunity. Men like Richard discovered that life in the services provided a fertile environment for exploring the contours of homosociability in an institution which relied upon physical and emotional interdependence. In this sense, the armed forces and the contexts that were created by the special conditions of service life were exceptionally conducive to same-sex expression and identity.

Homosex

Despite the staunch regulations against sexual acts between servicemen (or, in the case of women, moral distaste), sexual contact between personnel formed a distinct subculture in the armed forces. The most useful way of understanding this activity is through John Howard's concept of homosex, a term which designates same-sex sexual activity which makes no assumption about the sexuality of its participants. In the male branches of the services, perhaps the most frequent and widely accepted manifestation of homosex was mutual masturbation. Such activity was overwhelmingly viewed as a harmless source of sexual relief which was simply more satisfying than solo masturbation because the pleasure was controlled and directed by somebody else's hand. In reference to the Navy, John Beardmore, a queer former sub lieutenant, recalled: 'Sailors were a fairly randy lot and masturbation was not at all uncommon. You could go down in the middle watch which was twelve midnight to four and hear a whisper come from a hammock, someone saying "Give us a wank", which was just completely accepted by the lower deck ratings'.[28] On the lower deck, the act of masturbating a fellow sailor was known colloquially in naval slang as a 'flip', a term which suggests that it was an activity that was both understood and fairly commonplace.[29] In the Army and the RAF too, mutual masturbation was often viewed by officers and other ranks as a legitimate response to the absence of women and the need for safe sexual relief.

There can be little doubt that some of the organisational practices that gave shape to the three forces actually worked to facilitate homosex. In the Army and the RAF the system of employing young boys as batmen who acted as orderlies for their officers was sometimes rooted in sex. Indeed, it was not unknown for batmen to engage in homosex with their superiors. Both Richard Briar, who served in the Army, and Dennis Campbell, a former flight engineer in the RAF, described the relationships between officers and their batmen as part and parcel of the system.[30] Likewise, in his history of queer Britain, Alkarim Jivani claims that sexual relationships were 'enshrined in the structure of the Navy' through the 'wingers and oppos' system.[31] 'Wingers' were senior men who were assigned to mentor new recruits, whereas 'oppos' were seamen of a similar age and rank to recruits who were expected to guide them. 'Wingers' sometimes took advantage of this hierarchical, paternalistic relationship (and arguably, the vulnerability of their new crewmates) and conducted sexual relationships with their matelots. John Beardmore joined the Navy as a teenager and almost immediately became a target for young married officers who wanted to become his 'winger'. Beardmore also spoke of 'oppos' who conducted affairs with one another and later went on 'to become godfathers to each other's children'.[32] While there is no evidence to suggest that such relationships were sufficiently frequent to justify Jivani's assertion, it is obvious that senior men were well placed if they chose to become involved with their juniors and that the 'winger' system could be conducive to such activity. Moreover, the segregation and loneliness which accompanied life at sea could, in Beardmore's opinion, '[bring] on a certain degree of need for love and the expression of that love'.[33]

Some of the most common sexual transactions occurred between servicemen and their queer comrades. Before the onset of war, homosex between working-class, 'normal' men and their queer middle-class patrons was widespread.[34] As Houlbrook points out, the 'normal' men who engaged in these encounters did not conceptualise themselves as abnormal or in any way queer; the difficulty of finding a female sexual partner meant that their encounters represented a practical alternative to female company.[35] Accordingly, these exchanges were organised and constrained in order to counter any accusations of queerness. Commonly, this involved the unwillingness of heterosexual men to play a passive sexual role, since this would imply effeminacy and therefore queerness. Active, penetrative sex, on the other hand, involved the domination and penetration of a passive party, a role that reinforced rather than undermined masculinity.

While Houlbrook dedicates little attention to the practice and significance of homosex between 1939 and 1945, there is ample evidence to suggest that it continued, legitimated to a certain extent by wartime deprivation. As Frank Bolton observed, 'It [homosex] went on between friends. There were lots of ... liaisons between people who were not naturally gay. They [officers] turned a blind eye because they knew it helped people who would never dream of leaving their wives.'[36] Of all the men interviewed for *Queen and Country*, Richard Briar spoke with the most candour about the motivations of his sexual partners, all of whom defined themselves as heterosexual. During his service in the Army, Richard had several relationships with older and more senior-ranked men which began as soon as he arrived at his training unit. Almost immediately, Richard was singled out by a senior heterosexual sergeant, along with half a dozen other men who, it was thought, would make suitable partners for senior Army staff back at base:

> My sergeant walked me along the platform to the ticket barrier. We were collected together and taken out to outside of the station where an Army lorry was waiting, and what I remember was that my sergeant had developed his manoeuvre on me to the point that he was with me when we were boarding the lorry and he very kindly helped me, very unnecessarily, over the tailboard. He was very attentive and that meant that we were side by side when we were loaded into the back of this three tonne Army truck and driven the short distance to the park where the battalion was in camp. During the drive, I found that the jolting of the lorry was inclined to throw us together and at first I innocently assumed that it was accidental, but then I discovered that body contact was being made even when the movement of the lorry didn't require it. We were going through the blackout and so there was no possible observation of what was going on and the explicit sexual manoeuvre on me was made during that journey ... They had really got this absolutely worked out.[37]

Despite the predatory nature of the incident, Richard described it not in terms of sexual harassment but as a pleasurable and erotically charged inauguration into the sexual subculture of his unit. He maintained that he was picked off the train by the senior man based on attractiveness and the possibility that he would be a suitable sexual partner rather than because he exuded any indications, sartorial or otherwise, of queerness. He was chosen along with a few other men to be used as what Richard termed a 'receptacle'. The sergeant 'didn't view me any differently from a girl … the only women available to him were whores … and the clincher was that they had to be paid'.[38] It was a 'practical and pragmatic routine' that was replicated each time a new batch of recruits arrived at the unit.[39] Likely-looking men were picked out and senior officers, keen to avoid jeopardising their position, would send lesser-ranked friends to proposition potential sexual partners on their behalf. Partners would then be 'passed on' and shared between friends. During his time at the training battalion Briar was 'passed on' to two separate senior men, both of whom were married and preferred to have sex with other men because of the expense of local prostitutes and the threat of venereal disease. As Richard went on to say:

> Sexual activity between instructors and recruits was preferable to the heterosexual alternative which was available to them which was women who were whores and carried the increased risk of disease and also cost money. Looking back, I feel absolutely certain that various people in authority must have known what was going on and just chose to let it continue because, for their own reasons, they found it convenient and, after all, as they know from prisons, sexually satisfied men are easier to manage than sexually frustrated ones and that is a strong argument in favour of tacitly ignoring that it is happening.[40]

The deprivations created by the war legitimated this kind of sexual activity because, according to Briar and others, the absence of disease-free women and subsequent feelings of frustration needed to be overcome. Such liaisons were sometimes ignored by the authorities because they were deemed to be harmless activities, devoid of emotion and therefore not indicative of queer identity. This logic, which allowed otherwise heterosexual men to engage in homosex, was ruled by the same unspoken conventions which had governed activity between queer men and heterosexuals before the war, namely that the heterosexual participant had to be the 'top' or active penetrator and moreover that sexual acts were simply that – acts. As Richard Briar explained, there was little space for kissing or expressions of love during these liaisons because they would have imbued the sexual act with emotional meaning, thereby questioning the heterosexuality of the active partner.

Charles Pether, a low-ranking airman in the RAF, discovered just how fragile and transient these exchanges could be. During the war, Pether had experienced regular physical contact with his comrades, usually in the form of kisses and embraces. Upon bumping into one of his most needy partners on a train after the war, Pether recalled that the man 'couldn't get out of that compartment quick enough'.[41] Seemingly, once the war was over, these interactions were so taboo that they could not even be mentioned. This absence (or at least the fragility) of emotional attachment was also described by Dennis Campbell, a former flight engineer in the RAF, who recalled having sex with married men as an uncomplicated sexual transaction. Some of the men with whom Campbell had sex.

> [s]imply wanted their rocks off ... they had sexual feelings to satisfy ... In many places there was not a woman about. What did you do? Stations were usually in isolated places where you did not have access to a brothel or to a nearby city. There were no women available and you're growing up and you're feeling quite randy and quite horny and you need sexual relief and in many cases it was sexual relief rather than actual gayness.[42]

When asked if he ever felt that he was being taken advantage of by heterosexual men who initiated sexual contact purportedly out of desperation, Dennis Campbell replied: 'I wouldn't have minded being taken advantage of ... I don't think I ever was. I was quite happy. I didn't accept every offer that came my way'.[43] Similarly, Dennis Prattley, a rating in the Navy, did not frame his role as a sexual surrogate to his heterosexual comrades in terms of exploitation. On the contrary, he was aware that his operational duties during the day and his sexual activity at night made him an indispensable member of his crew. Moreover, Dennis's performance did not compromise his position nor the cohesion on board his ship; it actually facilitated his acceptance because it resonated with the memories that his comrades had of their wives and girlfriends, thereby providing a familiar, feminised space in which the hardships of war could temporarily be forgotten. The best example that Dennis gives of sexual surrogacy is his recollection that he was told that he reminded one sexual partner 'of my girl back home',[44] an acknowledgment that attests to the crucial emotional function that Dennis fulfilled on board his ship. It was a function that he was proud of, and one that he retrospectively conceptualised through the lens of patriotism. In claiming that he made 'a lot of boys happy' and that he 'did [his] bit for [his] country',[45] Dennis reversed the construction of the effeminate queer man as a disruptive, ineffective, social outcast in peacetime society and military rhetoric and reframed his experiences using discourses of integration and national obligation. This was also the case for John, who fought in the Army during the war and described himself as 'a sort of Evelyn Hove to the boys ... comfort for the troops ... they didn't confess their homosexuality to me, but they "used" me sexually occasionally'.[46]

The off-duty liaisons of John and Dennis mirror those of Richard Briar and Frank Bolton in that they all found themselves being sought out by their comrades for sexual relief. Although no heterosexual veterans chose to admit that they had taken part in such activity, their stories (and their motivations) were relayed to me by their sexual partners. These memories attest to the continued existence of homosex as a significant category of sexual activity in Britain between 1939 and 1945.

Publicly, the issue of venereal disease was deemed to be the primary motivation for homosex in wartime Britain. As we have seen, the threat of catching venereal disease and the unavailability of women was often used as a buffer against accusations of queerness, both by officers who discovered men participating in homosex and by participants themselves. Invariably, this angle was seized by social commentators in an attempt to explain what they saw as a lamentable increase in same-sex activity. The Public Morality Council, which was founded in 1899 to combat vice and indecency in London, believed that 'men may be turning to these practices [homosex] to avoid the scourge of V.D., of which so much is being made in the Press'.[47] This was also the view of the sex adviser George Ryley Scott:

> In men, the contraceptive element is not so strong a motive for perversion, although it has undoubtedly its effects. Here the fear is concerned with the risk of having either to marry against one's will or to be burdened with the cost of supporting a baby. A far stronger motivation for homosexualism [sic] in males is the fear of contracting venereal disease ...[48]

As the author of an extensive back catalogue that included *The Common Sense of Nudism* (1934) and *Phallic Worship* (1941), Ryley Scott was seemingly well placed to pass comment on the vagrancies of wartime Britain, and his observations are not quite as far-fetched as they might seem. Sexual resourcefulness certainly played a part as did the general need for intimacy during long, arduous and frightening conflicts.[49] However, Ryley Scott's construction of same-sex intimacy as a wartime aberration and of its participants as 'victims of the war' who would return to heterosexuality once the war was over[50] offers a rather one-dimensional interpretation of homosex, not to mention queer identity. Ryley Scott also neatly sidesteps any reference to love, an omission which demonstrates the antithetical relationship between love and queer desire in straight imaginings.[51] In reality, the homosex that was experienced by Britons at war in barrack huts, showers, tents and camp beds was motivated by a complex array of reasons, reasons which include convenience, desire, deprivation, comfort and love.

Homosex between 1939 and 1945 was fundamentally different from the encounters that had occurred between trade and middle-class men before the war. Where once, trade partners had often gained financially from their encounters with middle-class queers, commercial reward became less important, specifically in encounters that took place between comrades. Encounters were more likely to have been driven by the need for sexual satisfaction and emotional comfort. Homosex on the home front however continued to be driven by commercial reward. Middle-class queer men were judged to be a particular threat, largely because they were deemed to have the time and the money to seduce soldiers who were keen to supplement their meagre wages with money, alcohol and gifts. D. H. Blake, a heterosexual veteran of the Royal Navy, described how sailors facing a 'blank week' without pay, would deliberately visit pubs known to harbour queer men in the knowledge that they would be able to drink freely all night.[52]

In this sense, the war had a fundamental impact on sexual practices and on the formalised transactions between queer men and their trade partners which had been occurring since the late nineteenth century. Economic incentive became a secondary consideration. The particular exigencies of the war also created a space in which the congruency between same-sex activity and queer identity remained relatively malleable and, moreover, added a new dynamic to the practice of homosex, which, in effect, helped to fashion an environment in which it could continue. This malleability would be lost after the war, when queer men and those who framed their desires in the public domain sought to demarcate sexual identity more clearly through sexual activity and when the boundaries between queer and normal began to solidify. Finally, the onset of the conflict rendered permissible activity which had previously been conceptualised in popular imagination as the preserve of middle-class perverts, effeminate queans and impoverished guardsmen.

However, this should not be taken to infer that homosex was universally tolerated in the services. Each ship, unit and squadron possessed its own, often implicit, guidelines. Whether or not homosex was deemed permissible could depend on a myriad of factors which included location, the conditions in which the unit operated and the willingness of comrades and officers to ignore behaviour in the interests of morale, cohesion and the retention of valuable personnel. In this respect, units were closed societies, governed by their own moral guidelines. The willingness to turn a blind eye was not the only means by which men and women who desired members of the same sex could survive in the services. Many more made the conscious decision to veil their identity and pass their way through the war. Frank Bolton termed this 'playing it cool'; neither telegraphing desire overtly nor masking it completely.[53]

'Playing it cool': passing performances

By its very nature, the service environment was deeply heteronormative. Real soldiers were real men and by extension, heterosexual men. Accordingly, the antithesis of the martial male was the effeminate queer man. This binary relationship was reinforced through a process of implicit and explicit references. When asked how he knew that homosex was illegal in the Army, the queer veteran John Brierly replied, 'there were lots of unspoken things ... making jokes for example about these poofters and that sort of thing ... I can't remember it being discussed by anybody in authority ... you had to laugh at it or bash them [queer men] or something like that'.[54] These spoken and 'unspoken' indicators worked on the premise that heterosexuality was 'normal' and, to use Adrienne Rich's concept, the assumption that it was 'compulsory'.[55] In this sense, heterosexuality was (and is) both assumed and reinforced in opposition to the 'other' of queerness. Definitions of 'the other' were culturally commonplace and hung, as we have seen, on visible gender inversion. For example, when one Army veteran interviewed by the Imperial War Museum was asked to elucidate on the appearance of 'a pansy', he adhered to the pre-war stereotype of the queer man as an overstated caricature who wore 'a silk scarf, a flower in [his] button hole [and] funny clothes'.[56]

The cultural prevalence of this stereotype ensured that, overwhelmingly, integration depended upon conformity to heterosexual values and standards of performance. For men, these markers were hyper-masculine extensions of peacetime benchmarks which included honour, courage, physical strength and heterosexual virility.[57] Women were judged somewhat differently, that is, by their efficiency as workers but also their adherence to accepted sartorial conventions such as hairstyle and make-up, and, most importantly, their success with the opposite sex. Indeed, discussions about men helped to solidify the bonds between individual recruits. Almost immediately after she arrived at an RAF bomber station as a member of the WAAF, Pip Beck was informed by a more seasoned recruit that she could 'have a different boyfriend every night' if she wanted.[58] Similarly, one woman recalled that 85 per cent of the conversations held between herself and her friends were on the topics of men and dances.[59]

The opposite sex seemed to dominate much of the conversation between men too. In his wartime diary, the soldier W. A. Hill, who served in the Royal Army Service Corps, described having 'a very enjoyable and laughable evening on the topic of "My first girl"'.[60] More evidence comes from the soldier J. H. Witte, who served with the Army in Egypt. Witte's memoirs reveal the deeply heteronormative nature of life in the services. With his mates Mick and George, Witte visited a brothel in Jaffa and, unable to 'raise a gallop', he felt forced to lie.

> Mick and George were waiting for me when I came out. They were eager for details. I supplied most of them and made up the rest. I dwelt at some length on the Spaniard's anatomy and how she had her pubic hair shaved off. 'Cor', said Mick, 'they're not like that in Leeds'.[61]

References to heterosexual relationships formed the backbone of group solidarity because it was naturally assumed that the topic had a universal appeal; with few exceptions sex and romance were experienced or hankered after by everyone. For both sexes then, success in the field of dating, romance and sexual activity contributed to the maintenance of hegemonic military masculinity and femininity. As Tamara Shefer and Nyameka Mankayi indicate in reference to masculinity, 'The importance of visible sexual performance in "achieving" successful masculinity appears to be of great importance in the military context as it is elsewhere'.[62] Normative prestige and 'successful' masculinity and femininity were garnered not so much from the frequency of sexual activity but from success in the field of dating and, specifically, from dating members of the opposite sex. While serving in the ATS, Sarah Allen continued to date men in order to 'make an effort' and in the hope that she could eventually love a man and have a 'normal' life.[63]

This emphasis on heterosexuality could be both deeply stifling and profoundly exclusionary. From beautification rituals for women to conversations about desirable members of the opposite sex, markers of heteronormativity were everywhere, and virtually impossible to avoid. While this emphasis was as much to do with the majority presence of heterosexuals, it was an emphasis which played a deliberate role in dispelling any doubts about the gender identity of service personnel, not least because 'real' men and 'real' women were those who displayed an interest in the opposite sex.[64] Consistent with this focus on markers of heteronormativity, the armed forces directed the vast majority of their regulatory energies towards monitoring and controlling the sexual activity of the heterosexual majority. The two principal sex-related issues were venereal disease and pregnancy. As keystones of regulation, they preoccupied the authorities to such an extent that same-sex activity fell largely under the radar of surveillance. Inevitably however, such preoccupations also exerted additional pressure on men and women attempting to pass. Venereal disease, for instance, which was viewed by some servicemen as a rite of passage and therefore, as a marker of normative masculinity, provided those who caught it with a demonstrable marker of heterosexual success.[65] If then, sexual success was one benchmark of successful masculinity, the services helped to ratify this by encouraging men to use licensed brothels and by issuing condoms and treatment packets.[66] In effect, this was an acknowledgement of the inevitability that 'real' men would seek out sex with women.

In this way, recruits attempting to pass faced a barrage of normative discourses and most were forced to suppress any outward displays of their sexuality. 'Straight' mannerisms, fictional sweethearts and heterosexual banter with comrades were all faked in the name of integration. Frank Bolton recalled that he 'never let on. I was terrified of being found out when I was 18. You are brought up in a heterosexual culture and either adapt or you go under.'[67] Likewise Bert Bartley, a veteran of the Royal Corps of Signals, took his performance very seriously and 'worked hard to be ordinary':

> You've got to be as you would say, normal. You're facing a situation, your life has altered completely and you've got to sort of cope with it. It's no good going on about it and saying 'Oh I'm gay ... take pity on me' because I'd have probably got my papers straight away and been working down a coalmine or something ... you find that you make friends and they're straight and you've got to be straight with them and that's the point.[68]

Learning to adapt was often a natural extension of the discretion that tempered the performances of queer men and women in their pre-war lives. What many lost from their civilian lives, however, were crucial queer contacts and easy access to locations and venues where they might have expressed their sexuality. Most had no choice but to start this process again, quite often alone lest they jeopardise their own passing performances. For instance, Albert Robinson served as a cook within the Army Catering Corps attached to the Duke of Wellington's regiment. Much of his free time was spent alone, cruising for other men in locations far away from the rest of his unit. However, when he returned, he was, to all intents and purposes, a heterosexual serviceman who 'went along with it [the heterosexual culture] and made out you were the same as they were'.[69]

Ralph Hall's service life was characterised by similar discretion. Drafted into the RAF in 1940 as a storehand, Hall was forced to pursue a long-distance relationship with his lover Montague Glover. Three hundred letters passed between the couple over the course of the war and they offer an insight into the subterfuge and loneliness that characterised the wartime lives of some service personnel. In a letter to Glover on 1 December 1940, Hall described the extra-curricular activities of his comrades, writing 'the lads all go out after the cows that are down here. It's all women down here my dear. I go out on my own and think of the lads my dear. I went up to the Blackpool Tower and it was grand and I thought of you'.[70] By 1943, Hall was serving in Egypt and was still maintaining his heterosexual façade. In a letter to Glover written on 5 August 1943, Hall wrote, 'Only when I am in the dark I think of you'.[71] Following the end of the war, Hall was demobilised and the lovers were reunited. Freed from the RAF, Hall returned home to Glover and the couple were inseparable until Glover's death in 1983 at the age of eighty six.[72]

Like Hall, many men and women who desired members of the same sex compartmentalised their wartime lives into service life and sexual life. Francis Kennedy was acutely aware that separating his sexual identity from his career as a mechanic in the Corps of Royal Engineers was the only way that he could protect his position.

> [I was] … a closet gay. I had gay relationships before the war and during the war when I was on leave but not while I was in uniform or in the service … it would have been the end of your military career, it would have been a real bad time. You just had to take notice of it and conform to the rules. The dishonour … and the responsibility that I had prevented anything. I could have had an affair [with one colleague] but it didn't happen. I'm sure if I'd have dropped the guard it would have happened. The grip of the Army on you and the fear of being exposed [prevented it].[73]

This was also the case for Peter White, who trained as a gunner and later earned a commission with the 65th Field Artillery. Speaking of his service and his sexuality he recalled, 'It was a job and the friends I chose to make and activities [I did] in [my] spare time was something else. I have a sort of mind that … can compartmentalise things.'[74] Peter's ability to compartmentalise was tested to the limit when six of his men, including Dixie, a man with whom he was emotionally and sexually involved, were killed by a rocket. Unable to talk to anyone about the depth of his loss, White 'went on the bottle for a day' and maintained his silence for the rest of the war. 'I don't think anyone knew. One or two might have guessed. The matter was never mentioned. I was a monument of discretion.'[75]

Given that discretion was the order of the day, most straight-acting servicemen were careful to distinguish and separate themselves from self-evident queer men, the 'queans', 'poofs' and 'pansies', simply because they attracted too much attention. Peter White recalled the arrival of two self-evident queer men at his unit. White described them as 'feminine type inverts ... [not] my cup of tea' and sought to avoid associating with them for the duration of their service. In a similar way, Bert Bartley, a member of the Royal Corps of Signals described his conscious decision to 'have very little to do' with openly effeminate comrades.[76]

The queer author Rupert Croft-Cooke was certainly keen to pass during his service in the Intelligence Corps. He recalled arriving at an Intelligence school in Matlock, whereupon he discovered that most of the instructors were queer.

> It did not take much perception or experience to see that most of them were queers. No one has a greater admiration than I for the brazen invert, in the Army or out of it, or a stronger wish to identify myself with his resistance to conformity.[77]

While Croft-Cooke expressed his admiration for the honesty of his instructors, his description betrays a sense of discomfort and, more importantly, a disjuncture between queer men who were 'brazen' and those who adopted a more discreet performance. Both during his service in the Army and during his post-war life, Croft-Cooke was careful to project a masculine persona. Following his trial and imprisonment for homosex in 1953, Croft-Cooke wrote *The Verdict of You All*, a painfully honest account of his trial and subsequent spell in prison. In it, he defended his position and his opinion of queer men who performed effeminately. 'I did not mind in the least being thought a homosexual. I might have been irritated by any suggestion that I was a homosexual of the inverted, effeminate type, but that would have been because it reflected on my manhood, not because it reflected on my morals.'[78] In this sense, Croft-Cooke, like so many other queer men who grew up mindful of the need to pass unnoticed, eschewed the overtness of his instructors in favour of discretion. He actively dissociated himself from effeminacy and visible markers of transgression.

This need for discretion and dissociation did not, however, preclude the activities of those who wished to find sexual partners. Dennis Campbell mastered the art of telegraphing his availability to other men while to all intents and purposes acting as a heterosexual serviceman. 'We pretty well behaved normally. I was just myself ... but I didn't go around advertising it ... you didn't brag about the gay stuff.'[79] 'Normally' in this context seems to refer merely to Campbell behaving as a 'normal' person, that is, as himself. However, we might wonder to what extent Campbell's outward demeanour was implicitly influenced by the need to behave like a heterosexual. In any case, while Campbell did not brag about 'the gay stuff', he never lied about his marital status. Whenever he was asked, he always told others that he did not have a girlfriend, thereby obliquely confirming the suspicions of other men that he encountered during his service in the RAF. In this sense Campbell created his own rules of engagement, neither admitting nor lying about his sexuality. In doing so, he playfully manipulated his identity and the regulations of the armed forces. For Campbell, passing was a tool of empowerment which facilitated his integration and allowed him to slip between particular identities and performances.

Queerness and the 'people's war'

I want to finish this chapter by exploring the intersection between queerness and the 'people's war', and specifically, how that relationship was expressed by my interviewees. Conceived by the Ministry of Information during the Second World War, the 'people's war' was a carefully crafted piece of morale-boosting propaganda that espoused the virtues of tolerance, stoicism and equal sacrifice. It stressed unity and a homogeneity of morals and motivations and, in the post-war world, it has arguably become stronger and more impervious to criticism. Indeed, following the end of the war, both the 'people's war' and the myth of British civilian morale were, as Ian McLaine highlights, 'continually nourished by the tendency of politicians and others to call for a revival of the "Dunkirk spirit" whenever Britain faced a threat to her well being'.[80]

As I discussed in the introduction, the most recent revisionist work on the myth of the 'people's war' by Sonya O. Rose focuses on those who sat on the margins of wartime citizenship. As Rose observes, the British people rallied to the cause of war but it was a cause that could not entirely eliminate difference, not least within the arenas of class and morality.[81] While the 'people's war' may have existed as a unifying concept, the terms of that acceptance were carefully negotiated and delineated. Indeed, as soon as the foundations of its inclusionary rhetoric are interrogated, the limitations of the 'people's war' become all too apparent.

On the issue of queerness, the 'people's war' sits rather uncomfortably alongside the passing performances that these men felt compelled to pursue. As Frank Bolton said, 'There was no integration. You were a thing apart. You had to pretend. Ninety percent had to [hide it]'.[82] Another Frank, this time Frank Brown, who served as an engineer in the

RAF said, 'I used to keep my head down and if any jokes were made I kept quiet. I would laugh with the rest of them ... one had to.'[83]

It could be argued that true acceptance would have involved a willingness to accept each individual regardless of their sexual orientation. However, this is almost asking too much of the past. To demand that the 'people's war' should have been framed in this way, that it should have recognised and accommodated queer identity as one of its components, is anachronistic. Same-sex activity was not officially accepted in the armed forces, nor was it expressed openly by the vast majority. Rather than openness, the norm was discretion. As Albert Robinson, a cook in the Army said, 'queer people ... were very careful you know. And willing to make a great effort.'[84]

It was this stoical 'great effort' which facilitated the inclusion of personnel rather than an inclusion based on the acceptance of diversity. Indeed, Robinson's response may tune into the same discourse of collective sacrifice that constitutes the 'people's war' but it also explicitly delineates the parameters of wartime inclusion. In this sense, while the myth of the 'people's war' provides us with a powerful unitary discourse, its status *is* largely mythic. The wartime populace, and specifically the armed forces, may have been able to absorb some of the diversity which formed its emergency contingent, but the inclusion of those who were deemed to be 'peripheral' citizens or what Rose terms 'anti-citizens' was heavily negotiated. Whether an openly queer recruit was ostracised or accepted was subjective and often unit-specific; one openly queer recruit excluded by his unit might have been accepted in the next. What these conclusions point to is a subject-, context- and site-specific analysis of wartime cohesiveness. Given that acceptance also had to be earned, the concept of the 'people's war' does not convey accurately the place of those deemed as constituting the category of 'other' in wider discourses of wartime social inclusion.

As we will see in the next chapter, the fact that queerness often constituted a point of 'otherness' did not prevent queer veterans from absorbing the message of the 'people's war' and from feeling that they could form part of the wartime collective. As we saw earlier in the chapter, Dennis Prattley conceptualised his role as a sexual surrogate through the lens of patriotism. In doing so, he framed his experiences using discourses of integration and national obligation.

On the other hand, all of my interviewees agreed that integration could only be achieved through discretion and subterfuge. As Francis Kennedy said, 'nobody walked around saying "I'm gay". There was no problem integrating.'[85] Kennedy felt relatively comfortable with masking his sexuality because he did not view it as the defining feature of his identity. Jimmy Jacques believed that queer men and women integrated into the wartime community because they had to; 'you just had no alternative'.[86] Jacques felt part of the war because of a sense of shared hardship, and more specifically because he had been conscripted and therefore had little choice in the matter. Indeed, all of my interviewees viewed their passing performances as part of a wider, nationwide discourse of sacrifice, something which helps to explain why none resented serving a country which criminalised their sexual expression. This also has much to do with the fact that the queer population of Britain did not mobilise for war in order to agitate for social change and, specifically, for a change in the law. The queer 'community' (a term that must be used tentatively) responded to the call for service and it absorbed or rejected discourses of wartime togetherness just like the rest of the population. In this sense, queerness did not preclude the absorption of wartime and post-war rhetorics of inclusion but for some it worked to limit the depth of that absorption. In terms of queer servicemen themselves, it is clear that we cannot frame their experiences in terms of collective absorption; we need to think instead about subjective absorption and about the language and semantics of that absorption. While it would be unwise to completely denigrate the power of British unity and the power of the war in facilitating the acceptance of a wholly marginal subgroup of society, it is telling that all ten of my interviewees masked their sexuality and, moreover, that only ten of them felt brave enough to come forward and tell their stories. This seems evidence enough that the inclusivity of the 'people's war' was rather more nuanced than it has been imagined and, moreover, could be enacted quite differently by the various components of wartime society.

Conclusion

The armed forces bore witness to a wide spectrum of homosocial contact and desire which formed part of the fabric of life in the services. The inherent homosociability of the services encouraged some individuals to explore the limits of their camaraderie and use the close proximity of homosociability and same-sex desire to map the contours of their own feelings and identities. While there may have been certain institutional practices and traditions which facilitated sexual contact between personnel, the war seemed to legitimate these to an even greater extent. Take for instance the examples of the 'winger' and 'oppo' system and the Army tradition of giving each officer a batman. However if homosex occurred between an officer and a batman or in the Navy between a 'winger' and an 'oppo', it should not be assumed that there was always a direct association between those acts and the sexual identities of those who participated in them. In such instances, it is more constructive to consider the significance and motivation behind each encounter rather than seeking to determine the sexual identity of its participants. We have seen just how complex these motivations could be. Indeed, it is this sense of complexity which defuses the power of the sexual label and questions whether it is meaningful or accurate to classify individuals based purely on their sexual expression.

Notes

1 John Brierly, interviewed by Emma Vickers, 28 August 2006.
2 S. Cole, 'Modernism, male intimacy and the Great War', *English Literary History*, 68:2 (2001), p. 469.
3 Jimmy Jacques, interviewed by Emma Vickers, 21 July 2005.
4 John Booker, interviewed by Emma Vickers, 10 November 2006.
5 BBC PWA, A2829116, Len Waller.
6 John Brierly, interviewed by Emma Vickers, 28 August 2006.
7 John Brierly, interviewed by Emma Vickers, 28 August 2006. See also Fussell, *Wartime*, p. 82. The American services used the term 'chicken shit'.
8 J. Crang, *The British Army and the People's War 1939-1945* (Manchester: Manchester University Press, 2000), p. 76.
9 A. Barron, *From the City, from the Plough* (London: Pan, 1953), p. 24.
10 Royal Naval Museum Sound Archive, 23/1994 (1), Miss Isobel Holmes.
11 J. Bourke, *An Intimate History of Killing* (London: Granta, 1999), p. 141.
12 G. MacDonald Frazer, *Quartered Safe Out Here* (London: Harper Collins, 2000), p. 17.
13 London Metropolitan Archives (hereafter LMA), PH/GEN/3/19, Papers of Letitia Fairfield, Homosexuality, 1947-61, 'Homosexuality in women,' n.d.
14 R. Buckle, *The Most Upsetting Woman* (London: Collins, 1981), p. 181.
15 Holmes, *Acts of War*, p. 128.
16 IWM DD, 87/42/1, Len Waller. Acknowledgement is given both to the Trustees of the Imperial War Museum for granting me access to the collections and to the family of Len Waller for granting me permission to use his memoirs.
17 IWM DD, 89/1/1, R. H. Lloyd-Jones.
18 IWM DP accession number A30890. © Imperial War Museum.
19 S. Das, '"Kiss me, Hardy": intimacy, gender, and gesture in World War I trench literature', *Modernism/Modernity*, 19:1 (January 2002), p. 56.
20 Wotherspoon, 'Comrades-in-arms', p. 208.
21 Frank Bolton, interviewed by Emma Vickers, 19 June 2006. See also IWM SA, 872/4, S. Zeeland, *The Masculine Marine: Homoeroticsm in the U.S. Marine Corps* (New York: Harrington Park Press, 1996).
22 Frank Bolton, interviewed by Emma Vickers, 19 June 2006.
23 BOSA, S. Allen (pseud.), interviewed by Linda and Tom, Part 2, tape 49, 29 November 1990.

24 See John Alcock's account in Hall and Carpenter Archives Gay Men's Oral History Group, *Walking after Midnight: Gay Men's Life Stories* (London: Routledge, 1989), p. 45.
25 See Vick Robson's account in S. Neild and R. Pearson, *Women Like Us* (London: The Women's Press, 1992), p. 52.
26 Hamer, *Britannia's Glory*, p. 141.
27 The Second World War Experience Centre (hereafter SWWEC), Miss Edith Newman, 2844.
28 Transcript of interview with John Beardmore, 3bmtv, *Conduct Unbecoming* (Channel 4, 1996), p. 66.
29 TNA, ADM 156/193, Attempted gross indecency: W. A. Austin, Stoker 1st Class, C. Rice, Stoker 1st Class, enclosure no. 1 to Despatches Letter no. E. 623/23, 16 August 1936.
30 Richard Briar, interviewed by Emma Vickers, 9 November 2005, and Dennis Campbell, interviewed by Emma Vickers, 22 November 2005.
31 Jivani, *It's Not Unusual*, p. 65.
32 Jivani, *It's Not Unusual*, pp. 65-6. D. Hallsworth also insinuated that wingers had sexual relationships with one another. See IWM SA, 10702/4, D. P. Hallsworth.
33 Transcript of interview with John Beardmore, 3bmtv, *Conduct Unbecoming*, p. 15.
34 See Houlbrook, *Queer London*, p. 170. On the issue of trade see also P. Nardi, '"Anything for a Sis, Mary": an introduction to gay masculinities', in P. Nardi (ed.), *Gay Masculinities* (London: Sage, 2000), p. 3, and G. Chauncey, *Gay New York* (New York: Basic Books, 1994), p. 16.
35 Houlbrook, *Queer London*, p. 171.
36 Frank Bolton, interviewed by Emma Vickers, 19 June 2006.
37 Richard Briar, interviewed by Emma Vickers, 9 November 2005.
38 Richard Briar, interviewed by Emma Vickers, 9 November 2005.
39 Richard Briar, interviewed by Emma Vickers, 9 November 2005.
40 Richard Briar, interviewed by Emma Vickers, 9 November 2005.
41 Transcript of interview with Charles Pether, 3bmtv, *Conduct Unbecoming*, p. 5.
42 Dennis Campbell, interviewed by Emma Vickers, 22 November 2005.
43 Dennis Campbell, interviewed by Emma Vickers, 22 November 2005.
44 Dennis Prattley, *Timewatch*, 'Sex and war', BBC 2 (1998).
45 Dennis Prattley, *Timewatch*, 'Sex and war', BBC 2 (1998).
46 See John's account in Weeks and Porter (eds), *Between the Acts*, p. 178.
47 LMA, A/PMC/41, Public Morality Council: Patrolling Officers Reports, 1941-45, February 1944. Members of the PMC included representatives from the Church of England, Roman Catholic and non-conformist churches, leaders of the Jewish faith and leaders in education and medicine. It had no police powers, but it worked closely with the authorities and helped to prosecute, amongst others, importuners, prostitutes, racketeers and pornographers.
48 Ryley Scott, *Sex Problems and Dangers in War-Time*, p. 76.
49 Dennis Prattley believed that the frequency of men seeking him out for sex and physical intimacy increased following stressful missions and enemy attacks. Dennis Prattley, *Timewatch*, 'Sex and war', BBC 2 (1998).
50 J. Boyd-Carpenter, *A Way of Life* (London: Sidgwick and Jackson, 1980), p. 67.

51 M. Jolly, 'Love letters versus letters carved in stone: gender, memory and the "Forces sweethearts" exhibition', in M. Evans and K. Lunn (eds), *War and Memory in the Twentieth Century* (Oxford: Berg, 1997), p. 109.
52 Letter from D. H. Blake to Emma Vickers, 18 October 2006.
53 Frank Bolton, interviewed by Emma Vickers, 19 June 2006.
54 John Brierly, interviewed by Emma Vickers, 28 August 2006.
55 A. Rich, *Compulsory Heterosexuality and, Lesbian Existence* (London: Onlywoman Press, 1981). See also G. Rubin, 'The traffic in women: notes on the "political economy", of sex', in R. Reiter (ed.), *Toward an Anthropology of Women* (New York: Monthly Review Press, 1975) and R. W. Connell, *Masculinities* (Cambridge: Polity, 2nd eds, 1995), pp. 103-6.
56 IWM SA, 17286, D. Arnold.
57 T. Shefer and N. Mankayi, 'The (hetero)sexualization of the military and the militarization of (hetero)sex: discourses on male (hetero)sexual practices among a group of young men in the South African military', *Sexualities*, 10:2 (2007), p. 192.
58 P. Beck, *Keeping Watch* (Manchester: Goodall, 2004), p. 13.
59 P. Summerfield and G. Braybon, *Out of the Cage: Women's Experiences in Two World Wars* (London: Pandora Press, 1987), p. 205.
60 IWM DD, 85/2/1, W. A. Hill, diary entry, 30 July 1942.
61 J. H. Witte, *The One That Didn't Get Away* (Bognor Regis: New Horizon, 1983), p. 51.
62 Shefer and Mankayi, 'The (hetero)sexualization of the military', p. 198.
63 BOSA, S. Allen (pseud.), interviewed by Linda and Tom, Part 2, tape 49, 29 November 1990.
64 W. Arkin and L. R. Dobrofsky, 'Military socialization and masculinity', *Journal of Social Issues*, 34:1 (1978), p. 162.
65 Lawrence Harney served in the Navy and believed that catching venereal disease was a rite of passage. Lawrence Harney, interviewed by Emma Vickers, 5 October 2006. Kenneth Lovell also described catching venereal disease as 'a normal hazard of soldiering'. See IWM SA, 13251, K. C. Lovell.
66 Field Marshal Montgomery was the most high-profile advocate of controlled brothels and strongly encouraged his men to engage in 'horizontal refreshment'. He did, however, ask them to avoid local women: Hamilton, *The Full Monty*, p. 308.
67 Frank Bolton, interviewed by Emma Vickers, 19 June 2006.
68 Transcript of interview with Bert Bartley, 3bmtv, *Conduct Unbecoming* (1996), p. 14.
69 Albert Robinson, interviewed by Emma Vickers, 5 October 2005.
70 J. Gardiner, *A Class Apart: The Private Pictures of Montague Glover* (London: Serpent's Tail, 1992, repro 1999), p. 94.
71 Gardiner, *A Class Apart*, p. 111.
72 Gardiner, *A Class Apart*, p. 136.
73 Francis Kennedy, interviewed by Emma Vickers, 5 December 2005.
74 SWWEC, 519/520, P. White (pseud.).
75 SWWEC, 519/520, P. White (pseud.).
76 SWWEC, 519/520, P.White (pseud.) and transcript of interview with Bert Bartley, 3bmtv, *Conduct Unbecoming* (Channel 4, 1996), pp. 13-15.
77 R. Croft-Cooke, *The Licentious Soldiery* (London: W. H. Allen, 1971), p. 46.
78 R. Croft-Cooke, *The Verdict of You All* (London: Secker & Warburg, 1955), p. 68.

79 Dennis Campbell, interviewed by Emma Vickers, 22 November 2005.
80 I. McLaine, *Ministry of Morale: Home Front Morale and the Ministry of Information in World War Two* (London: George Allen and Unwin, 1979), p.1.
81 Rose, *Which People's War?* One of the most recent examinations of the 'People's War' counternarrative is by S. Brooke, 'War and the nude: the photography of Bill Brandt in the 1940s', *Journal of British Studies*, 45:1 (2006), pp. 118–38.
82 Frank Bolton, interviewed by Emma Vickers, 19 June 2006.
83 Frank Brown, interviewed by Emma Vickers, 10 November 2006.
84 Albert Robinson, interviewed by Emma Vickers, 5 October 2005.
85 Francis Kennedy, interviewed by Emma Vickers, 5 December 2005.
86 Jimmy Jacques, interviewed by Emma Vickers, 21 July 2005.

3

Playing away

The recollections of John Alcock, a queer man born and raised in Birmingham, begin this chapter. His experiences provide a crucial point of departure for mapping and exploring the arenas in which servicemen and women could play away. In 1945 John visited London for the very first time. Upon entering Leicester Square he experienced something of an epiphany; there, among a crowd of revellers, he saw 'young Air Force boys wearing make-up'.[1] It was a sight that encouraged him to move to the city permanently, a city that promised sexual freedom, ambiguity and possibility.

It is in this clash between queer bodies constrained by uniform and national obligation yet powdered and painted that *Queen and Country* was born. How did men and women satisfy both their obligation (or wish) to serve and their sexual desires? Was it possible to subvert the strictures of authority? To what extent were their comrades active conspirators in this process of subversion? And finally, did bodies play any differently on leave than they did on active service? The chapter begins with a discussion of leave, and it focuses in particular on London and on the experiences of servicemen. The city's status as the main site of commercial leisure in the UK ensured that bodies could experience unparalleled opportunities for pleasure and consumption. However, it was a consumerism which centred overwhelmingly on the queer man. While the mass mobilisation of women into the uniformed auxiliary services (some 612,000 between 1939 and 1945) certainly increased the visibility and the consumer status of queer women and temporarily fractured the explicit links between women, dependence and familial authority, the queer leisure market was still dominated by the male consumer.[2] This is not to say that lesbian venues did not exist between 1939 and 1945. The research conducted by Sarah Waters and by Gardiner, Oram and Turnbull, for instance, suggests that venues such as the Gateways Club in London provided a safe haven for queer women well into the 1950s.[3] 'Official' archival traces also attest to the spatial organisation of leisure for queer women in London in the 1930s and 1940s. In the wake of the raid on the Caravan Club in 1934, for example, an unnamed officer lodged a report on the raid which included the observation that 'Some of the women were ... lying about and embracing each other. One of the women was smoking a pipe.'[4] As Rebecca Jennings points out, lesbian sociability in the years leading up to the Second World War was a rapidly changing hotchpotch of 'unregistered nightclubs and illegal drinking dens ... coffee bars and the street' where queer women found themselves occupying the same social spaces as the city's hawkers, prostitutes, criminals and immigrants.[5] The scene would not develop any significant degree of coherence until well after the cessation of hostilities. In this sense, while it is possible to gain a tantalising glimpse into the fabric of London for queer women, the paucity of this material and the apparent reluctance of female veterans to render themselves visible in order that they might be interviewed means that the ensuing discussion focuses exclusively on the experiences of queer servicemen.[6]

'City of swarming, city full of dreams':[7] queer sociability and policing in London, 1939–45

For service personnel engaged in active service, leave was fundamental to the maintenance of good morale. Between 1939 and 1945, Britain's towns and cities became much needed boltholes, allowing personnel to throw off the masquerade of the militarised, disciplined body. Aside from Edinburgh, Brighton and Portsmouth, all of which found popularity with hedonists craving an escape, it was London that promised the most potent mix of alcohol, entertainment and sexual opportunity.[8] As the most vulnerable migrated out of the city – some 600,000 children, mothers and expectant women in September 1939, followed by smaller movements after the fall of France and the onset of the Blitz in 1940, and the arrival of V1 flying bombs in 1944 – new, uniformed bodies entered its blacked-out streets and alleyways.[9] Throughout the duration of the conflict, large numbers of servicemen and women from Britain, the Commonwealth and later the United States of America continued to drift in and out of London on leave, a movement which ensured a regular stream of bodies. The result, as the writer John Lehman described it, was that '[a]n atmosphere of heightened emotion dominated. Kisses were exchanged with those one would never in normal times have reached the point of kissing'.[10] Quentin Crisp took full advantage of this *carpe diem* attitude:

> The city became like a paved double bed. Voices whispered suggestively to you as you walked along; hands reached out if you stood still and in dimly lit trains people carried on as they had once behaved only in taxis ... once when I emerged from Leicester Square Underground station ... I asked an invisible passerby where I was, he kissed me on the lips, told me I was in Newport Street and walked on.[11]

A somewhat less overstated but equally evocative account is offered by a former Wren, Jean Gordon: 'the whole of London was full of men all in uniform, all going off somewhere or coming from somewhere, all eager to have a good time. Under the blackout, [the city] was a blaze of light.'[12] Gordon's vignette paints a familiar picture of wartime London; an eagerness for pleasure and a desire to forget the horrors of war. In the 'livid incandescence' of the Blitz, bodies came and went and the threat of death was a constant companion.[13] As a result, chances were taken and meetings were often fleeting and ephemeral. In the fug of the blackout, there was no knowing who might be around the corner.[14]

Queer servicemen such as Richard Buckle relished their time in the city. Out of uniform and 'disguised as a civilian', he 'ranged the blacked-out streets in search of adventure'.[15] Whether in uniform or out of it, service personnel who visited London had much of the city at their disposal. Despite the onset of war, London's bars, clubs and cafes, or to use Matt Houlbrook's terminology 'the commercial sites of queer sociability'[16] continued to flourish, bolstered by the continuous flow of service personnel spending their weekends and periods of leave in the city. Personnel could choose between the low-class and relatively inexpensive pub scene or the anonymity and privacy of the nightclub or hotel bar. Jimmy Jacques, a former gunner and projectionist in the Army, testified to the importance and frequency of these venues by making a point of mapping them out for me during our interview.

> I used to go to all sorts of queer places, there were a lot of queer places in London you know where we all knew, you could stand at the back, meet people and that. You could go and have a meal at the Lilypond which was the Lyons Corner House in Piccadilly ... so, there was a network of queer people and there were clubs, er, they were very, not like the clubs now, Heaven and all these places all over the place, these modern ones. They were rather scruffy out-of-the-way places you know but I have a list of them here. There's the B and B Club in

Water Street, the White Bear in Piccadilly, the Mouse Trap coffee bar, that was Lord Montague's place, and there was the Captain's Cabin, there was Napoleon's nightclub in Mayfair, there was the Champion at Notting Hill Gate, Lyon's Brasserie Corner House, the Fitzroy. The Fitzroy was the one opened ... you see, during the war.[17]

It was not just other ranks that were well-served by the city. Officers seeking an escape flocked in particular to the Arts and Battledress Club and Le Boeuf sur le Toit. Both were highly respectable queer venues opened during the Second World War in response to increased demand.[18] Patrick Trevor-Roper described Le Boeuf sur Le Toit as 'an eye opener. Officers would come back hoping to dazzle with their uniform', while in the background, a pianist would be 'banging away twenties tunes'.[19] The club was also one of Richard Buckle's favourites, described by the former Army officer as 'mainly homosexual'.[20] Another well-known venue was the bar inside the Ritz, known as l'Abri or, fittingly, the Shelter. Michael Wishart called the bar 'a shrine of pilgrimage to homosexuals on leave from active service'.[21] As John Hollister indicates, all of these sites possessed 'social recognisability ... critical masses of potential participants ... recognize[d] compatible possibilities in a particular location'.[22] In engaging in these processes of 'social recognizability' and patronage, queer men played a critical role in fashioning the perimeters of what was a vibrant, fast-changing metropolitan culture.

Although the surveillance of known queer venues was drastically curtailed by the war, the police were nonetheless forced to respond to growing concerns about the 'corruption' of servicemen. As early as 1939, the Metropolitan Police were asked to keep the military police informed of any cases involving soldiers and 'perverts' and any premises suspected of harbouring same-sex activity between soldiers and civilians.[23] If discovered, a pub or club could be closed down under the terms of the Defence Regulations and the Emergency Powers Acts (EPA) without any further legal process.[24] For example, the Swiss Hotel on Old Compton Street and the Crown and the Two Chairmen on Dean Street were warned about their perceived 'harbouring of sodomites'.[25] Before 1936, a landlord could not be prosecuted for allowing queer men into their premises and only men caught importuning inside a pub or club could be punished. Following complaints from the Admiralty and the Canadian military in 1936, the police were forced to use section 44 of the 1839 Metropolitan Police Act which prohibited landlords from knowingly allowing disorderly conduct.[26] However, the caveat to this rule hinged upon the notion of respectable conduct, and so even notorious venues could avoid closure if their patrons behaved discreetly.

Apart from bars, clubs and pubs, hotels and hostels were also popular sites of same-sex expression in wartime London. The exodus of natives out of London meant that most hoteliers 'didn't turn a hair' if same-sex couples requested double rooms.[27] Most charitable hostels were also willing to accept any serviceman looking for a bed. Of all the many hostels that operated in the city, the Union Jack Club quickly established itself as a haven for personnel who desired members of the same sex. Opened in 1907 and located in a well-known red-light district, the Union Jack Club was a keystone of sociability and sexual activity for servicemen visiting the city. Roy, a queer man who served in the RAMC during the war, described meeting a Canadian serviceman in London during a heavy bombing raid. Turned away by the Salvation Army because of the Canadian's drunkenness, Roy took the soldier over to the Union Jack Club where the two men managed to secure some accommodation. Under a cacophony of enemy shells and sirens, the men spent the night together.[28]

For a shilling, men could have their own, private utopia in the shape of an individual cubicle. It was understood that those seeking the company of others would rent a cubicle for the night and leave their door open. According to one queer ex-serviceman, there was 'no bother about anybody getting into trouble'.[29] In fact, the Union Jack Club was a site where men could take old partners and look for new ones. As John Alcock recalled, 'you just left your door open and somebody would come in and spend a couple of hours with you'.[30] Most men visiting the club did not think twice about being watched by its staff. Indeed, Houlbrook suggests that 'surveillance floundered at the cubicle wall and the staff's unwillingness to police sexual morality'.[31] In the case of Frank Bolton, this unwillingness had severe consequences. When he was eighteen he visited the Union Jack Club for the first time and was raped by a sailor. He suffered painful internal injuries but felt unable to talk to anyone about the assault. 'You couldn't scream. The walls didn't go up to the ceiling. There was a gap at the top. I was terrified of anybody finding out.'[32] Bolton's fear and the club's blind eye policy ensured that the sailor was never prosecuted.

Men who preferred to search for others in the open air could frequent one of London's parks or cruise particular streets in the city. Despite the constant threat of Luftwaffe bombs and the hazards presented by the blackout, this activity did not cease. Indeed, London's parks continued to grant servicemen the space and visibility to cruise while providing them with covered ground for privacy. This, along with their accessibility, made them very popular. Green Park, St James' Park and Hyde Park were all familiar locations, both to servicemen and to the police. For several years preceding the onset of war, Hyde Park was placed out of bounds for soldiers to discourage importuning between soldiers and civilians.[33] Such activity could be punished under the terms of the Parks Regulation Act of 1872 and the Criminal Law Amendment Act of 1885. During the war, however, the police and the military authorities had little interest in policing the parks too vigorously. It was also difficult to keep watch over areas that were so heavily used and most men knew that they needed to vary where they cruised and picked up. Sympathetic policing also played a role in these spaces. Patrick Trevor-Roper was caught in St James' Park with another man just before he was about to leave for a period of service with the New Zealand Army. He described how the police officer 'went away ... because I was in uniform, I dare say ... because he thought "What's the point?" He let us go.'[34]

In spite of the city's position as the prime target for German aerial aggression, London managed to maintain its leading position as a site of queer sociability. Its streets, parks, bars, hostels and hotels provided men with innumerable opportunities to participate in the city's sexual economy, an economy which provided consumers with a recognisable set of queer venues. However, this recognisability also had a flip side. It could also mean surveillance, something which positioned the city not only as a site of opportunity but also of danger. Henning Bech ties this surveillance explicitly to the queer man, noting that 'the minute the homosexual gets into town and wants to realize himself, he runs up against the police ... one cannot be a homosexual ... without feeling potentially monitored.'[35] Urban spaces have always been more heavily policed than rural ones and likewise there has always been a strong link between cities, immorality and surveillance which has been well documented by historians and geographers alike.[36] While the activities of the police were significantly hindered by the exigencies of the war, the possibility of being caught became greater in the city.

For example, particular streets in the West End, including Regent Street, Leicester Square, Charing Cross Road and Oxford Street, were well-known areas for cruising between 1939 and 1945. However, the city's guardians of morality also knew where same-sex activity was at its most prolific. In December 1941, the following report was made by an inspector on behalf of the Public Morality Council.[37]

> I beg to report that during the past month I have kept observation on the West End Streets, and find that there is a considerable number of males loitering, for the purposes of importuning. Some of these were wearing high-heel shoes. Many had in their possession, when arrested, compacts, powder [and] face paint.[38]

It is clear that the authorities viewed these painted and powdered working-class 'West End poofs'[39] as dangerous enticers of young, lonely servicemen on leave. On the whole however, arrests for homosex in the city were relatively rare. The natural diversion of labour from the police service to the armed forces resulted in a severe curtailment of their activities. Between 1939 and 1945, only one Division, C Division, which covered the West End, operated a vice squad.[40] Moreover, the blackout hindered any sustained attempts to observe indecent behaviour. It was easy for men and women to slip into pitch-black streets and alleyways or retreat into the nearest pub or club.

Surveillance was not the only barrier to sexual encounters. Lack of time and money could also prohibit the serviceman on leave. Forty-eight hour passes were only granted once a month and passes which granted eleven days of leave were usually authorised only once every three months.[41] Pay also circumscribed a serviceman's ability to travel. Cigarettes and extra rations usually consumed the vast majority of a soldier's wage, leaving very little for alcohol and amusement.[42] Given that the ability of a recruit to escape to the city was often constrained by finance, location and military obligation, most free time was actually spent in close proximity to camp. As a consequence, servicemen manufactured their own homosocial places while on active service at home and overseas. These individualised spatial 'niches' were safer, precisely because they were not organised into sites which had 'mass recognizability' and were therefore less heavily policed by official and unofficial guardians of morality. It is to these places that we will now turn.

Sex, service and memory

One of the only works which engages with the concept of what might be termed 'spatial sexual resourcefulness' is John Howard's study of queer men in rural Mississippi, *Men Like That*.[43] One of the many conclusions that Howard arrives at is that, while Mississippi lacked the same proliferation of organised queer spaces as, for instance, New York, queer men in Mississippi became 'resourceful sexual beings' who exploited a wide range of public, private and semi-private spaces including schools, cars and church halls in order to have sex with other men.[44] While Howard's study demonstrates the resourcefulness of queer communities in rural environments, it is less concerned with the importance and emotional meaning of ad hoc places to the formation of queer identity. My work with queer veterans of the war suggests that memory, place and sexuality are intrinsically linked. In the context of total war, queer men found places that were both private and semi-private and they used them not only for pleasure but also as spaces of defiance and rebellion.

Jimmy Jacques spoke with exceptional candour about his sexual history and was particularly keen to tell me about his sex life in the Royal Artillery. I asked him to give me a brief summary of his wartime service career, namely where he trained and where he was posted. It was during this summary that Jimmy, quite unprompted, decided to tell me about landing in Gibraltar.

> JJ: Now, when I got to the Rock [Gibraltar] and there were no guns, we were put on this job, erm, do you now want me to tell you about me having an affair there or not?
>
> EV: You can tell me ... I tell you what, you tell me what you want and then I'll start on my specific questions.
>
> JJ: Well, I met a boy, we'll call him Bud, who was a physical training instructor and I'd only been on there a few hours and, erm, er, we had sex, believe it or not, in the showers. I was, because don't forget, I was only twenty then. [Laughs.]
>
> EV: [Laughs.]
>
> JJ: And, erm, I had regular sex with him he done special favours and put me on special jobs and things like that and of course it was against ... very much against the law and if you were caught, you were court-martialled and sent home and things like that. Erm, there were, well, I had an affair with him until I was moved up to work with an entertainment group.[45]

Jimmy's wish to divert his narrative away from what was an admittedly bland but necessary summary of his service life attests not only to the importance of this initial encounter in shaping the contours of his wartime experiences (and the subsequent telling of those experience some seventy years on) but to his own understanding of my research agenda. It is also significant that he chose to emphasise both the speed of the encounter and its less than private location. The purpose of this was twofold; it served as a means of rooting his sexual identity in a contemporary narrative of sexual success and as an example of his disdain for authority. Jacques clearly enjoyed the subversion of military authority explicit in the act of having sex with a military superior in a communal shower.

The illicit excitement of these encounters emerges most strongly in the memories of Dennis Campbell, a former veteran of the RAF. Dennis's early memories of volunteering for service were explicitly connected to one of the first physical expressions of his queer identity at the age of eighteen.

> EV: Where did you join up? Can you remember?
>
> DC: Yes. We had to report to Lord's cricket ground in London [pause]. I

travelled down to London by sleeper, the first time I'd been on a sleeper and the first time I'd been out of Scotland. And with me on the train was another young man and we discovered that he too was going to join the Air Force. Now the two of us spent a lot of time chatting; I think we were too excited to sleep and in the early hours of the morning, he said 'I dare you to go into the corridor wearing your underpants'. Now when you're 18 and you're dared, you don't want to play chicken, so I went into the corridor, we were right next door to the little loo and the next thing, Eric had pushed me into the loo, snipped the door and there we had mutual masturbation. This was incredible! We discovered that we had to report to the same aircrew reception centre, we were billeted in the same block of flats on Abbey Road in St John's Wood. Not only were we in the same block of flats, we were in the same room. I think I spent more time in his bed than I did in mine.[46]

For Dennis, the moment of departure from his home town in Scotland and the mutual satisfaction that followed coalesced into a pivotal moment of change. On the cusp of understanding his own desires, the incident came to represent his transition from an adolescent into a queer man and his inauguration into a new world of sexual activity in the RAF. In beginning our interview with this vignette, just as Jimmy had done with his own story about Bud, Dennis was attesting to its formative role in his wartime experiences and to his queer identity.

As we saw in chapter two, Richard Briar, a veteran of the Army, also structured his recollections of being queer around two sites of travel and movement; the train station and the Army truck.[47] It should come as no surprise that transport featured so prominently in the recollections of Richard and others. From a purely practical angle, transport provided intimacy and seclusion and ensured that third-party surveillance was less likely both because of limited space and because such sites were, by their very nature, transient. Moreover, the rules of these semi-private spaces were very different to those which governed behaviour in more communal spaces, such as canteens for instance. They were sites where men could push the boundaries of homosocial contact and where notions of acceptable behaviour became blurred.

Apart from capturing the particular flavour and inherent eroticism of service life, the recollections of Richard, Jimmy and Dennis attest to the impact of the war on the spatial organisation of desire and the important function that was served by subjective individually forged sites of same-sex expression. Across Britain and in various locations on land, in the air and on sea, personnel fashioned their own, subjective existence. They 'played away' in both organised commercial arenas and subjective self-fashioned places. Born out of convenience, these latter spaces allowed recruits to extend the boundaries of same-sex sociability from recognised and familiar sites of patronage to individualised spatial niches.

For my interviewees, however, 'playing away' was not just confined to service in Britain; it also had resonance for those who served in overseas theatres of war. Far away from home, sexual expression invariably became easier. From Cairo and Italy to India and Malaya, service outside Britain offered a greater sense of spatial and sexual freedom, and provided men with an opportunity to explore queer life well away from the prying eyes of family and friends. Depending on location, overseas climates offered much to service personnel, not least the opportunity to escape the unpredictable British weather. Out in the field and away from the 'bullshit' of training camp, discipline was also often less rigorously enforced, familial constraints were further away, and such basic necessities as food and drink were cheaper and in greater supply. Although it would be unwise to over-emphasise the extent of sexual activity between service personnel and civilians overseas or give any credence to the claim that sexual mores were looser outside Britain, there is some evidence to suggest that servicemen were less sexually inhibited while serving abroad. If nothing else, their money went further and privacy was easier to obtain.

In Gibraltar (which according to the veteran Stan Maddocks was known as 'Hatters Castle' after the pejorative term 'brown hatters'[48]), men could cruise in the Alameda Gardens along concreted walkways and hide in the dense, tropical shrubbery if they desired privacy or protection. In the Middle East, one of the most notorious spots was Cairo, which was described by a cleric based within the city as 'the wickedest place morally that I have ever known'.[49] Cairo's famous street the Sharia-il-Berka was home to a multitude of queer bars and other venues, including the Taverne Français, a queer club for French officers, and various male and female brothels. Douglas Renwick, a veteran of the RAF, described seeing men in the Taverne Français dressed as women, dancing together.[50] One well-known venue for British officers was the Shepherd's Hotel, which according to John Costello was a rendezvous point for queer members of the military elite.[51] The freedom granted by Cairo was not just limited to commissioned officers, however. Other ranks were equally able to enjoy the city and all it could offer. Richard Briar certainly felt freer there.

> EV: In the Army, where were you most able to be a queer man?
> RB: In Cairo ... that's where I had the most opportunity.[52]

Away from organised venues overseas, foreign climes also provided opportunities for seclusion and privacy. Albert Robinson found that the rough, deserted roads and long grasses of North Africa offered ample privacy for regular sexual encounters with a corporal.[53] Similarly, John Booker thought that conditions in South East Asia were relaxed enough (and sufficiently far enough away from authority) that any open declarations of same-sex desire would have mattered very little.[54] It would seem that the further away a unit was positioned from its headquarters, the less relevant the stringent application of military rules and regulations became. Of course, overseas service did not always grant sexual freedom. Periods of frontline activity obviously put paid to extended periods of relaxation. Moreover, it was invariably easier for support staff and officers to explore their locales than frontline soldiers. The diaries of Myles Hildyard, a queer officer in the Nottinghamshire Yeomanry, certainly attest to the liberatory potential of the war and the privileges that could be granted by rank and regimental postings. When his regiment was shipped to Palestine in order to prevent the German forces from moving through Syria towards the Suez Canal, he found himself cut off from the action and spent most of his time in the area writing, sightseeing and socialising.[55]

For all of its disruption and dislocation then, the war heralded a period of change and opportunity. It facilitated travel and social mixing and gave recruits the chance to let loose and play away. In some cases, the war also prompted experimentation and a hedonistic attitude to life, love and sexual expression. In all of this activity, men who desired other men continued to organise their sexuality around commercial sites of queerness. But they also manufactured their own spaces, both out of choice and necessity. This spatial resourcefulness is a testament to the resilience of these personnel. It also attests to their determination that the illegality of same-sex activity should not inhibit their enjoyment of service life.

'What goes up my arse won't give you a headache': queerness and the 'good fellow'

The concept of playing away refers not only to geographical space but also to gender subordination. Self-evident queer men and women represented the most visible embodiments of same-sex desire in the services. Although they undoubtedly sat on the peripheries of martial culture, many were able to survive and even flourish. This section of the chapter will explore the experiences of these men and women and the dynamics of the relationships that they forged with their peers.

The story of John, a queer man who served in the Army, epitomises just how positively openly queer men and women could be treated. Most of John's comrades were aware of his queerness and were fiercely protective of him. He recalled: 'The attitude to homosexuality in the Army was protective. They [the men] used to send me up like mad. But if any stranger did it, he used to be kicked to death.'[56] One of the most obvious reasons which helps to explain why men such as John might have been protected relates to the notion of the 'good fellow', a designation which indicated that a person was accepted and valued. The benefit of 'good fellow' status was that, once it was imbued, it could override other issues that might otherwise threaten that recruit's position, including their sexual activity. To reiterate the words of R. C. Benge, a former major in the Army, 'one was either, within that military context, a good fellow or not. All other considerations were irrelevant'.[57]

Some queer men were accepted as good fellows because their outward performances defied the dominant model of same-sex identity; that of the pale, effeminate pansy. The surprise element of these 'normal' performances emerges quite frequently in the memories of some heterosexual veterans. A.W. Weekes incredulously described a storeman on board his ship who happened to be queer. According to Weekes the storehand was 'a huge chap', who despite his sexuality could lift heavy bags of flour.[58] Similarly, in reference to a queer comrade known as 'Cynthia' who worked at the Balloon Command Station in Orkney, George Sutcliffe said:

> [Cynthia] was very well liked for his 'free spirit' attitude, his cheeky tilt at discipline, [he was] very friendly and humorous, one of the lads ... he was very attractive, good looking, super fit and was known to swim in the Pentland Firth in very rough seas, sometimes pulling in a boat's drawline for anchorage. Cynthia was a 'one off'.[59]

Like the storeman described by Weekes, 'Cynthia' was admired for his strength, fitness and overall physical appearance, features which in themselves are desirable markers of masculinity. In addition, however, Cynthia possessed other characteristics that made him a welcome member of the crew at the balloon station, namely individuality, humour and an anti-authoritarian approach to military discipline. In Sutcliffe's words, Cynthia was both 'one of the lads' and a 'one off'. This is a curious, almost oppositional compliment. To be classed as 'one of the lads' implies that Cynthia fulfilled the norms of the group and was accepted as a member of it. He had, in the words of Dwight Fee, 'gender affinity' with heterosexual men.[60] However, being a 'one off' sets Cynthia apart from the rest in that it resonates with the idea that he was separate from the rest of his peers. This distance is telling, as is the fact that the man was known by a female name, a tactic of both affectionate mockery and also separation and denigration.

Some recruits were tolerated and accepted not because they conformed to hegemonic masculinity but because they openly defied those markers. John Beardmore was queer, and served as a sub lieutenant in the Navy. He spoke of the queer coder on his ship, a man known as Freddie, who, before the war, had worked as a chorus boy. Freddie would defuse the tension of battle by calling out 'open fire, dear' and would break into impersonations of Gracie Fields and Vera Lynn whenever the stress became too much.[61]

Likewise, Terry Gardener was unapologetically brazen about his sexuality, but he was also accepted by his shipmates because he was both a cook and an entertainer. 'I could be very entertaining. Everybody loves to laugh whatever the circumstances and … there were some dreadful, dreadful circumstances especially on the Western approaches. People were just thankful to get through the day and if I was there to give them a laugh, it was a bonus, wasn't it?'[62] Similarly, Frank Bolton remembered two effeminate queer men who worked in the cook house. 'Everybody knew and they knew and they camped themselves silly … they were friendly and everybody laughed and joked with them.'[63]

Men like Freddie and Terry Gardener were valued for their skills and personalities. Ironically, in providing comedic relief in moments of exceptional stress, they were displaying precisely the bravery and emotional self-control which were valued by the armed forces.[64] Jo Denith's description of two queer men under his command in the Army evokes a similar sense of emotional composure and an unselfish attitude towards others. Immediately before they disembarked from their landing craft during the D-Day landings, one of the men began to daub his lips with lipstick and, when asked to explain himself, said, 'I must look pretty for the Germans'. Denith recalled that everybody on board collapsed in fits of laughter. 'You couldn't help but laugh at them not because they were inadequate but because they had the bloody courage to laugh … they had this amazing capacity to see the ridiculous part of life. I think they felt they'd got to be brave in front of the straight lot'.[65] The notion of bravery was also discussed by John Beardmore, who commented that '[queer] men were very often much braver than straight men because they had … the feeling that they had to make a stand to prove themselves … I know many cases where queer men went, paid enormous risks and were totally without fear'.[66]

This process of over-compensation helped to align these men with military masculinity and bridged the gap between heterosexuality and queerness. It also helped to question culturally prevalent ideas about queer men, including the assumption that they were woman-like and effete and therefore, by extension, unable to protect their country's interests. The colleague described by Denith may have worn lipstick and preferred men to women but his presence on board a troop carrier just about to land on a D-Day beach is testament to his ability as a soldier. Like Sutcliffe's memories of Cynthia, however, there is an implicit sense of othering in Denith's recollections which, offset against his praise, hints that acceptance had its limits.

In addition to character, value was also measured by the efficiency and ability of a comrade. For instance, asked if queer men caused any disruption in the Navy, Weekes's response was unequivocal. 'You accepted the chap as he was. If he was a good messenger or a good pal. [Non-sailors] can't understand the passionate feeling about sailors collectively.'[67] The efficiency of an individual and the sense that sailors looked after their own kind meant that sexuality was, in some cases, irrelevant. Describing his ship's queer commander for instance, W. H. Bell spoke first and foremost of the man's skill as an officer. '[He] was a good seaman. [He wore] silk stockings. Whenever he did entertain anybody aboard it was always a man, never a woman ... when we got to sea he was there and when we were under attack he took over ... we never got hit ...'[68] Bell's deliberate juxtaposition of the commander's queerness and his ability is hugely significant. First and foremost, the commander excelled in his role as a leader, the success of which was gauged by the fact that none of his men were killed during his time in charge of the ship. Bell's anecdote suggests that the commander was able to override any distaste for his sexuality through his effectiveness in a highly technical, stressful and by association, masculine role. Bell also implied that he was able to accept the commander's sexuality because he was distanced from it.

This apparent willingness to tolerate openly queer comrades who did not pursue their interests on active duty was often critical. For instance, in addition to his queer commander, Bell also knew a steward who was queer. Bell tolerated the man because he 'didn't carry out anything on board ship. What he did ashore was his business.'[69] The same sense of comfort through distance can also be found in the memories of Elizabeth Reid Simpson. Reid Simpson served in the WAAF until 1942, during which time she encountered a female couple at her station who slept together. After complaining about the noise to 'Mary ... a good old East Ender', she was told: 'Where were you brought up? Don't you know anything? They're lesbians and they always manage to get posted together ... they don't fancy you so get back to bed and go back to sleep and don't bother about them'.[70] In fact, Reid Simpson admitted that people merely 'ignored' the couple. The possibility of ignoring the women was facilitated by their efficiency as workers, and because their sexuality was expressed within the confines of a committed relationship and was therefore deemed to be harmless to others.

Of course, the tolerance conveyed by these narratives does not tell the whole story. Some openly queer men and women were shunned by their peers, and others had to work harder to claim a space within their units. Often the most audacious and challenging responses came from those who were unable or unwilling to hide their queerness. If Terry Gardener was met with hostility on his ship, he would respond with 'What goes up my fucking arse won't give you a headache ... I had the cheek not to let anybody take advantage of me so if anyone said "Are you queer?" I would say, "Yes! So what?"'[71] In replying with his aggressive and humorous retorts, Gardener was making an assertion about his identity and claiming a space on board his ship.

Like Terry Gardener, Charles Pether faced hostility from some in his unit. As a young, effeminate male, Pether felt exposed and decidedly vulnerable, feelings compounded by what might be regarded as good-natured 'ragging', dished out by the unit's cook.

> I was being dolloped the porridge onto my plate. The cook said to me "Hi beautiful. How about it?" I just dropped my plate and ran out ... [I thought] I've got to stand up to this. The following morning the same thing happened and when he said "oh, good morning beautiful. How about it?" I said "well, there will be others before you but if you want to queue up, be my guest." [72]

As the antitheses of martial masculinity and the most obvious and unapologetic queer men in their units, it might be assumed that Pether and Gardener were exceptionally vulnerable to verbal and physical hostility. However, their feminine performances actually worked to protect them. While their difference may have singled them out as targets for banter, they were protected because of their feminine vulnerability. As Susan Brownmiller argues: 'Feminine armour is never metal or muscle but ... an exaggeration of physical vulnerability that is reassuring (unthreatening) to men.'[73] In imbuing their performances with aspects of femininity, both men were able to survive service life, countering any explicit questions about their performance and their presence with humorous and cutting retorts.

In part, the toleration of these men was created by a powerful 'for the duration' discourse and by the notion that the war was being fought by a diverse collection of individuals. Toleration and acceptance were also tied into notions of comradeship and a desire to protect the weak, including those who did not conform. More specifically, however, self-evident queer men who imbued their performances with elements of femininity could find themselves protected not only because of their difference or their skills but because their performances resonated with the memories that men held of their female partners, friends and relatives. Such performances could offer comfort through the evocation of what Goldstein calls the 'metaphysical sanctuary' that is necessary to reinforce the gender contract, that is, the notion that men protect their home and women stay within it.[74]

There is one final reason that helps to explain this unofficial toleration and that is the relationship between citizenship and service. Indeed, what renders the Second World War in Britain so inherently fascinating is that it led to a temporary loosening of pre-war prejudices and taboos which is linked to the fact that between 1939 and 1945, citizenship was predicated less on sexual orientation and more on individual service and sacrifice. For instance, Rose provides compelling evidence of the wartime perception that real men served their country and unmanly men 'pretend[ed] to believe in "peace"'.[75] On 2 June 1940, the *Sunday Pictorial* offered a damning indictment of the 'elegant sissies who fester in the restaurants of London, gossiping like girls … they've got more scent than sense'.[76] A week after Dunkirk, the *Sunday Pictorial* pushed its anti-pacifist stance even further with an article called 'Pacifists and Pansies'.

In this way, articulations of wartime masculinity were linked explicitly to military service. The decadent, perfumed 'sissies' who occupied the bars and restaurants of London were accused of gender inversion and by extension, same-sex desire, precisely because they were not fulfilling their masculine obligations to serve and protect the nation. Indeed, it is telling that the same accusations of effeminacy and sexual deviancy were levelled at Conscientious Objectors. Such an explicit rendering of the connection between 'sissies' and military service indicates that the fulfilment of military obligation could offer queer men, especially openly camp and flamboyant men, a point of access into the wartime collective which in peacetime was vehemently opposed to their presence.

Whatever the reasons for their retention and toleration, the presence, integration and effectiveness of these self-evident queer men is a powerful rebuttal of the opinion expressed most frequently by heterosexual veterans of the war that openly queer men did not serve in the forces. Moreover, their presence and effectiveness also challenges the claim made by the Ministry of Defence that the presence of queer personnel in the armed forces had a detrimental impact on morale. This was one of the major conclusions of the report by the Homosexual Policy Assessment Team which was used to retain the ban on queer personnel in the 1990s. The report's monochrome vision of morale denies the complexities of group membership and neglects to acknowledge the existence of what Derek McGhee terms 'compatible and non-disruptive' queer personnel,[77] a category which includes those who were openly queer yet tolerated by their comrades.

By necessity, because of conscription and the needs of war, the armed forces absorbed a significant plurality of masculinities into their ranks during the Second World War, a fact which confirms that hegemonic military masculinity represented little more than an unrealistic and unobtainable aspiration. Moreover, while the martial male was constructed in relation to the 'other', in which the effeminate queer man, the conscientious objector and the civilian were constructed as gender deviants, such prescriptions were effaced by the reality of the Second World War. Some heterosexual recruits may have used their queer comrades to confirm and demarcate their own heterosexuality, but this was not always the case. As we have seen, there are numerous examples of men who became models of queer military masculinity, effectively helping to refashion the attitudes of their comrades towards queerness by proving their effectiveness. Some of the queer men that have been described in this chapter were accepted because they displayed masculine characteristics such as physical and mental strength, leadership or bravery. Others facilitated their integration into the services through their humour, compassion and the personal qualities that they brought to their jobs.

In this sense, queer men, particularly those who made their sexuality an obvious part of their identity, provide a good litmus test of just how all encompassing and how credible nationalist discourse was in unifying Britain. This tentative attempt to map the extent of the inclusion experienced by openly queer personnel into the wartime collective illustrates just how fragile (and ultimately, subjective) the concept of the 'people's war' was between 1939 and 1945. However, given that articulations of masculinity (and to a lesser extent, femininity) were linked explicitly to military service this could offer openly queer personnel a point of access into the wartime collective, which in peacetime was rather less accommodating.

Playing away: rank and queerness

The toleration of an openly queer recruit, whether they were an entertaining addition to their unit or simply well-liked, could be withdrawn if it was coupled with force and especially if it was affected by assertions of rank. Exploiting the privilege of rank was sometimes central to the censure of, and yet also the expression of, queer identity. It is the purpose of this section to illuminate the often contested intersection between queerness and rank. The section focuses on the activities of queer officers as observed by those who served alongside them. In contrast to the 'good fellow', this section of the chapter discusses those who, by 'playing away', fractured the acceptance of their comrades.

In some cases, rank destabilised the regulation of the queer recruit by imbuing its holder with a certain degree of immunity from the law. The officer Crank Dyer was described by one of his battalion as a 'heck of a soldier'.[78] When Dyer moved from one battalion to another, William Brown recalled hearing one of his sergeants say '"Oh, we'll have to get him a lad fixed up". He had to have a boy, this fella. He was a very peculiar man. Great soldier and wonderful on parade but … that was one of his things … we had to provide this young lad to be his batman, for him to use'.[79] In this context, 'use' meant have sex with, yet Dyer was never punished. Indeed, the officers within the unit were willing (whether through fear of his seniority or his ability as an officer) to accommodate Dyer's sexual tastes and turn a blind eye to his activity. According to Brown, each batman was awarded with a gold watch, inscribed with the phrase 'For services rendered'.[80]

Major Peter Burke was also notorious for propositioning the soldiers under his command.[81] The recollections of those who served with Burke attest to his skill as a leader of men. He was described as 'a good officer' and 'a brilliant soldier' but also, by no fewer than a dozen men who were interviewed by the Imperial War Museum, as a devious sexual predator. Although he was later sent to a court-martial for indecency, purportedly for propositioning a member of the RAF, Burke had, until then, been protected not only by his status but by his unit.[82] Isolated from outsiders who might expose him, he was able to satisfy his sexual desires without fear of punishment. One of the techniques that he used most frequently was to accompany potential partners to the unit's operations post, deep in Eastern Libya. With little more accommodation than a slit trench, a crow's nest and an underground pillbox, Burke had ample opportunity for close physical contact and seclusion. He was also notorious for propositioning his drivers. Frank Penlington described driving the officer to Palestine and being ordered to take him to a secluded location.

> We stopped ... got out ... and the next thing I knew, he'd got his trousers off. I was a 19 year old lad ... I didn't know what the bloody hell was going on ... I says, because a famous place in Cairo was the Burka, a place where all the prostitutes were ... I says 'You want to get to the bloody Burka. Fuck off!' That was the end of that. Got in the truck and we went back and [he] never bothered with me at all after that.[83]

Burke's lengthy survival is a testament not only to the pragmatism that dominated the war years but also to the ways in which that pragmatism could both benefit and disadvantage a unit. Burke may have been an effective officer but his advances were often aggressive and hard to decline, given his position and the privileges he could grant or withhold. Harold Thompson described sleeping next to Burke who proceeded to touch Harold's groin. 'I nearly jumped out of my skin ... I just flung my arms ... he was a good officer, as brave as anybody [but] everybody was frightened.'[84] Burke's seniority and Thompson's respect for his skills as a soldier prevented him from telling anybody about what Burke had done and was doing to other men within the unit.[85]

There can be no doubt that seniority offered queer officers such as Dyer and Burke a greater degree of choice when it came to expressing their queerness, because they could actively request particular visits and choose particular men whom they could proposition in safe locations away from others. However, their stories also highlight the difference between acceptable and unacceptable behaviour. Acceptance was dependent not only on the behaviour and discretion of a serviceman or woman but also the nature of the relationship between an individual and his or her unit. Burke's exploitation of his men meant that, while he might have been accepted as a leader, he was not regarded as a comrade. Moreover, Burke's survival hinged on his seniority; had he been a lower-ranking officer or even an NCO, it is likely that those who rejected his advances would have reported him to a more senior officer.

The intersection between queerness and rank, and therefore the amount of contact that an officer had with lower-ranking personnel, could also influence the psychic comfort of a recruit. This was expressed very bluntly by a veteran of the Army, K. C. Lovell.

> I never came across homosexuality within the battalion but we did have one officer who we all reckoned was as queer as a nine bob note

... he became my company commander ... We looked on it ... as a bit of a joke. But if it came near home, he wasn't just a poufter [*sic*], he was a shit stabber and there was a difference. It wouldn't have been tolerated.[86]

Lovell's response betrays obvious elements of homophobia; he could accept the presence of an effeminate, non-aggressive officer whose position kept him away from direct contact with the lower ranks. However, he would not have been comfortable serving with a lower-ranking, active queer man, a duality hinted at by the contrast between the noun 'poofter' versus the aggressive implications of the term 'shit stabber'. Lovell's comments echo an underlying theme in the reactions of heterosexual servicemen to their queer comrades. Openly effeminate and, crucially, sexually passive queer men were visible and therefore less threatening to other men because the markers of their sexual transgression were visibly mapped on to their bodies through their gender performance. Such men could be viewed variously as amusing, different or, in Lovell's case, as a joke. However, active and less obvious queer men destabilised these constructions because, in the imaginations of some, their masculinity implied a desire for anal penetration and because they were often less easy to identify.

In particular contexts and spaces, the explicit or implicit queerness of a recruit could affect the comfort of his or her comrades. Showers, ablutions and sleeping arrangements were situations which required reciprocal negotiation. Trust and consent were essential. Greta Lewis for instance described communal bathing and the need to avoid 'funny women'. 'One used to always be saying "I'd love to go for a bath with [Greta]". "Oh", I used to say, "never put me down with her because I'll never go for a bath if you do'.[88]

Both Lewis and Lovell's narratives highlight the fragility of the 'good fellow' construct and more generally, the numerous conditions which granted an individual's acceptance into a unit, conditions which included the psychic comfort of others. If that comfort was violated, the consequences could be severe. Dennis Maxted, a seaman in the Royal Navy, described being on board a liner, The *Duchess of Richmond*, which was travelling from Glasgow to Suez. Hearing a commotion on the quarter deck one day, he discovered a man immersed in a forty-gallon drum of crude oil. The man was a member of the RAF and, according to those who had manhandled him into the oil, he was queer. Maxted maintained that the perpetrators did this as an alternative to tarring and feathering in order to display their disapproval of the man's sexuality.[89] While there is no indication that the victim had behaved inappropriately, the mere suggestion of queerness was not usually enough to invoke the withdrawal of a group's acceptance and provoke such an act of aggression.

Sexual exploitation was one of the reasons why acceptance was sometimes withdrawn. B. Millard, who served in the Army, recalled one young lieutenant who had tried to take advantage of his batman. The senior man was later cashiered.[90] Instances like this differ significantly from cases such as that of Crank Dyer, whose activity was accepted and understood. These differences in the way that personnel were treated occurred because each individual unit could possess a different moral code from the next. Activity deemed acceptable in one unit could be totally unacceptable in another. To this end, units were closed societies that were governed by their own unwritten codes of behaviour. As we shall see in the next chapter, such codes supplemented and sometimes surpassed the laws laid down in the King's Regulations.

Playing away on stage

One final arena that allowed some men and women the means to 'play away' was literally, performance. Both in Britain and elsewhere, there is a long and celebrated tradition of transvestism in the armed forces.[91] In the British armed forces, drag was a formulative part of the institution; a mainstay of good morale and hugely important element of off-duty entertainment. Both in formally organised entertainment groups such as the Entertainments National Service Association (ENSA) and Stars in Battledress and in more informal unit-based theatricals, the stage, whether literal or figurative provided a safe environment where performers could experiment with their gender and its expression. Many queer servicemen gravitated towards performance and volunteered to impersonate women in plays, skits and variety shows. Some, like Terry Gardener, became full-time performers and were partially or fully exempted from their other duties. As we saw in chapter one, Gardener was conscripted into the Navy despite his best efforts at his medical to secure an exemption through a deliberate display of outrageous effeminacy. Once in the Navy, he wasted no time in finding an outlet for his personality. Both at his training camp at Chatham and in Gibraltar, Gardener continued his pre-war occupation as an on-stage drag queen, his performances sanctioned, at least in Gibraltar, by the Admiral of the Fleet.[92]

Charles Pether found a similar acceptance. In the absence of anybody 'vivacious', and mindful that as an effeminate and androgynous young man he 'stuck out like a sore thumb' in his unit, Pether volunteered to take part in the concert parties as a female impersonator. 'I used to strut on the stage and I made costumes out of nothing, out of parachute silk, mosquito netting. I used to cut my plimsolls … cut the top part off where the shoe laces would be then someone in the workshop would silver them for me … I adored it.'[94] Unsurprisingly, the servicemen adored Pether and often followed him back to his quarters. By counting how many men were queuing outside his door following each performance, Pether was able to gauge just how convincing his impersonation had been.

In the Navy, impromptu theatrical performances were known colloquially as 'Sod's Operas' by virtue of the performers they attracted. Seemingly, there was never a shortage of volunteers for the female parts. Charles Stringer overheard one man claiming 'it's the only opportunity to be myself'.[95] This opportunity 'to be oneself' helps to explain why so many queer men chose to join informal entertainment groups and perform in plays, shows and dance routines. They allowed talented men and women to showcase their talents and, crucially, offered queer men a licence to perform, not necessarily always in drag. While serving in the RAF, Dennis

Figure 6: Hula-Hula 'girls' rehearsing their Christmas act on board a destroyer depot ship, Scapa Flow, 18 December 1942.[93]

Campbell entertained his squadron by dancing. Both he and Frank Bolton were able to construct a network of queer friends by joining different groups of entertainers. Asked if he thought that such entertainment groups attracted queer men, Campbell replied unequivocally, 'Oh yes. Look at the people like Stanley Baxter [and] Kenneth Williams. They started in concert parties.'[96] Indeed, Williams and Baxter served in Singapore, Malaya and Hong Kong alongside John Schlesinger and Peter Nichols just after the end of the Second World War. Nichols would later write a highly successful novel, *Privates on Parade*, which was loosely based on his experiences as part of a Combined Services Entertainment troupe.[97]

Organised concert parties were less frequent than impromptu performances put on to allay the boredom of war and lighten the mood of a unit. Richard Buckle's speciality was an 'obscene' song called 'My little pussy'. Dressed as a little girl with long hair, Buckle claimed that his performances 'boost[ed]' the morale of the Central Mediterranean Force and expedite[d] an Allied victory'.[98] Similarly, Lois Goossens, a former member of the ATS, described devising a dance with girls wearing long dresses 'partnered by some wearing male officers' uniforms'. Together the women danced to the tune 'Who's taking you home tonight?'[99] One of the most detailed accounts comes from R.C. Benge. Along with the men in his unit, Benge would create ad hoc officers' messes and nominate some of the batmen as waiters. Wearing cosmetics and christened with female names, the 'waiters' would serve the officers with vermouth – or whatever was available – in a bucket. Such parodies 'provid[ed] color [*sic*] to an existence which would otherwise have been emotionally drab'.[100] Whether queer or otherwise, these performances contributed to the *esprit de corps* of Benge's unit and provided a respite from the tedium, destruction and death of the war.

On the whole, such performances did not threaten or destabilise military masculinities and femininities because they were sanctioned, temporal and bounded to the stage, whether that stage was actual or improvised. The visible evocation of masculinity and femininity also worked to reinforce military masculinity and femininity. Additionally, however, these performances could expose the erotic tensions implicit within same-sex communities and, as Marjorie Garber points out, reveal a complex interaction of different issues.

> [T]he history of cross-dressing within the armed services attests to a complicated interplay of forces, including male bonding, acknowledged and unacknowledged homosexual identity, carnivalized power relations, the erotics of same-sex communities, and the apparent safety afforded by theatrical representation.[101]

Largely, however, far from questioning the sexuality of its performers, the stage (whether literal or, in the case of a table in a mess deck, figurative) offered a safe environment for performers where accusations of queerness were subsumed by the success or failure of the entertainer. Indeed, what renders these theatrical arenas so remarkable in the case of male-to-female cross-dressing is that they provided performative niches within which men could question (and often evade) the peacetime association between transvestism and same-sex desire. By making female impersonation a form of entertainment, the services were demarcating very specific boundaries of acceptable and unacceptable behaviour and demonstrating that in their inflated and aggrandized caricatures of women, female impersonators were acting outside their ascribed gender roles. However, they could be accepted because they did not permanently destabilise normative categories of gender and actually stabilised gender identities by reintroducing a female element into what was a male-dominated and sometimes wholly male environment. As Garber highlights, however, there was a more destabilising consequence of such performances. By their very transition into another gender, drag performers questioned the aesthetics of desire, something which elicited a range of responses from those who viewed such transitions.

From a less theoretical standpoint, the value of male and female impersonation in the services was that it provided an outlet for anxiety, tension and trauma, both for those who performed for the crowd and their spectators. What is more, any recruit who possessed the ability to entertain others was a valuable asset, regardless of their sexuality. Dennis Prattley and his two friends spent much of their naval careers entertaining their colleagues by dragging up as women. Their success encouraged them to want to leave the Navy and begin full-time careers as drag queens. Unfortunately the Navy did not want to let them go. After three appointments with naval psychiatrists, three declarations of queerness and three outright refusals, Prattley and his friends gave up trying and resigned themselves to the fact that the Navy would retain them until the end of the war because they were too valuable to discharge.[102]

Conclusion

The concept of playing away encapsulates moments of escape and the subversion of authority; periods of work and periods of leisure, moments where passing performances were discarded and inhibitions were cast to one side. In all of this activity, context played a hugely important role in facilitating or inhibiting same-sex expression. Proximity to the base headquarters, to locations where personnel could play away and to the surveillance of the family all influenced the extent to which personnel could play away. Away from training camp, attitudes towards homosex were often pragmatic. However, for all the perceived or actual freedom imbued by the overseas posting or the camp set far away from headquarters, the King's Regulations did not simply evaporate. Location was merely one factor; the unwritten moral codes of a particular unit, squadron or ship also dictated whose behaviour was accepted and whose was not.

Notes

1 John Alcock, interviewed by Paul Marshall, July 1985, Hall-Carpenter Oral History Project, BLSA, catalogue reference: C456/003 tape 1, © British Library.
2 Mellor (ed.), *History of the Second World War: United Kingdom Medical Series – Casualties and Medical Statistics.*
3 S. Waters, *The Nightwatch* (London: Virago, 2006), J. Gardiner, *From the Closet to the Screen: Women at the Gateways Club, 1945–85* (London: Pandora, 2003), Oram and Turnbull (eds.), *The Lesbian History Source Book.*
4 TNA, MEPO 3/758, Caravan Club, disorderly house, male prostitutes, 1934–41, Minute by unknown police officer, 16 August 1934.
5 R. Jennings, 'The Gateways Club and the emergence of a post-Second World War lesbian subculture', *Social History*, 31:2 (2006), p. 211.
6 See for instance BOSA, S. Allen (pseud.), 29 November 1990, I. 'Bubbles' Ashdown, 22 February 1993, and Barbara Bell's autobiography, *Just Take Your Frock Off* (Brighton: OurStory, 1999). While much has been written on lesbian sexuality and space – see for instance G. Valentine, '(Hetero)sexing space: lesbian perceptions and experiences of everyday spaces', *Society and Space: Environment and Planning D*, 11:2 (1993), pp. 395–413, and S. Munt, 'The lesbian flaneur' in D. Bell and G. Valentine (eds.), *Mapping Desire* (London: Routledge, 1995), pp. 114–25 – the only academic work that touches (albeit briefly) on the period 1939–45 is Jennings' monograph on the emergence of lesbian subcultures in post-war Britain, *Tomboys and Bachelor Girls: A Lesbian History of Post-War Britain, 1945–71* (Manchester: Manchester University Press, 2007).
7 This is the opening line from Charles Baudelaire's poem 'The seven old men': C. Baudelaire, *The Flowers of Evil*, trans. James McGowan (Oxford: Oxford University Press, 1993).
8 See Roy's account in Weeks and Porter (eds.) *Between the Acts*, p. 98.
9 A. Calder, *The People's War: Britain, 1939–1945* (London: Jonathan Cape), p. 36. For more on the nature of wartime London see A. Bell, 'Landscapes of fear: wartime London, 1939–1945', *Journal of British Studies*, 48: (2009), pp. 153–75.
10 J. Lehmann, *In the Purely Pagan Sense* (London: Gay Modern Classics, 1985), p. 130.
11 Crisp, *The Naked Civil Servant*, pp. 154–5.
12 Royal Naval Museum Sound Archive, 69/1994 (1*2), Mrs J. Gordon.
13 H. Green, *Caught* (London, Vintage, 1943, repr. 2001) pp. 95–6.

14 See Sam's account in Weeks and Porter (eds.), *Between the Acts*, p. 124.
15 Buckle, *The Most Upsetting Woman*, p. 196. In reference to London's guardsmen during the interwar period, it was acknowledged by General Corkran that 'only men of good character were allowed to go out without uniform, and that the concession as to plain clothes was regarded by the soldiers as a very valuable one'. However, just like the men under his command, Corkran certainly knew the value of civvies to men seeking out homosex. In 1931 he lamented that guardsmen out of uniform who engaged in sexual activity with civilian men were much harder to police because they were less visible in and around the city once they had surrendered their distinctive red jackets. See TNA, MEPO 2/8859, Activities of homosexuals, soldiers and civilians: co-operation between the army and the police (1931–50), notes on a Conference held 7 May 1931, Richmond Terrace, London, re Homosexual Offences, p. 1.
16 Houlbrook, *Queer London*, p. 68.
17 Jimmy Jacques, interviewed by Emma Vickers, 21 July 2005.
18 Houlbrook, *Queer London*, p. 83.
19 Patrick Trevor-Roper, interviewed by Margo Farnham, 8 January 1990, Hall-Carpenter Oral History Project, BLSA, catalogue reference: C456/089 tape, 1. © British Library.
20 Buckle, *The Most Upsetting Woman*, p. 196.
21 M. Wishart, *High Diver* (London: Quarter, 1978), p. 65.
22 J. Hollister, 'A highway rest area as a socially-reproducible site', in W. Leap (ed.), *Public Sex/Gay Space* (New York: Columbia University Press, 1999), p. 67.
23 TNA, MEPO 2/8859, Activities of homosexuals, soldiers and civilians: cooperation between the army and the police, 1931–50, letter from R. L. Preston (Assistant Provost Marshal) to Mr Howe (Met. Police), 7 June 1939.
24 Houlbrook, *Queer London*, p. 79.
25 *Ibid.*
26 Houlbrook, *Queer London*, p. 77.
27 See Sam's account in Weeks and Porter (eds), *Between the Acts*, p. 124.
28 See Roy's account in Weeks and Porter (eds.), *Between the Acts* p. 99.
29 Gerald in Weeks and Porter (eds.), *Between the Acts*, p. 10.
30 John Alcock, interviewed by Paul Marshall, July 1985, Hall-Carpenter Oral History Project, BLSA, catalogue reference: C456/003 tape 1. © British Library.
31 Houlbrook, *Queer London*, p. 122.
32 Frank Bolton, interviewed by Emma Vickers, 19 June 2006.
33 TNA, MEPO 2/8859, Activities of homosexuals, soldiers and civilians: cooperation between the army and the police, 1931–50, notes from a Conference held at New Scotland Yard, 20 October 1950.
34 Patrick Trevor-Roper, interviewed by Margo Farnham, 8 January 1990, Hall-Carpenter Oral History Project, BLSA, catalogue reference: C456/089 tape 1. © British Library.
35 Bech, *When Men Meet*, p. 99.
36 See for instance Cocks, *Nameless Offences*, Higgs, *Queer Sites*, L. Knopp 'Sexuality and Urban Space: A Framework for Analysis', in D. Bell and G. Valentine (eds), *Mapping Desire* (London: Routledge, 1995), pp. 149–61, L. J. Moran, *The Homosexual(ity) of Law* (London: Routledge, 1996), pp. 118–68. Also F. Mort, 'Mapping sexual London:

the Wolfenden Committee on Homosexual Offences and Prostitution, 1954–57', *New Formations*, 37 (1999), pp. 92–113, and 'The sexual geography of the City', in G. Bridge and F. Watson (eds.), *A Companion to the City* (London: Blackwell, 2000), pp. 307–15.
37 See chapter two, n. 47.
38 LMA, A/PMC/40 – Public Morality Council: Patrolling Officers' Reports, 1938–42, December 1941.
39 This is Matt Houlbrook's terminology. See Houlbrook, *Queer London*, p. 46.
40 Houlbrook, *Queer London*, p. 46.
41 IWM DD, 91/36/1, J. Wallace.
42 J. A. Crang, 'The British soldier on the home front: Army morale reports, 1940–45', in P. Addison and A. Calder, *Time to Kill: The Soldier's Experience of War in the West 1939–1945* (London: Pimlico, 1997), p. 68.
43 J. Howard, *Men Like That: A Southern Queer History* (Chicago: Chicago University Press, 1999).
44 Howard, *Men Like That*, p. 64.
45 Jimmy Jacques, interviewed by Emma Vickers, 21 July 2005.
46 Dennis Campbell, interviewed by Emma Vickers, 22 November 2005.
47 See chapter two, p. 76.
48 Letter from Stan Maddocks to Emma Vickers, 27 April 2006. The term 'brown hatter' is said to derive from 'brown hat' which was purportedly one of the sartorial indicators adopted by queer men in the early part of the twentieth century. It later developed into a pejorative term. See Houlbrook, *Queer London*, pp. 167–8.
49 Women's Library, 3/AMS/4/01 Box FL 314, Records of the Association for Moral and Social Hygiene, Armed Forces – Correspondence and Papers relating to Venereal Disease, Part 5, 1941-44, letter to Miss E. M. Turner at the Association of Moral and Social Hygiene from Llewelleyn Gurgune, All Saints Cathedral, Cairo, 17 November 1941.
50 BBC PWA, A4984581, Douglas Renwick.
51 The Army's General HQ was in the city. See Costello, *Love, Sex and War*, p. 168.
52 Richard Briar, interviewed by Emma Vickers, 9 November 2005.
53 Albert Robinson, interviewed by Emma Vickers, 5 October 2005.
54 John Booker, interviewed by Emma Vickers, 10 November 2006.
55 M. Hildyard, *It Is Bliss Here: Letters Home, 1939–1945* (London: Bloomsbury, 2006). Hildyard was later sent to Crete where he was captured by the Germans.
56 See John's account in Weeks and Porter (eds), *Between the Acts*, p. 178.
57 Benge, *Confessions of a Lapsed Librarian*, p. 25.
58 IWM SA, 21584/3, A. W. Weekes.
59 Letter from G. Sutcliffe to Emma Vickers, 8 September 2005.
60 D. Fee, "One of the guys": instrumentality and intimacy in queer men's friendships with straight men', in P. Nardi (ed.), *Queer Masculinities* (London: Sage, 2000), p. 57.
61 Arguably, Freddie's use of the well-known register of music hall gave his comrades a means of comprehending his humour and helped to facilitate his integration.
62 Jivani, *It's Not Unusual*, p. 65.
63 Frank Bolton, interviewed by Emma Vickers, 19 June 2006.

64 See for instance Connell, *Masculinities*, and O. Sasson-Levy, 'Individual bodies, collective state interests: the case of Israeli combat soldiers', *Men and Masculinities*, 10:3 (2008), pp. 12–13.
65 Jo Denith, *Timewatch*, 'Sex and war', BBC 2 (1998).
66 Transcript of interview with John Beardmore, 3bmtv, *Conduct Unbecoming* (Channel 4, 1996), p. 5.
67 IWM SA, 21584/3, A. W. Weekes.
68 IWM SA, 22585, W. H. Bell. There is some evidence to suggest that the Navy was one of the most tolerant services. George Melly, a veteran of the Navy, believed that the service had 'more of a tradition of tolerance than did the Army or the Air Force'. See *The Times*, Magazine (5 November 2005), p. 12, and G. Melly, *Rum, Bum and Concertina* (London: Weidenfeld and Nicolson, 1989).
69 IWM SA, 22585, W. H. Bell.
70 IWM SA, 18201, E. Reid Simpson.
71 Jivani, *It's Not Unusual*, p. 65.
72 Transcript of interview with Charles Pether, 3bmtv, (*Conduct Unbecoming* Channel 4, 1996), pp. 20–21.
73 S. Brownmiller, *Femininity* (London: Hamish Hamilton, 1984), p. 51.
74 J. Goldstein, *War and Gender: How Gender Shapes the War System and Vice Versa* (Cambridge: Cambridge University Press, 2001), p. 304.
75 *Sunday Pictorial*, cited in S. O. Rose, 'Temperate heroes: masculinities in wartime Britain,' in S. Dudink, Hagemann, and J. Tosh (eds), *Masculinity at War and in Peace* (Manchester: Manchester University Press, 2004), p. 189.
76 Ibid.
77 D. McGhee, 'Looking and acting the part: queers in the armed forces – a case of passing masculinity', *Feminist Legal Studies*, 6:2 (1998), p. 206.
78 IWM SA, 9951/16, W. P. Brown. Dyer is a pseudonym.
79 IWM SA, 9951/16, W. P. Brown.
80 IWM SA, 9951/16, W. P. Brown.
81 Burke is a pseudonym.
82 IWM SA, 12242/17, H. Thompson.
83 IWM SA, 16085/14, F. Penlington.
84 IWM SA, 12242/17, H. Thompson.
85 The officer was only prosecuted when he attempted to assault a member of the RAF. Daphne Brock, who served in the WRNS, found herself in a similar situation following an assault by a fellow Wren. She was advised by a friend, the novelist Henry Moss, not to complain about the incident because her First Officer was a well-known lesbian. See A. De Courcy, *Debs at War: How Wartime Changed Their Lives* (London: Weidenfeld and Nicolson, 2005), pp. 159–160.
86 IWM SA, 13251/28, K. C. Lovell.
87 P. Johnson, 'Haunting heterosexuality: the homo/het binary and intimate love', *Sexualities* 7:2 (2004), p. 191.
88 G. Lewis, in P. Summerfield, *Reconstructing Women's Wartime Lives* (Manchester: Manchester University Press, 1996), p. 178.
89 IWM SA, 18200/5, D. Maxted.
90 IWM SA, 20737/7, B. Millard.

91 Female impersonation as a form of entertainment has a long history in the services and Prisoner of War camps. See D. A. Boxwell, 'The follies of war: cross-dressing and popular theatre on the British front lines, 1914-18', *Modernism/Modernity*, 19:1 (January 2002), and for a discussion of cross-dressing in America during the First World War see G. Chauncey, 'Christian brotherhood or sexual perversion? Homosexual identities and the construction of sexual boundaries in the World War I era', in M. Duberman, M. Vicinus and G. Chauncey (eds.), *Hidden from History. Reclaiming the Gay and Lesbian Past* (London: Penguin, 1991), pp. 294-317. For a discussion of drag in POW camps see A. Rachamimov, 'The disruptive comforts of drag: (trans) gender performances among prisoner war in Russia, 1914-1920', *American Historical Review*, pp. 1-23. Laurel Halladay and Alan Bérubé both discuss female impersonators in the Canadian and American military during the Second World War. See L. Halladay, 'A lovely war: male to female cross-dressing and Canadian military entertainment in World War II', *Journal of Homosexuality*, 46:3-4 (2004), pp. 19-34, and Bérubé, *Coming Out under Fire*, pp. 75-7.
92 Jivani, *It's Not Unusual*, p. 64.
93 IWM DP, A13435.© Imperial War Museum.
94 Transcript of interview with Charles Pether, 3bmtv, *Conduct Unbecoming* (Channel 4, 1996), p. 8.
95 E-mail from C. Stringer to Emma Vickers, 29 November 2005.
96 Dennis Campbell, interviewed by Emma Vickers, 22 November 2005.
97 P. Nichols, *Privates on Parade* (London: Faber and Faber, 1977). See also The British Library Theatre Project, Peter Nichols interviewed by Jamie Andrews, 31 August 2005, p. 2. *Privates on Parade* was turned into a play and a film.
98 Buckle, *The Most Upsetting Woman*, p. 195.
99 IWM DD 92/30/1, L. Goossens.
100 Benge, *Confessions of a Lapsed Librarian*, p. 51.
101 M. Garber, *Vested Interests: Cross Dressing and Cultural Anxiety* (New York: Routledge, 1992), pp. 55-6. See also Boxwell, 'The follies of war', p. 16.
102 Dennis Prattley, *Timewatch*, 'Sex and war, BBC 2, 1998.

4

Make do and mend: military law and same-sex desire

Attempting to map out how homosex was regulated between 1939 and 1945 is a hugely complex task. Publicly, some veterans have made it clear that the criminality of same-sex expression meant that Britain would never have conscripted queer men into its ranks and certainly would not have retained them. Their attitude is summed up by John Clarke who, as we saw in the introduction, defiantly asserted that he did not serve with queer soldiers because it was illegal and un-British.[1] Clarke's reductionist assessment may be hugely misleading but it nonetheless highlights one of the central tenets of the King's Regulations; on paper, homosex between servicemen was a criminal act punishable by both civilian and military courts. Moreover, there is every reason to assume that the illegality of same-sex expression between men gave the armed forces more than enough of a reason to exclude those who displayed signs of it. In practice however, the services were neither draconian nor utopian. Out in the field, the stringent application of military law began to collapse and pragmatism rather than diligence became the dominant consideration. It was not in the interests of the services to search out or exclude all of the personnel who came to their attention because of homosex. Instead the policies of the armed forces were reactive and reflexive responses, deliberately formulated to ensure that only the most serious offenders whose conduct would impair military efficiency and who could not be usefully rehabilitated or reposted were removed from the services. In this sense, reading the experiences of same-sex desire and queer identity through the lens of its formal disciplinary code fails to acknowledge the complex and often contradictory ways in which legislation was actually applied. The purpose of this final chapter of *Queen and Country* is to map out the formal and informal disciplinary mechanisms that were used against men and women who were caught out and highlight just how pragmatic the services were prepared to be.

The Law

In British law, buggery and indecent assault were outlawed by the Offences against the Person Act of 1861. This was followed by section 11 of the Criminal Law Amendment Act of 1885 which defined any act of 'gross indecency', whether in public or private, as a punishable offence. In this way, the services could punish homosex committed by a serviceman under both civilian and military jurisdictions; as a civil offence, homosex was often framed under section 41 of the King's Regulations, which referred to offences punishable by ordinary law. If a serviceman were tried in a civilian court for an offence, he would not face retrial by a military court. However, a serviceman could be tried by a civil power following a conviction or even an acquittal in a military court.[2]

Under military law and specifically the 1879 Army Act and the 1881 Regulation of the Forces Act, homosex between men in the Army was punishable under section 18 (5) of the regulations by the key phrase 'disgraceful conduct of a cruel, indecent, or unnatural kind'.[3] As under civilian law, men could be punished for sexual contact (defined as 'buggery' or any other sexual act between males), any attempts to 'be party to the commission of any act of gross indecency with another male person', attempts to 'procure the commission of any such act [and] to do any grossly indecent act in a public place, or to publicly expose the person, or exhibit any disgusting object'.[4] In the Royal Air Force and the Royal Navy, the charges were laid in exactly the same terms, although Navy personnel could not be punished under naval law for homosex that occurred onshore.[5] They could, however, be punished under civilian law.

Officers discovered committing homosex could also be punished under section 16, that is, 'behaving in a scandalous manner unbecoming the character of an officer and a gentleman'. It was a charge used overwhelmingly against officers who had paid for goods with cheques that subsequently bounced. Couching an act of indecency as scandalous behaviour avoided any association with indecency even if the conduct of an officer was clearly indecent. Such cases are admittedly rare but they seem to suggest a deliberate attempt to avoid the ignominy or disgrace of a charge of indecency. In 1940 for instance, a captain was registered in the Judge Advocate General's charge book as having stroked the hand of a male soldier and slept in the same bed as another. In spite of these manoeuvres and their 'indecent' nature, the officer was only charged with scandalous conduct.[6]

An even more undefined charge was conduct, disorder or neglect to the prejudice of good order and military discipline. One example of how the charge was used comes from the Army's charge books. On 30 October 1939, a rifleman was taken to a court-martial charged with conduct to the prejudice of good order and military discipline because he had entered the bed of a colleague and handled the man's genitals.[7] While the recruit in question was not accused of indecency, it was common for a charge of an act to the prejudice of good order and military discipline to accompany one of indecency.

Unlike their male counterparts, servicewomen could not be punished for same-sex activity under either civilian or military law. In 1943 alterations to military legislation meant that the ATS and the WAAF could be disciplined for all offences outlawed by the Army Act whereas previously they had only been punishable for offences under section 15, the section dealing with absence without leave, and section 40 which covered conduct to the prejudice of order and discipline. (The WRNS was considered to be a civilian organisation and was therefore entirely exempt from service discipline.)[8] However, lesbianism could still not be officially punished under section 41, offences punishable by civilian law, simply because it was not illegal, nor could charges be brought under section 18, (disgraceful conduct of an indecent kind) which was the regulation used to frame offences committed by men.[9] Accordingly court-martial records for the WAAF and the ATS mostly document cases of theft, breaking out of barracks and absence without leave, which, as we shall see, were also some of the most common offences committed by servicemen between 1939 and 1945.

On paper, punishments for homosex between men appear to be deliberately punitive. Gross indecency, or the performance or encouragement of a sexual act between males, could be punished with two years' imprisonment, as could indecent exposure. Indecent assault on a male person involving the use of threat or force to commit a sexual act carried a maximum sentence of ten years in prison. Buggery could be punished by imprisonment for life.[10] These sentences offer a frightening indication that, if used to its full capacity, the law could be exceptionally savage. However, in practice, the King's Regulations were themselves little more than guiding principles designed to permit the law to be applied fiercely only if and when the actions of a serviceman were seen to necessitate it. To cite the Air Ministry, they were not 'hard and fast rules to be rigidly followed. Each case must be treated on its merits, regard being had both to the offences and punishment [and] to the future value of the airman to the service'.[11] As the military historian Gerry Rubin remarked, military law was 'applied strictly by the authorities in some cases ... less strictly in others; and perhaps not even enforced at all in some circumstances for reasons which might relate to practicality or to pragmatism or even to moral distaste with particular rules'.[12] Out in the field and away from the discipline of the training unit, regiments were closed societies, governed as much by their own codes of morality and behaviour as by the King's Regulations. Overwhelmingly, bodies on active service were policed not by 'official' regulators of the law but by their peers and their superiors. In all of this activity, pragmatism and morale were the determining factors in deciding if action should be taken and the form it should take.

Queering indecency

One of the fundamental problems which hinders an accurate quantification of how many men were taken to a court-martial for homosex is the use of the catch-all term 'indecency'. Every case that went to a court-martial was recorded in a force-specific register. Homosex was classified as indecency along with various other offences including indecent exposure and bestiality. There are obviously fundamental differences between each category of offence. Indecent assault, that is, the use of threat or force to commit a sexual act against the will of another person of either sex, is clearly very different from gross indecency, which refers to the encouragement or performance of a sexual act only between men. The registers do not include a column marked 'indecent assault' and accordingly there is no indication of the specific indecent act or acts for which a serviceman was being tried. Therefore, the generic category of indecency encompassed all offences between males and by males and indecent assault between members of the same sex and the opposite sex.[13] While this prevents an accurate quantification, it also adds further weight to the idea that there were fewer cases and convictions for homosex than is suggested by the registers.

A further methodological challenge lies in the nature of military discipline itself. In general, a court-martial was only invoked as a last resort when a particular incident could not be ignored or dealt with in other less formal ways. For instance, company commanders and commanding officers had the power to deal with cases summarily without any recourse to a court-martial. Medical and administrative discharges were also invoked against those who, for a number of reasons, were spared an official trial. Lastly there is some evidence to suggest that an unquantifiable number of cases of gross indecency involving servicemen and civilians may have been dealt with by the civil authorities.

Given that officers had the option of pursuing these 'alternative' disciplinary avenues, this chapter will focus both on 'official' figures pertaining to indecent acts convicted by court-martial and also on the multiple options that were available to commanding officers, including the reasoning which propelled particular decisions. The next section of the chapter will quantify how many servicemen were convicted by courts-martial for gross indecency and provide a context for a discussion of 'alternative' disciplinary responses which avoided the need for a court-martial.

Quantifying indecency

Official sources seem to suggest that indecency was comparatively rare. The War Office's official publication on army discipline states that 210,029 other ranks were convicted by courts-martial over the course of the war, a figure which does not include commissioned officers. Of this number, only 790 convictions were registered for indecency.[14] 'Absence without leave' was the most prevalent offence, for which there were 75,157 convictions, followed by 'desertion' (30,740 convictions) and 'theft' (18,599).[15] Compared with these, the 'official' figure for convictions of indecency seems relatively insignificant.

Of the 790 convictions for indecency recorded in these 'official' figures, 297 were for activity committed in the United Kingdom, 26 cases of which were delivered by district courts-martial (DCM) and 271 by field general courts-martial (FGCM). A further 493 convictions were delivered in overseas commands, 467 of which were given by field general courts-martial and 26 by district courts-martial. District courts-martial were convened for lesser offences and general courts-martial (GCM) generally dealt with commissioned officers and more serious cases involving other ranks. During times of war the latter were replaced by field general courts-martial which were courts held out in the field of operation.

While the data provided by the War Office represent one of the only 'official' sources that tabulates wartime criminality (and, crucially, convictions of other ranks for indecency) in the Army during the war, it does not include the number of commissioned officers who were convicted of indecency in any of the three services. This data, which I have compiled from registers at the National Archive, is summarised into table 2.[16] In the Army, the RAF and the Royal Navy, 1,813 cases of indecency were taken to courts-martial between September 1939 and August 1945, a figure which includes commissioned officers. 1,428 of these men

Table 1 Comprehensive summary of court-martial convictions (British other ranks, home and overseas), 1 September 1939–31 August 1945.

Offences	1939–1940	1940–1941	1941–1942	1942–1943	1943–1944	1944–1945	TOTAL
Cowardice	–	5	26	24	41	71	**167**
Offence against inhabitant	80	22	52	159	165	94	**572**
Sleeping on or leaving post	475	983	631	610	467	688	**3,854**
Mutiny	72	4	79	61	344	240	**800**
Striking or violence to superior	550	947	960	1,003	1,223	1,375	**6,058**
Threatening or subordinate language	369	856	746	952	1,089	1,251	**5,263**
Disobedience	554	1,618	1,689	2,148	2,676	2,725	**11,410**
Resisting escort	115	226	221	250	277	316	**1,305**
Desertion	552	2,724	4,322	5,113	5,719	12,310	**30,740**
Fraudulent enlistment	8	17	27	32	12	4	**100**
Absence without leave	1,488	12,358	15,091	13,936	14,167	18,117	**75,157**
Fraud	71	160	183	134	146	158	**852**
Theft	639	2,186	3,230	4,166	3,842	4,536	**18,599**
Self-inflicted wound	22	10	19	8	40	238	**337**
Indecency	48	76	92	116	134	324	**790**
Drunkenness	554	555	252	729	765	957	**3,812**
Allowing to escape	2	114	144	125	114	154	**653**
Escaping	184	1,132	833	697	643	576	**4,087**
Losing by neglect	679	5,104	5,189	1,472	849	634	**13,927**
Injuring property	30	150	165	160	166	141	**812**
Falsifying official document	25	84	123	128	181	182	**723**

Table 1 (continued)

Offences	1939–1940	1940–1941	1941–1942	1942–1943	1943–1944	1944–1945	TOTAL
Enlisting after discharge with ignominy	7	–	1	–	1	2	**11**
False answer on attestation	6	38	23	25	11	6	**109**
Ill-treating a soldier	65	130	126	139	144	161	**765**
Miscellaneous Military offences	860	3,251	3,811	4,738	4,880	5,545	**23,085**
Miscellaneous Civil Offences	228	654	1,140	1,307	1,276	1,436	**6,041**
TOTAL	7,683	33,404	39,197	38,323	39,372	52,141	**210,029**

Notes:
TNA WO 277/7: War Office, *The Second World War, Army 1939–1945: Discipline* (London: HMSO, 1950) 1939–1945).
Discrepancies in totals are original.

Table 2 Breakdowns of court-martial cases and convictions for indecent behaviour in the Army, RAF and Navy, 1 September 1939–30 August 1945.

Table 2.1 Breakdown of cases and convictions for all courts-martial recorded against commissioned officers and other ranks in the Army at home and abroad, 1939–45.

Army all ranks		Convictions and total cases (conviction rates in brackets)		
		Total	OR	CO
GCM	Home	57/68 (83.8%)	5/6 (83.3%)	52/62 (83.9%)
	Abroad	66/117 (56.4%)	15/18 (83.3%)	51/99 (51.6%)
DCM	Home	42/56 (75%)		
	Abroad	46/61 (75.4%)		
FGCM	Home	378/468 (80.8%)		
	Abroad	518/630 (82.2%)		
	Total	**1107/1400 (79.1%)**		

Table 2 (continued)

Table 2.2 Breakdown of cases and convictions for all courts-martial recorded against commissioned officers and other ranks in the RAF at home and abroad, 1939–45.

RAF all ranks	Convictions and total cases (conviction rates in brackets)		
	Total	OR	CO
GCM	Home 30/39 (76.9%)	15/16 (93.8%)	15/23 (65.2%)
	Abroad 25/31 (80.6%)	5/5 (100%)	20/26 (76.9%)
DCM	Home & Abroad 71/94 (75.5%)		
FGCM	Abroad 56/72 (77.8%)		
	Total 182/236 (77.1%)		

Table 2.3 Breakdown of cases and convictions for all courts-martial recorded against personel in the Royal Navy at home and abroad, 1939–45.

Navy all ranks	Convictions and total cases (conviction rates in brackets)	
	OR	CO
	119/145 (82.1%)	20/320 (62.5%)
Total	**139/177 (78.5%)**	

Table 2.4 Overall figures and conviction rates for all courts-martial recorded against personel in the Army, RAF and Navy, 1939–45.

Army, RAF and Royal Navy	Convictions and total cases (conviction rates in brackets)
Other Ranks	**1270/1571 (80.8%)**
Officers	**158/242 (65.3%)**
Grand Total	**1428/1813 (78.8%)**

Key:
GCM – General Courts-Martial
DCM – District Courts-Martial
FGCM – Field General Courts-Martial
OR – Other ranks
CO – Commissioned officers

were convicted of indecency, a conviction rate of 78.8 per cent. While the overall conviction rate across all three services was fairly consistent (between 73 and 79 per cent) the conviction rate for officers, 65.3 per cent, is surprising low. This seems to suggest that officers were much better positioned to excuse their behaviour than the average other ranker. In the Navy alone for instance, 32 officers were taken to courts-martial for indecent offences between September 1939 and August 1945. One officer's sentence was annulled on the grounds of insufficient evidence and eleven others were acquitted.

However, by way of a comparison, officers in the Army appear have escaped punishment rather less frequently than officers in the Navy. 161 cases were brought against officers in the Army, of which 103 resulted in convictions. These convictions represent 9.3 per cent of the total number of convictions in the Army as whole; a number which needs to be offset against the proportion of commissioned officers in the Army. Over the course of the war, commissioned officers constituted between 6.6 and 7.6 per cent of overall personnel of the Army.[17] Statistically then, convictions of Army officers for indecency were more prevalent than convictions for indecency among other ranks. Seemingly, Army officers were held up to a higher standard of decorum which seemed to result in a higher rate of convictions. In the absence of any detailed case notes for each court-martial that was held in the Navy, it is difficult to explain exactly why the conviction rate was so low. However, the high rate of officers who were acquitted of same-sex indecency suggests that it was difficult to obtain evidence that could be used to secure a definite prosecution. For example, one of the only cases of indecency between males that is documented in The National Archives involves an acting sub lieutenant on HMS *Jamaica*. In 1943, the officer was accused of indecent assault and an act to the prejudice of good order and naval discipline. He was subsequently acquitted based on lack of evidence, specifically, that the accused had failed to identify the officer (who had supposedly touched his body and genitals) with any certainty.[18]

In terms of the locations where courts were formed, the court-martial registers for the Army offer a good sense of the extent to which overseas service contributed to higher instances of indecent behaviour. Over the course of the war, 808 cases of indecency involving Army personnel were heard overseas versus the 592 cases that were heard in courts-martial on British soil.[19] This should be understood in the light of more men being sent overseas rather than as evidence that instances of indecency increased exponentially in overseas theatres. As the war progressed, increasing numbers of servicemen were redirected to overseas locations, thereby outnumbering their counterparts serving at home. In the Army alone, 2,620,000 men (out of 3,788,000) served outside the UK during the war.[20] This suggests that the increase in overseas convictions can be largely explained by the rising strength of the overseas contingent rather than by an explosion of indecency. And while I suggested in chapter two that some servicemen were less sexually inhibited while serving outside Britain, the figures warn against assuming that this was the case for all.[21]

Unfortunately, the one fundamental flaw in any interpretation of the data is the use of the catch-all term indecency which, as I have already highlighted, encapsulated a whole raft of 'deviant' heterosexual and same-sex behaviour including bestiality, indecent exposure, receiving indecent material through the post and indecent assault. It is therefore nearly impossible to quantify with any real accuracy how many of the indecency charges that were recorded in the registers for the Army, the RAF and the Navy referred to same-sex offences between men. The only way to establish whether a case involved heterosexual or same-sex activity is to cross-reference each charge in the register against the corresponding charge in the charge book, thereby establishing a clear link between act, charge and punishment. By way of a sample, I examined all of the charges contained in the charge books that were lodged against men in the Army between 1939 and 1945. The books appear incomplete in that they do not appear to document all of the courts-martial that occurred between 1939 and 1945. In this sense, while they cannot be used to quantify cases of same-sex indecency they are nonetheless useful in highlighting the relationship between indecent acts and the charges that were subsequently filed against an offender.

Of the 178 cases which involved Army personnel being charged for indecency in these charge books, 51 dealt with heterosexual offences and 127 dealt with same-sex offences.

As table three indicates, unspecified acts of gross indecency, buggery and groping appeared most frequently in the charge books. Gross indecency was usually used as a generic category when, for whatever reason, a more specific offence could not be cited against an offender. Most of these charges would have involved non-penetrative sexual acts because if penetration was involved, a charge would normally have been classed as buggery rather than gross indecency. Likewise indecent assault was also used as a generic category even though some of the charges specify that a victim was groped.

This small snapshot provides us with a crucial insight into the behaviours that might reasonably result in a formal charge versus a

Table 3 Charges documenting same-sex offences in the Judge Advocate General's charge books for the Army, 1939–45. Compiled from INA WO 84/52–72

Charges	
Attempt to procure	15
Attempted buggery	7
Buggery	24
Found in a toilet together	1
Found in the same bed	5
Groping	24
Gross indecency (unspecified acts)	26
Indecent assault (unspecified acts)	17
Masturbation in front of Army personnel	4
Mutual masturbation	1
Request to get into the same bed	1
Spent the night together in same room	1
Undoing fly	1

more informal punishment. Even the suggestion that two men had slept in the same room or had performed an indecent act with one another was sometimes enough evidence to propel a charge to a court-martial. As we might expect however, there are anomalies in the records. I discovered an additional six men who were charged with scandalous conduct and behaviour which prejudiced good order and discipline whose offences with other men were very clearly of an indecent nature. Interestingly, one of these cases – that of a lieutenant who propositioned his male staff – was framed as scandalous behaviour and conduct to the prejudice of good order and discipline in the charge book and later appears as indecency in the court-martial register, which in itself suggests that charges could be reframed before the onset of a trial. It is therefore possible that a number of charges which were entered in the registers as scandalous behaviour or conduct to the prejudice of good order and discipline were actually masking incidents which were indecent (and vice versa). This potentially increases the number of courts-martial for indecency, making any quantitative approach at best an indication of trends rather than an accurate quantification.

In this sense, the data both from the registers and from the charge books are far from accurate. With regard to the latter, while the charge books illuminate the specifics of particular offences and charges, they represent only a fraction of the cases of indecency that were brought to court-martial during the course of the war. It would therefore be inaccurate to claim that the greater frequency of charges lodged for same-sex offences (127 out of 178) represents unequivocal evidence that same-sex indecency outnumbers heterosexual indecency, not least because this particular sample is too small and its representativeness is difficult to judge. Moreover it is entirely possible that the higher figure for acts of same-sex indecency versus heterosexual indecency relates to the exigencies of the war, namely the segregation of the sexes and the health risks associated with local women and prostitutes rather than any wholescale explosion in homosex. It could also relate to 'official' military intolerance of same-sex activity.

In spite of the uncertainty that obviously affects the accuracy of the data, it is still possible to make the claim that indecency, however it was manifested, did not constitute a major problem for the Armed Forces. 1,813 servicemen of all ranks were tried by courts-martial for indecency in the Army, the RAF and the Navy, yet a total of 5,896,000 men served in the three forces between 1939 and 1945.[22] There are a number of factors which go some way to explaining why instances of indecency appear relatively infrequently in comparison to other offences. As I will go on to explore, unofficial tolerance and the nature of wartime policing undoubtedly played a part. It is also possible that fear of the consequences deterred some men from seeking out suitable sexual partners. There are also other, more tangible explanations. For instance, the civil courts had the power to deal with cases in which a serviceman had committed a crime against the person or property of a civilian.[23] Certain offences such as treason, rape and manslaughter had to be tried by a civil court and commanding officers were specifically required to report serious offences such as treason, murder, sexual assault and any cases involving a civilian or their property to the police.

The main factors which determined whether a case was dealt with by the civil authorities were, first, whether the case involved a serviceman committing an offence against a civilian or their property and, second, the circumstances surrounding the detection of the offence. If, for instance, a soldier and civilian were caught in a civilian environment by a member of the civil police, it was usually dealt with by the civil authorities.[24] One case from 1943 involving a low-ranking airman and a telephone operator found committing an unspecified 'indecent act' in the toilets of London's Trocadero cinema demonstrates this. It was dealt with entirely by the civil authorities, beginning with Tower Bridge Magistrates' Court and

Table 4 Homosexual offences known to the police and proceedings taken in England and Wales, 1939–45.

Date	Homosexual offences known to the police	Persons proceeded against
1939	1,192	595
1940	1,156	545
1941	1,324	616
1942	1,788	721
1943	2,076	886
1944	1,912	806
1945	2,000	782
Total	11,439	4,951

Compiled from Home Office, *Committee on Homosexual Offences and Prostitution* (London: HMSO, 1957), pp. 130–1.

ending with the Central Criminal Court.[25] The serviceman would not have faced a retrial by a court-martial and his case would not have been included in the registers which recorded courts-martial.

The tabulation above is taken from the Wolfenden Report and provides an indication of how many incidences of homosex were known to the police and how many were proceeded against (but not necessarily convicted) over the course of the war.[26] Some of these would certainly have involved servicemen and civilians but it is impossible to determine how many servicemen might have fallen under the jurisdiction of the civilian courts.

A sample analysis of all the 'indecent acts' that were heard at one London borough court, specifically the Tower Bridge Magistrates' Court between 1939 and 1945, reveals 49 arrests for importuning, masturbation (by individuals and between couples) and other less specific acts of indecency. Only four of those cases involved servicemen.[27] In this sense, there is no reason to assume that these additional figures (if, that is, they could be separated from offences between civilians) would have had a significant impact on the number of cases brought against servicemen by the armed forces or on the number of convictions. However, they might help to explain why there were so few convictions for indecency recorded by the registers, given that cases between servicemen and civilians were not dealt with by a court-martial. To clarify, cases dealing with gross indecency between servicemen and civilians that were tried by civilian courts could have reduced the number of cases coming before courts-martial, thereby reducing the number of cases that would be documented in the Army, RAF and Navy registers. However, even taking this unknown number into account, there is little evidence to suggest that the total number of cases would have constituted a significant problem for the services.

The relatively small number of convictions in the services also relates to the nature of military justice. Courts-martial were the last disciplinary option at the end of a broad spectrum of options, all of which were less inconvenient and less public than a court-martial. Military courts were time-consuming to organise and expensive to convene, and these were factors which sometimes worked to persuade commanding officers that they should be avoided. As John Carrington Spencer noted, '[the] expenditure of time and labour which the system involves is prodigious especially in time of war'.[28] For example, a written summary of the evidence had to be provided and each court required a specific number of officers to be present. A district court-martial had to be presided over by a field officer and required at least three officers from different corps to be present, all of whom had to have held a commission for at least two years. General courts-martial required five officers with no less than three years' commissioned service, and the president of a general court had to be a general or a colonel.[29] Accordingly, because of the cost and the organisation involved in convening a court-martial, they were not ordered unless there was a significant chance that a serviceman would be convicted. This attests to the value of summary action and also suggests that offences had to hit a particular benchmark of seriousness and convictability before they were considered for a military trial.[30] Moreover, whether a trial was subsequently ordered depended on 'the prevalence of the particular offence charged, the general state of discipline in the corps or district' and 'the character of the accused',[31] all factors which would seem to suggest that courts-martial were used only when they were unavoidable and that they were used as exemplary mechanisms of control.[32]

It is clear then that courts-martial were used as a deterrent both because of their relative rarity and because of the way that they were publicised. Internally within the services, sentences which had been confirmed were 'promulgated in the orders of all of the formations in which the convening of the court had appeared and in every case in the orders of the unit concerned'.[33] The confirming authority could also recommend that cases and verdicts were read out on parade as a warning to the other members of the unit. Externally, courts-martial were open to the public and the press.[34] While there is little evidence to suggest that the press were a consistent presence at every court-martial, *The Times* did publish small articles of particular court-martial cases as 'News in brief' and in lists of official appointments and notices under the heading 'London gazette', which included men who had retired, been appointed or left one of the services.[35] Such notices sometimes included men who had been court-martialled, usually with their name, rank and date of their dismissal.

During the whole of the war, however, *The Times* only documented two cases of gross indecency involving servicemen, presumably because of the notoriety of the men involved. One case was the court-martial of Captain Sir Paul Latham of the Royal Artillery. The former MP for Scarborough and Whitby was found guilty of indecency in September 1941 and was cashiered and sentenced to two years' imprisonment. In summing up the case, Sir Patrick Hastings spoke of 'the horrors of publicity given to a case of this sort. Sir Paul Latham's life is now pretty well damned'.[36] Even though the register book and the particulars of Latham's crimes as described in *The Times* both confirm that Latham was charged and found guilty of homosex, *The Times* did not make any reference to gross indecency.[37] Instead, the newspaper used the vague term 'disgraceful conduct', thereby drawing a veil of secrecy over the specifics of the case.

The only other case of same-sex indecency reported in *The Times* was the hearing of Captain Ian Colin Maitland, Earl of Lauderdale, who was arrested in 1943 for 'engaging in an act of impropriety' with a kitchen porter.[38] Although I will discuss Maitland's case in more detail later on in the chapter, it is worth noting *The Times*' ambiguous description of his offence. The earl was caught engaging in mutual masturbation yet this is almost impossible to decipher from the press report.

If reporters happened to attend a hearing, they could generate a great deal of unwanted publicity for the service, the offender and his family. The Air Ministry were so perturbed by this that they requested that 'wherever it is possible, cases should be disposed of summarily, and that no-one is brought before a court-martial if it can possibly be avoided'.[39] In the RAF, the sentence passed at a court-martial remained secret until it was disseminated to the man's unit. The press would not be furnished with any general details about a court-martial but if they asked for them, the RAF was obliged to check the facts and confirm them. In the Navy, the press could ask the naval information officer at each port if there were any cases about to be heard. Moreover, a court-martial flag was flown by the commander-in-chief when a court was sitting.[40] In the Army, the policy was similar to that of the Navy. The finding and sentence of a court-martial were usually given to the press if they made a specific enquiry about a particular case. Lists of courts-martial were not made available for the press until 1948 when the Army began to answer press calls about cases and began posting lists of forthcoming trials at each Army command.[41]

In the event that the press turned up for a court-martial, Army officers were advised to make it clear that:

> Although there is no wish to interfere with the publication of proceedings of trials held in open court, it should be borne in mind that publicity of a soldier's trial may be harmful to him on return to civil life, and it is desirable that it should be carefully considered whether the soldier deserves such publicity, especially for a purely military offence.[42]

Moreover, officers were requested to handle the press tactfully and ask them to exclude from their report 'matters which it is not in the interests of the Service to publish or which would cause unnecessary pain and suffering to innocent parties'.[43] However, as a member of the Judge Advocate General's office argued in the following memo from 1942, when the power of a deterrent was required, the press was a powerful weapon:

> It is the fear that those with whom he normally has to associate will know of his misdoings, that keeps the average citizen (including an officer or a soldier) on the straight and narrow path. It may be brutal, but it seems to me essential to retain in these difficult days the maximum deterrent effects possible. No soldier will suffer if it is known in his local circle that he has been absent without leave; but he will, and in my view should, suffer if he has been found guilty of, say, some disgraceful conduct of an indecent kind under section 18 (5) of the Army Act, which is a military offence.[44]

The public shaming of men through public court cases had to be carefully negotiated. Too many public cases of indecency would have harmed the image of the services and the British overseas, thereby undermining the war effort and the ongoing recruitment drive. Too few and the armed forces might have faced accusations that they were harbouring 'criminals'. In the event that a case of indecency threatened to undermine the public face of the armed forces, it could be held in camera away from the public's gaze. Courts were usually held in camera when they involved 'a thoroughly unsatisfactory state of affairs in a unit, such as a general state of indiscipline, that can fairly be ruled as one providing information of value to the enemy because it gives food for enemy propaganda or shows a state of bad morale in our Army'.[45] Usually these were political cases involving spies or the ill-treatment of prisoners of war, for instance. In such cases the War Office would usually become involved if it believed that a case should not be disseminated to the public.[46] When such an order was made, only the sentence would be read in open court; the finding would not be declared unless the person had been acquitted.

Another more underhand technique used by the armed forces was to hold serious cases of indiscipline in forbidden or hard to reach areas, thereby excluding the press and the public and frustrating the efforts of reporters. The Army's Director of Public Relations denounced this as 'discreditable subterfuge'[47] because, although such cases were still technically public, they could not be attended by those outside of the establishment. Overseas court-martial hearings also offered the offender and the service a greater degree of privacy because it was less likely that the press would know about the case and be able to attend the trial.

The value of a judicious court-martial and, more importantly, a heavy sentence awarded to a serviceman who had committed an act of indecency (that was subsequently read out to an offender's unit) was that it was intended to encourage discreet behaviour and, in some cases, discourage sexual activity altogether. Richard Briar remembered meeting one soldier who was awaiting a court-martial for having been discovered conducting a sexual relationship with a young soldier. The recruit

> made a point of telling me that what I was doing was illegal and a court-martial offence in the Army and I said 'yes, I was perfectly well aware of that' but I trusted my own discretion and common sense to make sure that I was not going to be running the risk myself … court[s]-martial deterred people but it didn't stop people … it just made them extra discreet about being detected.[48]

While the threat of a court-martial was less an incentive not to pursue desire and more of an incentive to pursue it inconspicuously, some men made a conscious decision not to conduct relationships with others in case they were caught out. Frank Brown limited himself to cruising and little more during his service in the RAF for instance.[49] There is ample evidence to suggest that he was not alone in abstaining from sexual and emotional relationships with other men while on active service.

While it is clear that trials were sometimes used judiciously by the Armed Forces in order to deter would-be offenders, for the most part the services were keen to avoid too much undue publicity in case it harmed their reputation and undermined the confidence and trust of the general public. For these reasons, officers sometimes chose to avoid courts-martial altogether and deal (away from the courts) with men deemed to have committed homosex. It is, therefore, likely that many more 'offences' than appeared in the court-martial registers were ignored or dealt with away from official channels for reasons of discretion, efficiency, morale and the conservation of manpower. If the services were reluctant to bring the accused to court, they could choose from a number of alternative responses. Summary punishments were the least serious disciplinary response, followed by options which included relocating an offender and discharging them through medical channels or as 'services no longer required.' The purpose of the following section is to illuminate why, in the first instance, a commanding officer made the decision to discipline a serviceman or woman.

Confirmation, consent and competence: taking the decision to discipline

At the most basic level, disciplining homosex for both genders hinged upon the notion of absolute proof, that is, the positive identification of men and women whose activity was too self-evident to be ignored. In the ATS, for instance, officers were advised by Letitia Fairfield, the retired chief medical officer of the ATS, to act only on 'definite evidence'.[50] In practice, however, this 'evidence' often proved difficult to obtain. Fairfield herself was astute enough to warn officers that sartorial styles and forms of self-presentation amongst queer women were more nuanced than they were popularly constructed. In her opinion, neither a 'masculine physique [n]or the adoption of male clothing or pursuits' constituted evidence that a woman was queer.[51] Likewise, officers were warned that even women sharing beds 'may be doing so for warmth and because they have slept with their sisters all their lives' and, moreover, that women demonstrating their affection for one another 'may be following the normal customs of factory life'.[52] Fairfield also displayed a remarkable unwillingness to link queer desire to its physical expression. 'Even consciously homosexual friendships between women are usually kept entirely on a mental plane. Perverted physical practices ... are fortunately rare. Where this occurs it is usually among women of a depraved type or among the self-conscious intelligentsia, who are probably more actuated by craving for excitement than any real desire.'[53]

In this way, physical and sexual intimacy between women was framed as the furthest pinnacle of female deviancy rather than as a simple manifestation of desire. It was also deemed to belong to intelligent women and certainly not those from the working classes, whose bed-sharing was rooted in poverty rather than perversion. Fairfield's willingness to deny 'physical practices' and, moreover, explain behaviour that might otherwise have been taken as confirmation of lesbianism, gave officers a very limited and ultimately prescriptive definition of 'definite proof' that in all likelihood required women to be caught in the act on a number of occasions. However, in never making this explicit and moreover, in suggesting to officers what did not constitute 'definite proof' rather than what did, Fairfield effectively sidled away from the issue, her criteria of identification offering numerous loopholes but little else. While this ensured that only those against whom there was unflinching evidence were disciplined, it also meant that most women would probably have been given the benefit of the doubt. It is perhaps also telling that the ATS did not have any guidance on dealing with same-sex attraction until 1943 when Fairfield, who had retired as chief medical officer a year earlier, was asked to produce her secret memo, 'A Special Problem'. Even after its publication, there was still an unwillingness to lecture women openly on the subject in case it occasioned 'too much talk'.[54]

In the Army there was a similar emphasis on 'confirming' that a man possessed a queer identity. In a memorandum written in 1942, the psychiatrist John Bowlby, who worked for the Royal Army Medical Corps, advised officers and particularly those attached to training battalions to identify 'feminine types and confirmed homosexuals' along with other servicemen who displayed character traits such as bedwetting, insomnia and nail-biting. Bowlby warned officers that such characteristics 'may indicate mental defect or temperamental instability', and men displaying any one of them would be 'very liable to break down in action … the majority (although not all) will make bad front-line soldiers'.[55] This memorandum, written more than two years into the war, was clearly a pragmatic response to the problem of wastage. 'Confirmed homosexuals' were identified as a possible source of loss and, in identifying them, Bowlby was suggesting that they might not be valuable to the Army in a combat capacity. However, the memorandum contains a number of key caveats. If these men had to be 'confirmed', what kind of evidence was required? It might be assumed that Bowlby was referring to men who performed effeminately and incompetently and possibly those who were caught in the act with others. Moreover the term 'confirmed' strongly hints at a distinction between men deemed to possess a queer identity and those who had merely engaged in homosex, suggesting that incidents that could be constructed as 'isolated' or 'deprivational' might be ignored.

On the whole, the memorandum offers a narrow construction of queerness. To be identified as such, soldiers would have to appear as they were conceptualised in popular culture, that is, as flamboyant and effeminate. Those who were passing and those who adopted more masculine forms of self-presentation were conspicuously absent from Bowlby's instructions, as were those whose sexual activity was discreet or infrequent enough to avoid confirming that they possessed a queer identity. Accordingly, discretion was often pivotal in helping a serviceman or woman to remain in the services. What is more, it appears fairly consistently in the recollections of queer men and women when discussing their own conduct and that of others less willing to conform. Dennis Campbell summed up its importance in reference to his service in the RAF when he said, 'it [queerness] was never a source of contention just as long as you did your job properly [and] you were discreet about your behaviour'.[56]

The other major issue that dominated the discussions of officials attempting to define the contours of disciplinary action was efficiency. In both the WAAF and the ATS it became a fundamental benchmark in the identification of, and action against, queer servicewomen. In the WAAF, for instance, Violet Trefusis-Forbes, the Director of the service, believed that only lesbians who were disrupting their own work and that of other servicewomen should be dealt with.

> In approaching an airwoman or officer who we are fairly convinced is a Lesbian, or in approaching one whose behaviour is such as to suggest she is, we should point out to her that her behaviour is that of a schoolgirl and that these sentimental attachments are not what we expect from airwomen who must necessarily always set a good example to others. That unless she can behave herself as a sensible adult we consider that she will have a detrimental effect on discipline generally [and] we would have to dispense with her services.[57]

This extract alone reveals just how pragmatic Trefusis-Forbes was prepared to be. According to the memo, an airwoman would only be approached if her behaviour was sufficiently 'convincing' and if there was ample evidence that it was adversely affecting the discipline of others. As a scribbled note by Trefusis-Forbes on the bottom of the memo attests, such women were classed as 'misfits', that is, recruits who did not fit into life in the WAAF. This emphasis on efficiency was drawn on fairly consistently by Trefusis-Forbes. In one instance, she became involved in the case of two women at RAF Upwood who had been accused of being in a relationship after some of their correspondence was discovered by their commanding officer.

> In view of the fact that the writers of both letters are obviously in a highly temperamental and peculiar state of mind and are miserable if parted for a few hours at a time leads me to suppose that their work

is unlikely to be as efficient as it would otherwise be. Since these two airwomen appear to be unable to behave like grown-up people who belong to a fine service and that their childish conduct cannot be overlooked any longer, they must be separated.[58]

Once again, the root of the issue was not the mere presence of the women but their inefficiency and the detrimental impact of their behaviour on the 'fine' reputation of the WAAF. In positioning efficiency as the foremost consideration, Trefusis-Forbes suggested that it was not the presence of queer women that was the problem. All women regardless of their sexual preferences would be retained by the service and by their units if they were sufficiently mature and competent. If they were not, however, they would be separated, not excluded. In the ATS, Letitia Fairfield also underscored efficiency and discipline as the guiding principles when it came to dealing with queer women. Women 'sharing an excessive attachment' were separated by reposting only if they could not be 'diverted by other interests'. Moreover the exigencies of war meant that only more serious cases of 'perverted practices or [women who] attempted [to] corrupt other women by talk or example' were considered for discharge.[59]

Crucially, both Fairfield and Trefusis-Forbes encouraged disciplinary action only when the work of a servicewoman was thought to be impaired or if there was evidence to suggest that a woman was 'corrupting others'. These were stipulations that worked in the favour of women who became involved in relationships with others. In effect, queer servicewomen would be ignored on the condition that their conduct was neither deemed to be affecting their ability to work nor viewed as detrimental to discipline and the reputation of their respective service. Anecdotal evidence gleaned from oral testimony substantiates this approach. We have already heard from a former member of the WAAF, Elizabeth Reid Simpson, who was told by a fellow recruit to ignore a female couple in the bunk above her on the grounds that 'they don't fancy you' and were therefore not a threatening presence.[60]

One reason which explains why some known queer service personnel were ignored while others were disciplined can be explained by the attribute of the 'good fellow'. As we have seen, the quality of being a 'good fellow' could work to neutralise the activities of an individual. Take, for instance, the case of Richard Briar, who, as we have seen, discovered a well-organised system of sexual activity between recruits and instructors at his training battalion. On one occasion Briar was seen by his commanding officer in a compromising position with his company's sergeant major, Ted. Briar was only partially hidden from view by a bush and found himself staring directly at his commanding officer, who promptly looked away and walked on. When Briar questioned Ted about the officer's lack of reaction, Ted commented, 'Billy Boy never does see anything that it's inconvenient to see'.[61] In explaining this scenario, Briar invoked an implicit understanding of the 'good fellow'. Ted was a valuable member of Briar's training battalion and, if the commanding officer had chosen to 'see' the men as opposed to ignoring them, he would have been forced to undertake costly, time-consuming and morale-deflating disciplinary proceedings against two men who possessed skills which were more important than their off-duty relationships. Their indiscretion was therefore counterbalanced by their 'good fellow' status and the understanding that sexual activity between recruits and senior ranks might be an important part of the training battalion. Such pragmatism was less likely to occur in the city because regulatory agencies, and those whom they policed, were anonymous entities, unknown to each other. While men discovered committing homosex in the city were defined and judged by those activities, men in the armed forces could often avoid prosecution because of their value to the war effort and because they were known to their units. Moreover, the cost and organisation involved in calling for a court-martial often meant that it was easier to ignore such activity. This quiet accommodation was rather more commonplace than we might imagine. Moreover, rather than expressing ignorance, it more commonly demonstrated a willingness to ignore.

One individual who could not be protected by the 'good fellow' attribute was the writer George Green, who was court-martialled for indecency while serving with the Army. Green's case offers an explicit example of how the absence of the 'good fellow' designation could work against a serviceman discovered committing indecency. Green edited and produced magazines for the forces in Ceylon. His free time was spent in the pursuit of 'verandahism', 'a compound of drink, sex, benzedrine and cigarettes', so called because it took place on a verandah which Green had taken over as his own.[62] According to his colleague Ronald George, Green's 'abandoned and happy' off-duty behaviour was a source of contention with two officers within his mess who vowed to catch Green out. In 1944, they achieved their goal. Green was seen 'on his bed, all lights on, in the wrong place, at the wrong time with someone whose company ... could only be regarded as by the military authorities as conduct unbecoming'. The mess servant who witnessed the scene had spread the story 'more in a sense of amusement than hostility', but this reached one of the officers who disliked Green. The result was a court-martial and a sentence of two years' imprisonment with cashiering.[63]

The officer's personal vendetta against Green was as much if not more to blame for his activity being reported as the indiscreet nature of his offence in the first place. Had Green been a well-liked and respected member of his mess, he might have avoided prosecution altogether.

Discretion, efficiency and professionalism were therefore hugely important. This is confirmed by Charles Pether, a queer man who served in Alexandra with the RAF. Pether described two 'absolutely brazen' queer men in his unit in Alexandria who were put on a troop-ship back to Britain. According to Pether the men openly cruised for men and 'had a ball':

> [T]hey were called into the adjutant's office and apparently they knew what it was about because David put a little lipstick on and fluffed up his hair. [The officer] said 'Ball and Parker, we have had some complaints about you.' And one of [them said] 'Well I'm sorry to say sir, we've had no complaints.'[64]

It is reasonable to assume that it was not the knowledge that same-sex activity was occurring which influenced the decision of the adjutant, but the knowledge that the camp was being disrupted by two soldiers who were not prepared to behave discreetly and who were adversely affecting the discipline of their unit.

On the other hand, behaviour which was deemed to be harmless was often ignored. In his memoirs, the heterosexual veteran R. C. Benge described being sexually assaulted on two separate occasions by soldiers in his unit. In the first incident, he was groped by the platoon sergeant when he was half-asleep, something he attributed to the sergeant's drunkenness. On the second occasion, Benge recalled being groped by a private during a 'stand to inspection'. The soldier later came to apologise prompting Benge to dismiss him and inform him that 'the incident would be forgotten'.[65] The willingness of Benge to forget the incidents can be explained by his understanding of wartime deprivation and his uncompromising acceptance of the queer men who served in his battalion, one of whom was a company commander and a 'much admired' officer. The knowledge that same-sex activity was occurring and that 'a percentage of homosexuals much higher than the national average had somehow found its way into our Battalion' was understood and ignored because it was deemed to be harmless.[66]

Benge's recollections also reveal the importance of the presence of an understanding third party, whether it was an officer called upon to deal with a case or a hut full of comrades. They could be pivotal in determining whether an offence was ignored or what level of punishment was metered out. Joan Wyndham served in the WAAF and was forced to report the activities of a sergeant and a fellow WAAF following information from Wyndham's 'busybody' NCO that the two women were sleeping together. Wyndham was reluctant to pass the complaint on, not least because she felt intimidated by the sergeant who she described as 'big and tough with an Eton crop'.[67] She was, however, forced to report the couple because her NCO had displayed less willingness to ignore their activity than Wyndham herself, something made evident by Wyndham's reference to the NCO being a 'busybody' who unnecessarily meddled in the affairs of others.

The ability of a recruit to avoid detection and prosecution could then often depend on the willingness of his or her comrades to turn a blind eye. During his service in the Army, Jimmy Jacques dated men and would sneak out at night to visit them. He maintained that his fellow recruits in the barrack room realised what he was doing: 'I think it was pretty obvious because the guys in the barrack room used to say "Oh we know what you're up to" and all that sort of thing'.[68] Jacques was never challenged however and continued to date other Army personnel until he was demobbed. In choosing not to report their suspicions, Jacques' barrack hut displayed a willingness to protect and collude with him. Likewise, in the following passage, a veteran of the Army describes a case of mutual masturbation that was 'hushed up' before the Battle of El Alamein:

> A soldier in our brigade was discovered masturbating with a private in a tent and they were both put on a charge by the sergeant major. Our colonel, who was himself a homosexual, was absent, and so the case went right up to the brigade headquarters. The brigadier, who had been a boy soldier promoted through the ranks and to whom nothing in army life was a surprise, dismissed both men with a reprimand. The colonel was absolutely furious that it had got as far as it did. 'The battalion's been out here for two years, these two youngsters had never had home leave,' he stormed afterwards in the mess. 'Out in India when I was in the ranks, reveille brought every man tumbling out of everyone else's bunks. What the hell do they want the men to do for sexual relief, go down the brothels in the bazaar, chase Arab women and catch syphilis?'[69]

Given that the soldiers were put on a charge by the sergeant major, we might assume that he was somewhat less accepting of homosex than his superiors. The willingness of both the brigadier and the colonel to disregard the incident has a great deal to do with the status of mutual masturbation as an activity that was not indicative of a queer identity and possibly suggests that the officers believed that the two men were sexually frustrated, fatigued and unwilling to engage in heterosexual sex because of the likelihood that they would catch venereal disease. Finally the colonel's reaction and his sympathy for such cases was no doubt a deterrent to those who might consider reporting cases of indecency in the future.

One reason which helps to explain why disciplinary action was sometimes instigated relates to activity which occurred against the consent of an individual. Moreover, it was usual for incidents which involved officers to be viewed more seriously and subsequently treated more punitively by the courts, because senior-ranked men were required to set an example to others and there were often questions of abuse of power to be considered. However, seniority could also afford a degree of protection. We have already heard the case of Major Peter Burke,[70] an officer who was notorious for assaulting his men. Burke's activities were never prosecuted. However, the testimony of those who worked alongside the officer, which can be found at the Imperial War Museum, provides unequivocal evidence of his aggressive attempts to facilitate sexual contact with the men under his command.[71]

The five drivers who were assaulted by Captain Charles Bernard, an Army officer with the Oxford and Buckinghamshire Light Infantry, provide yet more evidence of the privileges granted by rank.[72] All of the drivers were members of 52 Division of the Royal Army Service Corps. In 1940, Bernard was found guilty of three charges of indecency. It was alleged that he had placed his hands on the thighs of three drivers, undone one driver's flies and placed his fingers into two of the drivers' flies with intent. Bernard's defence rested on the assertion that the jolting vehicle with its small dimensions and Bernard's oversized map board had forced him to rest the board on the thighs of his drivers and touch their thighs whilst reaching for his map case.[73] The officer did not attempt to explain why he had inserted his fingers into the drivers' flies. One of the men admitted that he did not report the assault until well after the event because it was 'my word against his'.[74] However, seniority could work both ways, that is, as a means of protection or as an assurance that disciplinary action would have to be taken.

To summarise, formal disciplinary procedures were usually invoked against individuals and couples because of a combination of factors which included inefficiency, indiscretion, the absence of consent and the absence or disintegration of the 'good fellow' attribute. It is highly likely that each individual unit treated homosex and the presence of queer personnel in a different way, depending on various factors which included its operational status, location in the field and the appropriateness of proceeding with a formal court-martial. This latter factor was strongly dependent on the certainty that a conviction would be achieved. As we have seen, there were also more subjective factors to be considered including the value of an individual, the disruption caused by their activity and the extent to which they had violated their unit's unwritten codes of morality and behaviour. Despite the stock response of the King's Regulations, disciplinary responses to same-sex indecency were rather more nuanced. Having explored the factors which could influence the decision to either invoke formal disciplinary action or avoid it, the chapter will now examine the range of summary punishments available to officers in dealing with same-sex activity.

Summary punishment, reposting and discharge

Overwhelmingly, pragmatism and the needs of the war effort were the two main factors in determining how a recruit should be disciplined. Accordingly, summary action was sometimes the best approach; it was immediate and it avoided the removal of a recruit from the war effort except for a short period. Officers had the power to invoke any punishment within the King's Regulations including detention (for a maximum of 28 days), fines (up to £2 for drunkenness only), pay deductions (up to £4), confinement to barracks (up to 14 days), extra guards and piquets (duties), and admonition.[75] It is probable that some of these punishments were meted out to offenders instead of more serious disciplinary action taken through a court-martial. Ultimately, it was the officer in charge who had the final say as to how a recruit should be disciplined. Alan Shaw served in India with the Army and recalled how a senior NCO was accused of an unspecified indecent act with a boy soldier. Instead of a formal trial, the NCO was offered a voluntary reduction in rank to corporal which he accepted. The need for manpower was so great that a year later, the man's rank was restored.[76] In this way, the decision of an officer to invoke summary punishment depended on the value of an offender and the impact that their absence might have on the strength of a unit, but also on the seriousness of the offence and whether or not the individual was a valued member of his or her team. In the story told by Shaw, the NCO's value to the war effort was regarded by his commanding officer as significantly more important than his actual offence.

Aside from summary punishments, reposting an offender was also an option, either as a means of separating two recruits or in order that an individual could pursue his or her interests in private. One unnamed psychiatrist believed that during the war 'the conservation of manpower was an essential priority ... it was often considered practical and realistic to post known homosexuals of good intelligence and proved ability to large towns, where their private indulgences were less likely to be inimical to the best interests of their service'.[77] In the WAAF and the ATS, the 'judicious posting' of an individual as a means of separating a couple was one of the primary disciplinary techniques invoked against queer women.[78] Sometimes this was preceded by a period of observation and an imposed separation during which time a couple would be forced to work in separate locations or on separate shifts. The covert observation of queer women and their co-workers may also have been pursued in the WRNS. Margaret Lane, a former member of the Voluntary Aid Detachment, was asked to observe two Wrens and 'find out what I could' about them. After listening to complaints from their co-workers that the women were 'sleeping together and cuddling etc', Lane informed the matron in charge and the women were separated.[79]

On the whole, Trefusis-Forbes, the Director of the WAAF, was keen to give women 'the chance to pull [themselves] together after a talk or two' before she would consider reposting them. Similarly, Letitia Fairfield encouraged officers to separate a couple only if 'they cannot be diverted by other interests'.[80] Such references to the remedial value of talks and diversionary interests attest to a common cultural discourse or what Oram terms 'a loose Freudian typology' which constructed lesbianism as an emotional throwback and something which, consistent with prevalent ideas about same-sex boarding school environments, adolescents usually grew out of.[81] This was the line taken by the sexologist Havelock Ellis whose study of lesbianism through the lens of boarding-school friendships and in particular, relationships between older and younger women, dominated popular and sexological typologies of same-sex relationships well into the 1950s.[82] For instance, the sex adviser Rennie MacAndrew believed that public schools created particularly favourable conditions for the spread of lesbian desire, a 'habit' that he deemed to be both 'innocent and passing'.[83]

Given these fairly consistent understandings, it is not surprising that Fairfield described lesbianism as 'essentially the persistence of an immature mental and emotional phase'. Trefusis-Forbes followed Fairfield's lead and interpreted it as a 'silly schoolgirl craze'. Essentially, such women were viewed as immature anomalies who in failing to progress into adulthood, had become permanently trapped in a phase of adolescent infatuation.

It may be argued that nothing more is involved than a highly developed 'schoolgirl craze' between two foolish and ill-balanced young women … grown-up women do not usually indulge in these silly 'schoolgirl crazes' which are only indulged in by young girls and which most people learn to despise as they grow older and more sensible.[84]

As Rebecca Jennings highlights, such attachments were 'both deviant and normative' in that they were considered to be part and parcel of adolescence.[85] Indeed, as Jennings goes on to discuss, the phenomenon of the schoolgirl crush or 'pash' had provoked considerable debate among educational commentators, doctors and youth workers since the nineteenth century. It was also a popular and established theme in adolescent fiction up until 1928.[86] Arguably, the prevalence of this discourse of 'boarding school desire' offered a degree of license for the expression of same-sex desire. Indeed, it is perhaps not surprising that some women who were caught in the act invoked the very same discourse to affect a degree of sympathy. When Stevie Rouse discovered two women in the same bed using a dildo, the couple's first line of defence was the claim that it was the first time they had used it, and the first time that they had acted on their feelings.[87]

In general, officials in the WAAF were keen to repost a recruit, and continue to repost them at regular intervals (to make it harder for them to form new relationships), only if 'there is no clear proof of perversion and where the woman is efficient at her WAAF trade'.[88] Discharge from the service would only occur in the event that a woman was deemed to be a corrupting influence on others or what Lieutenant Colonel Albertine Winner, consultant to the women's services, called 'a promiscuous psychopath'.[89] Winner maintained, however, that only 'some half-dozen women had to be discharged [from the services] on these grounds … it was not due to ignorance of the possibilities, though there certainly was a very sensible awareness of when action was and was not required'.[90] This 'sensible awareness' offered a degree of protection to those who were astute enough to mask their behaviour. If 'promiscuity' and 'psychopathic' behaviour were used as benchmarks to identify serious cases, it was not hard to beat the system, characterised as it was by a degree of uninterest and a willingness to ignore all but the most obvious and disruptive.

For men and women who were deemed to be 'psychopaths', one of the options available to the services was a medical discharge on the grounds that an individual was indeed a psychopath or a neurotic, a route which bypassed the courts and prevented any undue attention both for the individual and their respective service.[91] This was the preferred choice of the British Army which often chose to 'quietly invalid [homosexual offenders] out of the service, with appropriate medical advice'.[92] The Royal Air Force also discharged men in this way. Arriving at an accurate estimation for how many men and women were medically discharged for their sexuality is impossible, however. We know for instance that in labelling recruits arriving in the United Kingdom following service overseas, the Emergency Medical Service classed 'sexual perversions' as a form of neurosis along with other 'illnesses' including alcoholism, hysteria and neurasthenia or nervous exhaustion.[93] The label psychosis was, on the other hand, used to identify such illnesses as post-traumatic psychosis, manic-depressive psychosis, melancholia, paranoia and schizophrenia. It is likely, however, that queerness fell under both of these categories. For instance the 1948 publication *The Statistical Health of the Army* summarises, among other things, the number of psychiatric cases treated in military psychiatric hospitals under the generic headings 'psychosis' and 'psychoneurosis and psychopathic personality'.[94]

If we are to accept that same-sex desire was deemed to be either a form of neurosis or an indication of psychopathy, the implications of such labels are problematic, though entirely plausible to doctors in the 1940s. As categories of mental illness 'neurosis' and 'psychosis' cover a multitude of afflictions; their generic non-specificity means that although we can ascertain how many members of the armed forces were discharged under these headings, we will never know how many of those were actually discharged for actual or alleged queerness.[95] Moreover as diagnostic typologies, the labels are bound to the notion that same-sex desire was abnormal, and manifested itself in mental abnormality or abnormal behaviour. This in turn tunes into culturally prevalent ideas about the visibility (in both dress and behaviour) of queer men and women, namely that they were uniformly effeminate and, in the case of women, masculine in appearance.

However, it seems unlikely that a medical officer diagnosed queerness very frequently. Unless that information was volunteered or discovered, we have to assume that very few men (and women, for that matter) were diagnosed as suffering from neurosis that was directly traceable to their sexuality. It is more likely that they were diagnosed as suffering from a mental condition, of which sexuality may or may not have been viewed as a contributory factor. This is suggested by Charles Anderson's 1944 article 'On certain conscious and unconscious homosexual responses to warfare', based on his work at the Wharncliffe Neurosis Centre. Of the 209 'conscious homosexuals' seen by Anderson between 1939 and 1945, 153 had been admitted for anxiety states, 19 for hysteria, 15 for paranoid attitudes, 15 for depression, four for attempted suicide and 12 for anti-social behaviour.[96] Anderson's 203 'unconscious homosexuals' were divided in a similar way, although 169 were thought to be suffering from anxiety states; 33 of those were for anxiety states with 'mourning patterns' which Anderson assumed were reactions to the death of friends and lovers.[97] None of these men were admitted to Wharncliffe purely on account of their presumed queerness but for symptoms that were later attributed to it. We might also question the extent to which Anderson's awareness of same-sex desire was matched by other psychiatrists working in connection with the Armed Forces during the war.

In the event that a serviceman or woman required psychiatric help, whether voluntarily, following the recommendation of an NCO, or before a court-martial, they would have been assessed by the unit medical officer and then referred to the command's psychiatrist. In the Army, command psychiatrists were expected to assess each case that came before them and recommend a course of treatment or suggest that a patient should be transferred to a military mental hospital or an Emergency Medical Service hospital. Patients deemed to be psychotic were sent to one of thirteen military hospitals set aside specifically for their treatment. Cases of psychoneurosis were sent to Emergency Medical Service (EMS) neurosis centres, and after 1941 discharged neurotic patients were placed into supervised jobs where they could still be useful to the Army.[98] There were EMS neurosis centres at Mill Hill, Sutton, Shotley Bridge, Cardiff, Southport, Dudley, Whitchurch, Borocourt, Bromsgrove, Woodside, Nuneaton, Reading (for women only) and Sheffield.[99]

In the overseas commands, resources were sparser. In 1942 three consultant psychiatrists were sent to India, Gibraltar and North Africa. North Africa was also given an adviser in psychiatry during 1943, and the 10th Army had one consultant and two psychiatrists.[100] By January 1944 there were 171 psychiatrists working for the Army in the UK and 85 working overseas including 15 in North Africa and 21 in India. By 1944 the RAF was employing 36 psychiatrists.[101] Both overseas and at home commands the system was strained. According to John Bowlby, there were only 'a few psychiatrists on each command. Medical specialists have independently remarked that their physicians would at once be swamped if they sent every patient on whom they would like an opinion'.[102] Such a shortage placed the system under a great deal of pressure. Under such circumstances only individuals demonstrating acute or dangerous levels of psychiatric instability would have been investigated and, for that matter, discharged.

It might reasonably be assumed that command psychiatrists and their staff possessed neither the time nor the compulsion to treat queer men and women who displayed no visible signs of mental illness or who had not been caught engaging in homosex. It is more likely that they assessed and treated patients who were sent to them because they were identified as suffering from mental health problems rather than because they were known to desire members of the same sex. There is a further point to be made here too; understandings of queerness were simply too undeveloped in medical and psychiatric circles for there to be any coherent scheme of identification, let alone treatment. Indeed, the treatment in itself was dependent on over-worked medical officers and psychiatrists diagnosing a mental illness and attributing it to queerness in the first place. Those who did send personnel for curative therapy were probably in a minority. It is far more likely that psychiatrists took a more practical approach to the problem, especially in the case of service personnel who admitted their queerness without having been caught committing indecency.[103] For instance, Dudley Cave served in the Army and, during his demobilisation medical, informed the medical officer that he was queer. Cave was then sent to see a psychiatrist at Millbank EMS hospital and fully expected to undergo a period of treatment. Instead the psychiatrist recommended that Cave should endeavour to find a suitable male partner with whom he could settle down.[104] Evidently, Cave's psychiatrist understood that his sexuality could not be altered. This was also the opinion of Charles Anderson who, in reference to the treatment of soldiers accused of committing homosex, was also acutely aware of the war and the limitations it imposed. In his 1944 article he remarked that 'under present circumstances the only practicable approach to the overt homosexual is to remove as far as possible the anxiety, paranoid or hysterical superstructure. [T]o convert a fully developed homosexual into a heterosexual is not much more promising than to do the reverse'.[105] With this in mind, it is unclear what kind of treatment the two women at RAF Upwood were receiving when Trefusis-Forbes commented that they were 'under medical treatment'.[106]

A positive avowal of queerness could secure a discharge on medical grounds or at least a period of 'treatment' which would remove personnel from active service, a fact that some men and women decided to work to their advantage. John Alcock, a queer veteran of the Army, had been conscripted into the service in the late 1940s. However, on becoming tired of Army life he chose to admit his queerness to the medical officer, thereby securing his own discharge through medical channels. He termed this admission 'taking the veil', a religious analogy which, in Catholicism and Islam, alludes to taking a vow of obedience or chastity.

In reclaiming this phrase and playfully inverting its meaning, Alcock signalled that his obedience to the Army was over and that he was both coming out of the organisation and out to the authorities.[107] While this policy of automatic dismissal may have been invoked more often in the post-war period of national service, given that manpower was less desperately required, Alcock was not the only one to secure a discharge in this way. Pat James, a driver in the WAAF, secured her own discharge after she declared her sexuality to a psychiatrist. 'I happened to hear that people were getting out of the WAAFs by being lesbians. So I thought that I would. I went to a psychiatrist, and I got out very easily. He just asked me how I felt when I saw a woman, about my reaction, I told him and I was out very quickly.'[108]

Others were less successful in convincing the authorities of their queerness, either because it was assumed that they were feigning their feelings to effect their own discharge or because their commanding officer was keen to retain them. We have already seen how Dennis Prattley attempted to force his way out of the Navy by admitting his queerness to a psychiatrist on three separate occasions, only to be turned down because he was too valuable to lose.[109]

Why then might an admission of queerness force a discharge given that it was unlikely to preclude a recruit's recruitment at their medical assessment? It is possible that discharges were granted because the 'straightening out' of an individual had failed to rectify their sexuality, something which, as we shall see, was probably more likely if the admission came from an older serviceman as opposed to a younger and therefore more 'redeemable' recruit. Moreover, as the war in Europe began to wind down and post-war national service began in 1945, there was no longer a need to recruit and retain personnel as urgently as before. In this sense an admission of queerness was more likely to result in a discharge if it occurred towards the end of the war.

A significant but unquantifiable number of men and women who desired members of the same sex were discharged through medical channels, either because they were deemed to be neurotic or psychotic or because it was an easy way of avoiding undue attention for someone who had admitted their queerness, truthfully or not. Based on the figures given by Anderson, who admitted 412 'conscious and unconscious homosexuals' into the Wharncliffe Neurosis Centre between 1939 and 1944, it is probable that many more queer men were hospitalised for a condition somehow attributed to their sexuality. These men are another unknown figure, invisible simply because the action taken against them was not a court-martial. Another 'invisible' statistic pertains to men and women who were discharged as 'services no longer required', otherwise known by the acronym SNLR. Often this catch-all term was deliberately used to discharge recruits who had engaged in homosex because as an administrative discharge it did not leave a paper trail. It was also sufficiency vague to cover a multitude of offences. In the WAAF and the WRNS, discharge was the final and most serious action that could be taken against a queer woman. Accordingly, discharges under SLNR were a valuable deterrent. Trefusis-Forbes was convinced that periodic discharges of women under 'services no longer required' would 'undoubtedly act as a warning on the Station that she [a suspected lesbian] came from'.[110] However, SNLR discharges were not quite as neutral as they appeared to be. Indeed, if such a discharge followed a good service record, it was often more desirable, in the WAAF at least, to give a 'fictitious cause' since the implicit message of an SNLR discharge to a future employer was that a particular woman was not worthy of retention.[111]

Summary punishments were obviously preferable to a court-martial and it is probable that they were invoked more often in the women's services in relation to queer offences because while same-sex acts between women were not illegal, officers had to respond to women whose activities were too disruptive to ignore. In the male services on the other hand, discharges and repostings were discreet alternatives to formal proceedings. This in itself renders it impossible to quantify how many men and women were disciplined because such activity did not leave a paper trail. What we can attempt to quantify, however, are the 'official' punishments that were meted out at court-martial.

Official disciplinary responses

This section of the chapter relies largely upon my work with the Judge Advocate General's charge books which record some of the charges laid against Army personnel during the war. By matching this data with the court-martial register and specifically identifying which cases of indecency were for homosex rather than heterosexual acts, it is possible to identify trends in sentencing. While this data can only be correlated for general courts-martial at home (an unrepresentative register in that it overwhelmingly documents charges against officers and more serious cases involving other ranks) it will at least offer an insight into the types of charges that were levelled against men discovered to have committed homosex.

Out of the sixty-eight entries for indecency recorded in the registers for general courts-martial in the Army at home, fifty-one can be traced to the Judge Advocate General's charge books. Of these fifty-one, six refer to offences against women which leaves forty-five indecent offences which were committed by men against men. In terms of sentencing, the most common sentence which followed a conviction for same-sex indecency was cashiering with imprisonment, usually with a sentence of hard labour. This sentence was recorded fifteen times. Hard labour usually involved heavy, physical and repetitive tasks such as rock-breaking and sewing mail bags. If an officer was cashiered, he also lost his commission and faced a dishonourable dismissal from his service. Cashiering was considered to be a more 'ignominious form of dismissal',[112] because once cashiered, former officers lost various rights of citizenship, including the right to work for the Crown and the opportunity to apply again for a commission. Additionally, officers who were cashiered faced the added embarrassment of explaining to their friends and family why they had been dishonourably discharged in the first place. Plain dismissal on the other hand avoided this indignity and allowed a convicted recruit to be re-employed by their respective service.

Of the forty-five cases of same-sex indecency that are documented in the charge books, plain cashiering was the second most common sentence delivered at courts-martial, occurring twelve times. Of the charges that are left, seven men were acquitted, seven were dismissed, two were severely reprimanded and a further two received eighteen months' hard labour. It is surprising that we see any severe reprimands for indecency at this level of courts-martial since the register from which the sample is taken is for general courts-martial which overwhelmingly dealt with commissioned officers and senior NCOs. The two officers in question were lieutenants; one was found guilty of an attempt to procure the commission of an indecent act and the other of indecent exposure and inappropriate physical contact with a prisoner of war. Severe reprimands were verbal warnings which were usually awarded because of a professional failing. However, they were usually given out for small-scale offences committed by other ranks and therefore it is unclear why two commissioned received such a lenient punishment.

The figures suggest that the majority of cases were dealt with more compassionately than the King's Regulations might lead us to expect. Officers who were acquitted, cashiered and dismissed outnumber those who received sentences of imprisonment. In addition five men had their sentences reduced by the Judge Advocate General during the confirmation of their cases. The confirmation process itself was deliberately designed to offer a fair appraisal of a case and the sentence that had been awarded. Sentences were rarely overturned but it was not uncommon for them to be significantly reduced.[113] For instance, one lieutenant was sentenced by general court-martial to two years' hard labour with cashiering for grasping the buttocks of a male sergeant. His sentence was later commuted to eighteen months' hard labour.[114]

Similarly, appeals could be submitted by convicted servicemen and cases were automatically reviewed every two or three months, the result of which was sometimes the reduction or suspension of a sentence. Often these decisions were driven by wartime necessity. One such example is that of Company Sergeant Major Firminger. He joined the Army in 1934, and in 1939 he was found guilty by general court-martial of attempted buggery and attempted suicide. He was sentenced to a reduction of rank, two years' imprisonment with hard labour and discharge with ignominy. The Army Council later remitted the discharge with ignominy and part of the unexpired sentence. In 1942, he was recommended for re-promotion, and it was subsequently decided that he had been 'suffering from a disease and was now practically cured' following a period of psychiatric treatment.[115]

While none of the officers in the sample received sentences of detention, this was a fairly common response to instances of indecency among other ranks and NCOs. In the registers for district courts-martial and field general courts-martial, sentences of detention are by far the most prevalent. Detention was one means by which an offender could be retained within their respective service and differed from imprisonment, which involved no such rehabilitation. Indeed, the War Office preferred to rehabilitate offenders found guilty of indecency. It advised that only 'confirmed homosexuals whose rehabilitation is unlikely should be removed from the Army by the most expeditious and appropriate means'.[116] This was not medical rehabilitation but disciplinary rehabilitation administered by military detention centres. Such 'treatment' was pursued not for the benefit of the individual but for the needs of the country.

> The offender is very often retained in the Service, not because we look on his crime any less severely but because with conscription for the forces and civil labour the country needs his services in the capacity for which he has been trained. In other words, we have more regard for the country's benefit than for that of the individual offender. [117]

Detention, as opposed to imprisonment or penal servitude which usually implied automatic dismissal, was usually reserved for offenders who were thought to be redeemable and could be returned to the armed forces following a sharp injection of discipline, training and education. This is made explicit in the following memorandum from the Air Ministry:

> Imprisonment should, as a rule, be reserved for offenders convicted of serious offences, or of grave Air Force offences, which, in the opinion of the court, renders their discharge advisable. If the nature of the airman's offence does not warrant discharge, detention, rather than imprisonment, should, as a rule, be awarded.[118]

Men sentenced to detention underwent a process of training including military instruction, assault courses, industrial work and courses of education. Consistent with the 'healthy body, healthy mind' ethos, there was also a heavy emphasis on sporting activities including athletics, boxing and team games.[119] This approach also fell in line with criminological understandings of same-sex desire which posited it as a moral failing. Men sentenced to such periods of detention were, in effect, being 'retrained' in the hope that a sharp injection of military discipline would straighten out their tendencies or at least encourage them not to indulge in them.

On the whole, officials within the Air Ministry were keen to rehabilitate men convicted of gross indecency as long as they were judged to be redeemable, that is, to quote one official, 'if the offender is young and there seems to be a reasonable prospect that he will respond to punishment and not repeat the offence'. (In a later revision, the word 'punishment' is crossed out and replaced by 'corrective treatment'.) Moreover, a comment scribbled in the minutes by one official concludes: 'I am prepared to consider individually those in category A (ii) (a) [homosexuals], provided that they are the passive parties and not the active'.[120] Evidently, therefore, the official viewed passive participants as less threatening than active ones. However, this willingness to retain those deemed to be the passive party in an offence runs contrary to notions of active and passive roles in military culture. Indeed, it was often the active or penetrative male who was elsewhere in the services viewed as the more excusable party, because his active role was seen to mimic heterosexual intercourse and was considered to be more normative (and more deprivationally motivated) than a passive sexual role. In wartime, such active behaviour could easily be passed off as an aberration motivated by heterosexual desperation. The reversal of this construction is, however, easily explained. Presumably, the official in question hoped to retain younger, passive partners in the hope that any same-sex activity was an adolescent phase that might be 'straightened out' by physical training and military discipline. This was certainly the opinion of the sexologist Desmond Curran. Writing in 1938, Curran believed that doctors should not:

> [c]onclude that the case is one of fixed or congenital inversion until at least the age of twenty-five has been reached, and sometimes, until even later ... the guiding principle is perhaps that these manifestations [in adolescents] should not be taken too seriously or too tragically ... many of the conflicts and fears of congenital inversion may be avoided or overcome by sensible explanation and sexual instruction. [121]

As we have seen, policymakers in the ATS and the WAAF were also keen to connect same-sex expression between women with immaturity or as a throwback from adolescence. Fairfield for instance believed that lesbianism was an 'immature mental and emotional phase',[122] and, likewise, Trefusis-Forbes viewed queer women as youngsters indulging in 'foolish school-girl crazes', most of whom would grow out of the habit. In advising her officers to redeem women displaying these 'crazes' through a stern 'talk or two', Trefusis-Forbes was tuning into popular discourses about situational homosex and moreover the difference between recruits whose queerness was 'true' and those who, to quote the Admiralty, had been 'led astray by youth or ignorance'.[123] Overwhelmingly, the latter faced a more sympathetic audience.

For those who could claim neither youth nor ignorance, there were other arguments that could be invoked to defend an offence. For some, this involved a claim of victimhood, that is, that a second party had forcibly coerced an individual. Bill Tawse, for instance, is queer and served as a naval medical orderly. He was caught having sex with an American soldier and, in desperation, jumped into the Mersey River. Sensing Tawse's regret, the orderly's senior officers decided to defend him based on the claim that the GI had coerced Tawse to have sex with him. All that was required was for Tawse to deny that he had invited the soldier's attention.[124] He was eventually found not guilty.

Interestingly, however, remorse did not always work to neutralise the verdict of a court-martial. We saw earlier how Captain Sir Paul Latham of the Royal Artillery was cashiered and sentenced to two years' imprisonment without hard labour. He too attempted to commit suicide by driving a motorcycle into a tree. However, perhaps the crucial difference between the case of Tawse and that of Latham rests on the latter's seniority both within the Army and in his peacetime role as a Member of Parliament. Moreover, it would seem that the severe punishment awarded to Latham and the extensive publicity which surrounded the case was in part a deliberate attempt to deter would-be offenders.

Wartime deprivation was another argument which was often invoked in the defence of an individual. Homosex that could be constructed as isolated or motivated by the deprivations of war was usually treated more sympathetically than those which took place between persistent or 'confirmed' individuals. As we have seen, when Stevie Rouse discovered two women in the same bed using a dildo, the couple's first line of defence was the claim that it was the first time they had used it and the first time that they had acted on their feelings for one another.[125] While this did not prevent them from being reposted, similar arguments were successful in convincing those in authority to take a sympathetic approach. In 1944, for instance, John Boyd-Carpenter appealed on behalf of an Army officer who had been found guilty of gross indecency with his driver and had been sentenced to be cashiered with two years' imprisonment. Boyd-Carpenter defended the officer by claiming that he was a 'happy family man of unblemished reputation … a victim of war'. His sentence was subsequently reduced to one of discharge.[126] This reference to victimhood is a telling cultural reference to ideas about the effect of war on sexual behaviour. As we saw in chapter two, George Ryley Scott's 1940 tirade against wartime immorality, *Sex Problems and Dangers in Wartime*, blamed a perceived rise in homosex on the conditions created by the conflict, namely the risk of catching venereal disease and the burden of 'supporting a baby'.[127]

On a similar vein, Ryley Scott attributed same-sex desire between women to the 'the sexual emancipation' engendered by the war, the 'comparative lack of men', 'the fear of heterosexual alliances resulting from pregnancy' and the 'masculinization of feminine fashions'.[128] Accordingly then, once the war was over and normality was restored, this 'abnormal' and, crucially, situational activity between men and between women would cease to occur. Ryley Scott was not the only advocate of this opinion. The sex adviser G. L. Russell, author of *Sex Problems in Wartime*, believed that most instances of wartime homosex were 'due simply to the segregation of men in large groups cut off from their womenfolk. There is no question of any permanent psychological disorder; it is simply that men seek relief from both sex-starvation and the strain of warfare by the only means that are available – masturbation and homosexual relations.'[129]

Such arguments were often used to defend charges of same-sex indecency. Captain Charles Bernard, the officer charged with five counts of gross indecency with his drivers, certainly invoked this premise of normality. When he took the stand at his court-martial, the officer was quick to present himself as a heterosexual male. He cited his good educational background at Wellington and then Sandhurst and stated that he was a first-time offender who was happily married.[130] When they took to the stand, his witnesses, Major Doyne and Private Brann, continued this line of defence, claiming that Bernard was a 'brilliant athlete ... a very good soldier ... [and] a very great asset'[131] with no 'developmental abnormality', no 'abnormal or vicious ... friends' and no 'abnormal tendencies'.[132] It is evident then that Bernard's defence rested on the premise not only of his value, but his normality. He was depicted as a heterosexual male who came from a stable background and possessed a happy marriage, a circle of 'normal' friends, a good career with a clean record and no signs of 'abnormality'. In short, he was viewed as a victim of the war and was subsequently dismissed from the Army without any further disciplinary action.

Similar arguments were also used to defend Captain Ian Maitland, Earl of Lauderdale, who was attached to the Queen's Own Cameron Highlanders. In 1943, he was caught having mutual masturbation with a kitchen porter in London's West End. Like Bernard, Maitland's defence rested on three factors; his heterosexuality (as evidenced by the fact he was 'happily married'), his drunkenness and his emotional instability owing to the death of his son.

> I'd like to say that I've had a lot of worry lately. My son was killed and I thought I'd have a binge on my own. I was drunk and didn't realise what was happening. It has sobered me up. Isn't there anything you can do? I am happily married and hate this sort of thing, boys and buggery you know. I had no idea you had men out watching for this sort of thing.[133]

Much like Lauderdale, Maitland was also saved by the pledges of his eminent colleagues at the War Office, notably Major General John Hay Beith who claimed that he had never met 'a more normal and natural person'.[134] Following a trial that lasted three days, the officer was found not guilty and acquitted.

Although Maitland was tried by a civilian court, both his case and that of Bernard demonstrate that alcohol, isolated incidents, deprivational behaviour, 'clean' service records and suggestions of an otherwise heterosexual lifestyle could all work in the favour of a serviceman discovered committing homosex. These are telling caveats which suggest an overwhelmingly criminological understanding of same-sex desire rooted in the exigencies of the war. Diagnostically, definite proof or confirmation that a recruit possessed a queer identity usually came from their 'criminal' acts rather than their outward performance. However, acts were not in themselves enough to prove this conclusively. Indeed wartime conditions allowed men in particular to claim that their activities were deprivationally motivated, episodic aberrations rather than indicative of a 'true' queerness. There were of course those who were viewed as 'true' or 'confirmed' for whom there was little defence once they were caught in the act. For the most part, however, the armed forces were willing to consider retention and rehabilitation for those who they deemed to be valuable and receptive to 'treatment'.

Conclusion

While the King's Regulations demarcated the official perimeters of indecent behaviour, the application of the law and the ways in which individuals experienced it differed significantly. Moreover, while the flavour of this chapter has been dominated by the clinical and quantitative nature of the sources from which it is constituted, behind an entry in a register in many cases lay a serviceman who was simply caught out for expressing a desire which the law interpreted as abhorrent. The registers themselves attest to the prosecution of couples and partnerships. Often, brackets were used to unite a pair of names, usually from the same unit, thereby indicating that two men had been caught together. It does not take a great leap of imagination to wonder how many relationships were forcibly ended following a charge of indecency.

Those who were unlucky enough to be caught out by the system were treated in myriad different ways, of which a court-martial was only the last line of action. Officers had the power to decide whether an offender could be ignored or whether more formal disciplinary action should be taken. In these negotiations, not all recruits were submissive recipients of military law. On the contrary, some, like Captain Bernard, took an active role in negotiating the perimeters of the law by, for instance, invoking arguments about normality to reduce the severity of their sentence. Others, such as John Alcock successfully avoided the disciplinary spotlight and yet were able to work the system to their advantage and force their own discharge.

While each service adopted similar techniques of identification and pursued a similar policy of expediency, there are significant differences between prosecution rates in the Royal Navy compared with the Army and RAF. All three of the services did, however, display a distinct uncertainty about same-sex activity, both in terms of how it was manifested and how it might be dealt with most effectively. On one hand, a clear distinction was starting to be made between homosex and queer identity, the latter being conferred upon men by the frequency and sexual role adopted by a particular individual. As we have seen, the Air Ministry were prepared to consider the rehabilitation of young and sexually passive offenders and the Army were largely interested in rooting out men 'confirmed' as queer. In the WAAF and the ATS, the identification of queer women was built upon the visibility of their activities and the notion of 'definite proof'. On the other hand however, understandings see-sawed precariously between a remedial, criminological approach which positioned same-sex desire as an acquired vice influenced by environmental factors, and one which stressed the irredeemability of certain congenital 'psychopaths'. The services were rather more willing to retain the 'redeemables' and only discipline and discharge those who could not be 'straightened out' or those who committed criminal acts which were too visible, disruptive or distasteful to ignore. Overwhelmingly though, and as the musings of military officials throughout the war demonstrate, queerness had yet to make the full transition from an act to an identity. Until it did, policy would continue to be constructed as a crime that was committed rather than as an identity that was possessed.

Notes

1 Letter from J. Clarke to Emma Vickers, 10 October 2005.
2 War Office, *Manual of Military Law* (London: HMSO, reprinted 1939), p. 567.
3 The Army Discipline and Regulations Act 1879, chapter 33, subsection five, within Incorporated Council of Law, *The Law Reports: The Public and General Statutes*, 16 (London: William Clowes and Sons, 1881), p. 116.
4 The Army Discipline and Regulations Act 1879, chapter 33, subsection five, within *The Law Reports*, 16, p. 116, and War Office, *Manual of Military Law*, p. 115.
5 TNA, ADM 105/104, Homosexuality in the Royal Navy in connection with security and blackmail 1957-69, Unnatural offences, circular letter N.L. 5773, 18 December 1913.
6 TNA, WO 84/55, Judge Advocate General's Office: Court-martial charge books, 1 March 1940-16 April 1940, 6 April 1940.
7 TNA, WO 84/53, JAG charge book, 30 October 1939.
8 V. Laughton Mathews, *Blue Tapestry* (London: Hollis and Carter, 1948), p. 117.
9 TNA, AIR 2/6486, Review of WAAF disciplinary cases in the light of the Markham Committee Report, letter from D P S, 16 October 1942.
10 War Office, *Manual of Military Law*, pp. 132-4.
11 TNA, AIR 2/9485, Discharge of airmen for reasons of misconduct during the war, 1940-50, Air Ministry File No A92339/40, Minute Sheet, signed Group Captain Joopan, 9 September 1941.
12 G. R. Rubin, *Murder, Mutiny and the Military: British Court Martial Cases 1940-1966* (London: Francis Boutle, 2005), p. 19.
13 See for instance TNA, WO 93/55, summaries of court-martial, 1939-69. The records for offences of indecency committed between 1952 and 1954 include 'indecent assault

upon males and females, acts of gross indecency between male persons, buggery and attempts ...'
14 TNA, WO 277/7, The War Office, *The Second World War, 1939-1945, Army: Discipline*, (London: HMSO, 1950), appendix 1 (a).
15 TNA, WO 277/7, The War Office, *The Second World War, 1939-1945, Army: Discipline*, appendix 1 (a).
16 TNA, WO 86/97, District Courts Martial: Register, Home and Abroad, Army, 1938-40, TNA, WO 86/98, District Courts Martial: Register, Home, Army, 1940-45, TNA, WO 90/8, General Courts Martial: Register, Abroad, Army Officers, 1917-43, TNA, WO 90/9, General Courts Martial: Register, Abroad, Army, 1943-60, TNA, WO 92/4, General Courts Martial: Register, Home, Army, 1917-45, TNA, WO 213/35-66, Field General Courts Martial (Home and Abroad), Army, 1939-45, TNA, AIR 21/1B, Field General Courts Martial Abroad, RAF, 1918-49, TNA, AIR 21/2, General Courts Martial Abroad, RAF, 1918-60, TNA, AIR 21/3, General Courts Martial Home, RAF, 1918-60, TNA, AIR 21/4B, District Courts Martial Home and Abroad, RAF, 1938-42, TNA, AIR 21/5, District Courts Martial Home and Abroad, RAF, 1942-45, TNA, ADM 194/59, Return of Officers tried by court martial and disciplinary court during the quarter ended 30 September 1939, to TNA, ADM 194/84, Return of Officers tried by court martial and disciplinary court during the quarter ended 31 December 1945; TNA, ADM 194/277, Return of Petty Officers, Seamen and Marines tried by court martial during the quarter ended 30 September 1939, to TNA, ADM 194/301, Return of Petty Officers, Seamen and Marines tried by court martial during the quarter ended 31 December 1945.
17 In 1939 the proportion of officers to men was 1:15 and in 1945 the ratio was 1:13. See D. Fraser, *And We Shall Shock Them: The British Army in the Second World War* (London: Cassell, 1999), p. 52.
18 See TNA, ADM 156/258A, Report of Court Martial, indecent assault on board HMS *Jamaica*: remarks by Naval Law Branch, 1944.
19 The same tabulations were not possible for the RAF or the Navy.
20 J. Ellis, *The World War II Databook* (London: BCA, 1993), p. 229.
21 One of the best known proponents of this view is Ronald Hyam. In *Empire and Sexuality* he argues that young Victorians who went overseas experienced 'an enlarged field of opportunity ... greater space and privacy [and relaxed] inhibitions'. See R. Hyam, *Empire and Sexuality: The British Experience* (Manchester: Manchester University Press, 1990), p. 88.
22 Mellor (ed.), *History of the Second World War: United Kingdom Medical Series—Casualties and Medical Statistics*, p. 829.
23 J. Stewart-Smith, 'Military law: its history, administration and practice', *Law Quarterly Review*, 85 (October 1969), p. 491.
24 For evidence that servicemen and civilians were punished by the civilian authorities for homosex during the First World War, see A. D. Harvey, 'Homosexuality and the British Army during the First World War', *Journal of the Society for Army Historical Research*, 79 (2001), p. 313. See also LMA, A/PMC/40, Public Morality Council, Patrolling Officers Reports, 1938-42, December 1941.
25 The case may be found at London Metropolitan Archives (hereafter LMA), PS/TOW/A/01/213, Tower Bridge Magistrate's Court Registers, April 1943 – February 1944, 19 May 1943 and 27 May 1943. For the Central Crown Court Records see TNA,

CRIM 5/13, Central Criminal Court of Indictments, September 1936 – December 1944, 92 June 1943, case no. 35, and for a slightly more detailed record of the case see TNA, CRIM 4/1700, Central Criminal Court, Indictments, 29 June 1943. Both men received a suspended sentence.

26 See the conclusion for a discussion of the Wolfenden Committee.
27 See LMA, PS/TOW/A/01/203-19, Tower Bridge Magistrates' Court Registers, September 1939 – May 1945. Masturbation and mutual masturbation were punishable under the terms of the Common Law and Byelaw of 1900 which outlawed the outraging of public decency. The latter offence could also be punished under the 1885 Criminal Law Amendment Act.
28 J. Carrington Spencer, *Crime and the Services* (London: Routledge and Kegan Paul, 1954), p. 3.
29 War Office, *Manual of Military Law*, pp. 45-6.
30 War Office, *Manual of Military Law*, p. 48.
31 War Office, *Manual of Military Law*, p. 48.
32 This is the line of thought taken by Connelly and Miller. See M. Connelly and W. Miller, 'British courts martial in North Africa, 1940-3', *Twentieth Century British History*, 15: 3 (2004), pp. 217-42.
33 Connelly and Miller, 'British Courts martial in North Africa', p. 228.
34 TNA, ADM 1/9837, Holding of Courts Martial in Camera, Amendment of BR II – Admiralty Memorandum and Naval Courts Martial Procedure, 1939, minute sheet number 3, 27 September 1939.
35 See for instance 'Quartermaster reduced to the ranks', *The Times* (25 March 1940), p. 8, 'Sapper released by court-martial', *The Times* (10 August 1940), p. 8.
36 'MP to be tried by court-martial, Commons informed of his arrest', *The Times* (1 August 1941), p. 4, 'Sir Paul Latham resigns', *The Times* (20 August 1941), p. 2, 'Court-martial of Sir Paul Latham', *The Times* (5 September 1941), p. 2, 'Court-martial of Sir Paul Latham, not guilty on three of 14 charges', *The Times* (6 September 1941), p. 2, and 'Sir P. Latham sentenced', *The Times* (24 September 1941), p. 2.
37 TNA, WO 92/4, General Court-Martial Register Home, 1939-45, court-martial of Sir H. P. Latham Bart., case heard 4-5 September 1941.
38 'Lord Lauderdale acquitted', *The Times* (24 November 1943), p. 2.
39 TNA, AIR 2/13907, RAF, Courts Martial, Press Questions and Policy, 1926-62, memo by DPS for AMP, 1 April 1938.
40 TNA, AIR 2/13907, RAF, Courts Martial, Press Questions and Policy, 1926-62, minute by Chief Information Office, 1 November 1948.
41 TNA, AIR 2/13907, RAF, Courts-Martial, Press Questions and Policy, 1926-62, minute by Chief Information Office, 1 November 1948.
42 TNA, WO 32/5225, Press Publicity for Courts Martial, 1940-66, memo by DPS, 26 March 1942.
43 TNA, WO 32/5225, Press Publicity for Courts Martial, 1940-66, memo by DPS, 26 March 1942.
44 TNA, WO 32/5225, Press Publicity for Courts Martial, 1940-66, memo from JAG's office, 13 March 1942.
45 TNA, WO 32/5225, Press Publicity for Courts Martial 1940-66, memo by DPR, 13 April 1942. This was sanctioned by the 1939 Emergency Powers Defence Act.

46 TNA, WO 32/5225, Press Publicity for Courts Martial, 1940-66, memo from DPS through JAG, 16 April 1942.
47 TNA, WO 32/5225, Press Publicity for Courts Martial 1940-66, memo by DPR, 13 April 1942.
48 Richard Briar, interviewed by Emma Vickers, 9 November 2005.
49 Frank Brown, interviewed by Emma Vickers, 10 November 2006.
50 LMA, PH/GEN/3/19: Fairfield, 'A special problem,' 1943.
51 LMA, PH/GEN/3/19: Fairfield, 'A special problem,' 1943.
52 LMA, PH/GEN/3/19: Fairfield, 'A special problem,' 1943.
53 LMA, PH/GEN/3/19: Fairfield, 'A special problem,' 1943.
54 LMA, PH/GEN/3/19: Fairfield, 'A special problem,' 1943. Such an attitude reveals a veiled allusion to the notion of lesbianism as an infectious epidemic that would sweep through barrack huts and units and produce legions of lesbian servicewomen. This was certainly an idea advocated by Marie Stopes (1880-1958), a prolific writer of advice manuals and a passionate advocate of birth control. In *Enduring Passion*, Stopes put forward the idea that the opinion that lesbianism was a 'corruption' derived from 'laziness and curiosity' that 'spreads as an underground fire spreads in the peaty soil of a dry moorland'. See M. Stopes, *Enduring Passion* (New York: Blue Ribbon, 1931), p.38.
55 Wellcome Library, John Bowlby collection, PP/BOW/C5/23, Army memo, 1942.
56 Dennis Campbell, interviewed by Emma Vickers, 22 November 2005.
57 National RAF Museum, AC 72/17, Box 5, memo on lesbianism from DWAAF to DDWAAF, P and MS, 8 October 1941.
58 National RAF Museum, AC 72/17, Box 8, letter from DWAAF to DPS, re a case of lesbianism, 2 December 1941.
59 LMA, PH/GEN/3/19: Fairfield, 'A special problem,' 1943.
60 IWM SA, 18201, E. R. P. Simpson.
61 Richard Briar, interviewed by Emma Vickers, 9 November 2005.
62 R. George, 'A disaster, 1944', in G. F. Green, *A Skilled Hand: A Collection of Stories and Writing by G. F. Green*, C. Green and A. D. Maclean ed. (London: Macmillan, 1980), p.106.
63 George, 'A disaster', in Green *A Skilled Hand*, p.108.
64 Transcript of interview with Charles Pether, 3bmtv, (*Conduct Unbecoming* Channel 4 1996), p.11.
65 Benge, *Confessions of a Lapsed Librarian*, p.53.
66 Benge, *Confessions*, p.53.
67 Wyndham, *Love is Blue*, p.103.
68 Jimmy Jacques, interviewed by Emma Vickers, 21 July 2005.
69 Costello, *Love, Sex and War* p.163.
70 Pseudonym.
71 IWMSA, 12242/17, H. Thompson, and 9951/16, W. P. Brown.
72 Bernard is a pseudonym.
73 TNA, WO 71/1049: General Court-Martial of Captain (Temporary Major) C. B. A. Bernard, Oxford and Buckinghamshire Light Infantry, 1940.
74 TNA, WO 71/1049, General Court-Martial of Captain (Temporary Major) C. B. A. Bernard, C. Melville re-examined by Major Marlowe, p.25.
75 TNA, WO 277/7, *The Second World War 1939-1945, Army: Discipline*, p.25.

76 BBC PWA, A3224350, Alan Shaw.
77 Costello, *Love, Sex and War*, p. 164.
78 A. Winner, *Homosexuality in Women*, reprinted from *Medical Press*, 3 September 217:5652 (1947), part of LMA PH/GEN/3/19: Papers of Letitia Fairfield, Homosexuality, 1947-61. See also P. Summerfield and N. Crockett, '"You weren't taught that with the welding"': lessons in sexuality in the Second World War', *Women's History Review*, 1:3 (1992), p. 446.
79 Letter from M. Lane to Emma Vickers, 30 April 2006.
80 LMA, PH/GEN/3/19, Papers of Letitia Fairfield, 'A special problem', 1943.
81 Oram, *Her Husband Was a Woman!*, p. 141.
82 See Ellis, *Studies in the Psychology of Sex* and M. Vicinus, *Intimate Friends: Women Who Loved Women, 1778-1928* (Chicago: University of Chicago Press, 2004).
83 R. MacAndrew, *Encyclopedia of Sex and Love Technique* (London: Wales Publishing, 1941), p. 331.
84 National RAF Museum, AC 72/17, National Box 8, letter from DWAAF to DPS, re a case of lesbianism, 2 December 1941.
85 Jennings, *Tomboys and Bachelor Girls*, p. 17.
86 Jennings, *Tomboys and Bachelor Girls*, p. 21, and Oram and Turnbull (eds), *The Lesbian History Sourcebook*, p. 130.
87 Stevie Rouse, interviewed by Emma Vickers, 17 June 2006.
88 TNA, AIR 2/13859, WRAF, Treatment of immorality, 1945-68, memo to AMP from DPS, 8 September 1942.
89 Winner, *Homosexuality in Women*. See also Summerfield and Crockett, '"You weren't taught that with the welding"', p. 446.
90 Winner, *Homosexuality in Women*.
91 TNA, WO 32/15251, Offences of an indecent or unnatural kind, Army Act 1953-60, L. M. to D. A. L. S. 4/891/ALS4, 23 May 1960.
92 Costello, *Love, Sex and War*, p. 164. See also TNA, AIR 2/12407, Government Committee on homosexual offences, Air Ministry evidence, record of discussions in the Select Committee, 17 February 1953.
93 TNA, MH 76/397, EMS Instruction booklet Supplements No. 7 with 58, Emergency Medical Services Instructions Part 1, Medical Treatment and Special Centres, p. 13.
94 The report refers to psychiatric outpatients in the UK from 1943 until 1944 under the categories of 'psychoneurosis', 'mental defect', 'psychosis' and the ambivalent 'other diagnoses'. War Office, *The Statistical Health of the Army 1943-45* (London: HMSO, 1948), p. 227.
95 118,000 men were discharged from the services on psychiatric grounds between September 1939 and July 1944. Nearly one third of all discharges from the Army were caused by mental illness, and psychiatric disorders were the largest cause of manpower wastage in the British Army. See Salusbury MacNalty and Mellor, *Medical Services in War*, p. 180.
96 C. Anderson, 'On certain conscious and unconscious homosexual responses to warfare', *The British Journal of Medical Psychology*, 20:2 (1944), p. 168.
97 Anderson, 'On certain Conscious and unconscious homosexual responses', p. 168.
98 TNA, WO 222/8, Notes on the administration of Army Psychiatry for the period September 1939-May 1943, p. 4.

99 TNA, CAB 21/920, Psychological Statistics: Out Patients at EMS Neurosis Centres, 1944, memo re EMS Neurosis Centres, 24 February 1944.
100 TNA, WO 222/8, Notes on the administration of Army Psychiatry for the period September 1939–May 1943, pp. 4–5.
101 TNA, CAB 21/2549, Validation of psychiatric procedures in the Services, 1943–45.
102 Wellcome Library, PP/BOW/C5/2/3: Box 109, Notes on selection and diagnosis in the Army, 1942, lecture notes from R. H. Lecture, 1942.
103 TNA, WO 222/1452, Medical Quarterly Report, No. 3 Corps Psychiatrist October–December 1944, p. 2.
104 Hall, Carpenter Archives and Gay Men's Oral History Group, *Walking after Midnight*, p. 33.
105 Anderson, 'Homosexual responses to warfare', pp. 173–4.
106 National RAF Museum, AC 72/17, Box 8, minute on disciplinary cases in the WAAF, 8 December 1941.
107 John Alcock, interviewed by Paul Marshall, July 1985, Hall-Carpenter Oral History Project, BLSA catalogue reference: C456/003 tape. © British Library.
108 Neild and Pearson, *Women Like Us* p. 59.
109 Dennis Prattley, *Timewatch*, Sex and war, BBC 2 1998. This may also have been the case with John Fraser, whose feigned admission of queerness was recalled in the autobiography of the Irish playwright and poet Brendan Behan. Fraser was a seaman working on board a destroyer, a job he disliked. Behan recalled how Fraser was informed by an American naval rating that queer men were automatically discharged as soon as they were discovered. Determined to get off his destroyer and out of the Navy, Fraser approached the captain of his ship and pretended that he was attracted to his oppo. The captain's response was one that Fraser did not expect. 'Pretty nice looking lad. I couldn't blame you for fancying him, but you know how it is. The course of true love never runs smooth. Try and concentrate on your work a bit more'. See B. Behan, *Confessions of an Irish Rebel* (London: Arrow, 1991), p. 129.
110 TNA, AIR 2/13859, WRAF, Treatment of immorality, memo from DWAAF, 2 February 1940.
111 TNA, AIR 2/13859, WRAF, Treatment of immorality, reply to DWRAF's memo by DG.M8, 6 March 1940. Not until 1971 did the Air Ministry consider dropping 'SNLR', because it was preventing women discharged for being lesbians from gaining further employment and therefore penalising the women in civil life for activities not illegal but an offence in the eyes of the military. See TNA, AIR 2/18644, Moral Welfare, unnatural friendships (homosexual practice, 1970–73), loose minute, 'Lesbianism in the WRAF', A. P. Doran, 13 October 1971.
112 War Office, *Manual of Military Law*, p. 465.
113 Connelly and Miller, 'British courts martial', p. 228.
114 See TNA, WO 92/4, General Courts Martial: Register Home, 1939–45, trial date 2 July 1941 and TNA, WO 84/62, Judge Advocate General's Office Court Martial Charge Books, 16 May 2 – August 1941, entry for 16 June 1941.
115 TNA, WO 32/18997, Recommissioning of officers discharged through misconduct or as result of civil court proceedings, 1941–51, confidential Memo from C. J. Wallace, DSP, 13 November 1942, re. CSM Firminger.

116 TNA, WO 277/7, War Office, *The Second World War 1939-1945, Army: Discipline*, p. 96.
117 TNA, AIR 2/9485, Discharge of airmen for reasons of misconduct during the war, 1940-50, King's Regulations, Air Council Instruction, paragraph 1280, clause 7, cited in Minute Sheet Enc. 39A, memo signed by Group Captain Joopan, 12 March 1942.
118 *Ibid.*
119 TNA, WO 226/8, Administration and Organisation of Military Detention Barracks and Military Prisons, 1943, part 1, The Development and Organisation of Military Detention Barracks and Military Prisons, n.d., p. 9.
120 TNA, 2/9485, Discharge of airmen for reasons of misconduct during the war 1940-50, Air Ministry Draft Confidential Order 7A, A.92339/40/P.I., Discharges in War for Disciplinary Reasons, 1941, p. 2.
121 D. Curran, 'Homosexuality', *The Practitioner*, 141 (1938), pp. 285-6.
122 LMA, PH/GEN/3/19, Papers of Letitia Fairfield, 'A special problem', 1943.
123 TNA, ADM 105/104, Homosexuality in the Royal Navy: connection with security and blackmail, 1957-69, Unnatural Offences, circular letter N. L. 5773, 18 December 1913.
124 Jivani, *It's Not Unusual*, p. 71.
125 Stevie Rouse, interviewed by Emma Vickers, 17 June 2006.
126 Boyd-Carpenter, *A Way of Life*, p. 67.
127 Ryley Scott, *Sex Problems and Dangers in War-Time*, p. 76.
128 Ryley Scott, *Sex Problems and Dangers in War-Time*, p. 76. This particular argument was also used in 1928 by the *New Statesman*. 'Now it [lesbianism] is a comparatively widespread social phenomenon, having its original roots no doubt in the professional man-hating of the Pankhurst Suffragette movement, but owing very much to wider causes, arising out of the war and its *sequelae*.' See 'The vulgarity of lesbianism', *New Statesman* 25 August 1928.
129 Russell, *Sex Problems in Wartime*, pp. 53-4.
130 TNA, WO 71/1049, General Court-Martial of Captain (Temporary Major) C. B. A. Bernard, charge sheet, 11 October 1940, examination of Bernard by Mr Humphrey, p. 51.
131 TNA, WO 71/1049, General Court-Martial of Captain (Temporary Major) C. B. A. Bernard, charge sheet, 11 October 1940, Major R. H. Doyne examined by Mr Humphreys, pp. 61-2.
132 TNA, WO 71/1049, General Court-Martial of Captain (Temporary Major) C. B. A. Bernard, charge sheet, 11 October 1940, Pte Brann examined by Mr Humphreys, p. 66.
133 TNA, MEPO 3/2331, The importance of legal aid in cases likely to cause publicity, 1943, minute to S. D. Inspector from Inspector H. Smith, 4 November 1943.
134 'Lord Lauderdale acquitted', *The Times* (24 November 1943), p. 2.

Conclusion

As the Second World War continues on an unstoppable trajectory from memory to history, the obligation of historians to capture the memories of those who bore witness to the conflict becomes ever more urgent. In part, *Queen and Country* represents a response to this sense of urgency. It has told a story about a group of people marginalised and criminalised by the historical record, yet who served and, in some instances, died protecting their country. At its heart lie the experiences of service personnel, such as Jimmy, Frank, Dennis, Richard, Albert, Francis and John. Their stories of love, hope, tenacity and bravery have driven *Queen and Country* on, even when others deemed that they should remain silent.

I began *Queen and Country* by examining the cultural landscape of pre-war Britain and the extent to which stereotypes and understandings of same-sex desire were reflected in the attitudes and behaviours of recruiters during the war. There is little evidence to suggest that men and women who desired members of their own sex were systematically identified for rejection by the medical boards, owing to the emphasis on physical health and because there was neither the knowledge nor the inclination to exclude recruits on the grounds of their sexual preference. To fuel the war, the services needed as much labour as possible. The British did not have such a large recruitment pool as their American counterparts, and so the luxury of being able to exclude those that were judged to desire members of their own sex was simply not an option.[1] Accordingly, the medical boards had one, fundamental prerogative; to process and direct as many men and women into the services as possible, including those who presented bodies and minds that they judged might be improved by the armed forces. While there were clear societal references to a supposed connection between same-sex desire and effeminacy in men and masculinity in women, these typologies were blind to the diversities of identity and the willingness of men and women to pass their way into the services. What is more, any suggestions of same-sex desire were also drowned out by necessity and, at that point in time, the dominance of criminological models which positioned it as a crime rather than an identity.

Two of the major priorities in writing this book have been on the one hand, to uncover how personnel who desired members of the same sex behaved in the services and on the other, to gauge the impact of their presence on the services. It is clear that they experienced the services in vastly divergent ways. Some expressed their sexuality openly while others chose to pass their way through the war. Passing may have been used overwhelmingly as a mechanism of defence but there is something inherently subversive and erotic about passing men and women who fooled the system yet still found the space to express their sexual identity, whether in a barrack hut, on a stage or in a city-centre bar. Moreover, even if most recruits passed their way through the war, there is evidence to suggest that a significant minority were able to express their sexuality more openly. There are complex reasons which help to explain why this latter group was tolerated and retained. Some were considered to be 'good fellows' while others were able to use their seniority to their advantage. Many were also undoubtedly aided by the criminological approach adopted by the services in dealing with homosex. The actual *presence* of men and women who openly identified as queer was largely unimportant because proof of a clear identity (and any disciplinary action that was meted out) came overwhelmingly in response to evidence that homosex had taken place. Even then, absolute proof did not always create enough momentum to provoke disciplinary action. The presence of men and women discovered to be committing homosex only became problematic if those activities were deemed to be detrimental to discipline and military efficiency. Whether or not any such activity was considered to be disruptive depended on a number of factors including its visibility and the seniority and value of the personnel involved.

These factors were explored in the final chapter in relation to the legal action (or, in the case of women, disciplinary action) that could be invoked against an individual accused of committing homosex. The chapter discussed the range of official and unofficial disciplinary mechanisms that were available to the services and explored the data on court-martial proceedings and convictions recorded in court registers and by the War Office. It also further examined understandings of same-sex desire as revealed by the approaches taken by senior officials tasked with disciplining personnel. On the whole, the services pursued a policy of maximum retention whereby only those who were considered to be persistent, 'confirmed' and disruptive were discharged. This unofficial policy represented an ad hoc response to the requirements of the war which demanded that, whenever possible, trained (and therefore valuable) recruits should be retained. However, while this may have indicated pragmatism rather than real acceptance, it still lay somewhat uncomfortably next to King's Regulations. Indeed, there is very little evidence to suggest that military law was applied consistently. One man caught for indecency could be sent to a court-martial and imprisoned while another caught for the same offence might be ignored or verbally chastised. The remarkable malleability of the rules is partially explained by the nature of military justice in the Second World War but it also implies a knowingness and a collusion which goes far beyond the mere turning of a blind eye. We saw for instance how Richard Briar's training battalion coordinated, sanctioned and ignored homosex between instructors and recruits which directly contravened civilian and military laws and how known queer women were retained in the services on the grounds of their ability. Conversely, we also saw the 'official' side of military discipline and in particular, how some men were caught and pilloried in order to serve as an example to others. Underlying all of this disciplinary action was the need to retain as many recruits as possible. This was a prerogative that the services pursued with vigour, even to the extent of re-employing men who had been discharged for indecency.

What then was the impact of the Second World War? In the widest of senses, the war represents an exceptionally important juncture in the history of queer Britain. It is a moment of both transition and crystallisation; a period when queer sexuality was variously comprehended as both acts and identities.[2] Similarly, in medical and criminological circles, understandings of same-sex desire oscillated between an innate and incurable condition and an environmentally induced symptom of loneliness, fear and desperation. It is perhaps not surprising then that policy makers within the armed forces were unwilling to classify queer bodies as irredeemable. It was an unwillingness that suggests not only a fissure between sexual acts and identities but a strong belief in the notion that military service would straighten out even the queerest of bodies. For the men who engaged in sex with other men during the war, sexual labels would never again be as indeterminate. After 1945, and without the heighted state of emergency, the Armed Forces were rather less pragmatic. The laissez-faire attitude that had prevailed between 1939 and 1945 was replaced with a solid doctrine of treatment and expulsion, a doctrine which was strengthened by the Wolfenden Committee's decision not to recommend the decriminalisation of same-sex acts between servicemen.[3] In British society more widely, the post-war period witnessed what Matt Houlbrook has described as a 'hardening' of 'the boundaries between queer and "normal"'.[4]

In this sense, Quentin Crisp's lament that the 'the horrors of peace were many' is, for some, an accurate epitaph for the end of the Second World War.[5] Demobilised and re-equipped with civvies, servicemen and women returned home and began their post-war lives. As Dennis Campbell recalled, making the transition from service life to home life could be traumatic. 'After I was demobbed, I felt kind of lost because I [was] away from this all-male environment and back into ... family life'.[6] Like Dennis, many had revelled in the opportunity to escape the gaze of their parents and relatives, make new friends and see new places. The end of the war meant a return to an old life and for some, a familiar routine. Jimmy Jacques was demobbed and returned his job as a projectionist at the British Picture Corporation. Richard Briar moved to America and became a radio broadcaster. John Brierly went to university and eventually became a sociologist. Albert Robinson joined the civil service. Francis Kennedy resumed his career in engineering, married and had two children. Dennis Campbell and Frank Bolton both became teachers. John Booker was employed as a proofreader at Cambridge University Press and Frank Brown came out of the RAF and missed it so much that he later rejoined the service.

When I asked my interviewees to assess the place and importance of the war in their lives, they all agreed that it was a deeply formative experience. Richard Briar believed that he developed 'socially and sexually' as a result of the war,[7] and likewise John Booker emerged from his Army service with a better understanding of himself and his sexuality. Without the war and his service within it, Booker believed that he would have 'continued at Cambridge and probably been even more closeted. I developed subsequently.'[8] In this sense, the war played a significant role in accelerating the sexual maturity of my interviewees. They met other men, formed social circles, patronised formal queer spaces together and manufactured their own. They fell in love (and out of it) and some became surer and more secure in their identities. Others, however, emerged from the war confused and frightened. For both Frank and John, the advice given by their doctors that their desire for other men could be straightened out by marriage merely hastened the inevitable.

Apart from the importance of the war, another theme that I explored with my respondents was the extent to which they felt part of the wider wartime collective. While most agreed that queerness did not prevent their inclusion, they also agreed that integration could only be achieved through discretion and subterfuge. As Francis Kennedy said, 'nobody walked around saying "I'm gay". There was no problem integrating.'[9] As we saw in chapter two, Jimmy Jacques believed that queer men and women integrated into the wartime community because they had to; 'you just had no alternative'.[10]

Aside from the clear subjective impact of the war on individual lives, the Second World War failed to invoke any real change in understandings and perceptions of same-sex desire which remained in something of a cultural stasis. During the war, and due to a complex mix of obligation, necessity and value, openly queer men (and to a lesser extent, women) were accepted into the emergency contingent. In such conditions, every individual, regardless of their sexual orientation, would be retained as long as their behaviour did not breach the conventions of their particular unit. In the post-war period, this capacity for tolerance was lost. In fact, there is no evidence to suggest that the presence of queer personnel in the armed forces between 1939 and 1945 had any significant impact on the peacetime services or on societal prejudice as a whole. There is, for instance, no sense of a linear narrative in which we can trace the gradual opening of the services to queer personnel based on their effective service during the war.

Proof of the war's limited impact on societal attitudes comes from the 1950s. The decade that followed the end of the Second World War was a period of social reconstruction and consolidation. Propelled by concern about the decline of Britain's population, discourses of pro-natalism and welfarism dominated the political agenda.[11] Chief among these concerns was the apparent decline in sexual morality, which some observers ascribed to the disruptive effects of war, mass mobilisation and the separation of families. Indeed, in a speech given by the Archbishop of Canterbury, Britons were called upon to reject 'wartime morality' and return to living 'Christian lives'.[12] Invariably, the focus of this public discourse fell disproportionately on one figure, the queer man, who became a scapegoat for social angst and international fears about the burgeoning influence of Communism. Rates of detection and prosecution for same-sex offences appeared to confirm that the war had indeed encouraged same-sex activity. In 1938, 719 men were proceeded against for same-sex activity in England and Wales. In 1952 the figure had increased to 2,109.[13] As Houlbrook has pointed out however, the presumed increase in activity was largely a result of the shift from wartime to peacetime operations rather than any whole scale attempt to target same-sex activity.[14] Similarly, Patrick Higgins has shown that there was no 'top-down' order to pursue offenders and moreover, that the increase in arrests and prosecutions in London during the 1950s was due to the zealousness of two or three police districts rather than part of a synchronised effort.[15]

Nonetheless, the Home Secretary Sir David Maxwell-Fyffe was quick to single out the queer man as the main source of social disruption. 'Homosexuals ... are exhibitionists and proselytizers and a danger to others ... so long as I hold the office of the Home Secretary, I shall give no countenance to the view that they should not be prevented from being such a danger.'[16] Maxwell-Fyffe's apparent zealousness plunged queer men into a climate of fear and loneliness. The writer Colin Spencer described living in a 'police state' where letters from friends would arrive with sticky labels affixed to the back to indicate whether they had been opened.[17] Similarly Peter Wildeblood found himself playing along with the heterosexual majority. 'It was necessary for me to watch every word I spoke, and every gesture that I made, in case I gave myself away. When jokes were made about "queers" I had to laugh with the rest, and when the talk was about women I had to invent conquests of my own. I hated myself at such moments but there seemed nothing that I could do'.[18]

As the number of arrests and prosecutions in Britain increased, doctors and psychiatrists reacted by producing a plethora of medical studies which discussed same-sex attraction and how it might be dealt with. These included Michael Schofield's 1952 study *Society and the Homosexual* (written under the pseudonym Gordon Westwood), D. J. West's *Homosexuality*, published in 1955, and two later studies by Clifford Allen and Michael Schofield.[19] Overwhelmingly these studies were sympathetic and progressive. One notable exception was the 1955 work *They Stand Apart: A Critical Survey of Homosexuality* which spoke of queer men and their sexual practices as 'evil', 'corroding' and 'filthy'.[20]

Amid this general climate of fear and revulsion, science was offering a curious means of redemption in the form of so-called 'curative' treatments. This trend towards medical intervention marks a significant shift in the conceptualisation of same-sex desire. In 1948 the World Health Organisation classed homosexuality as a mental disorder, which signified a revision of the perception that homosexuality was a crime to be punished.[21] Queer men and women were therefore classed as treatable subjects whose tendencies might be cured by physical, psychiatric and pharmaceutical intervention.[22] As we have seen, John Brierly and John Brown both saw psychiatrists who advised them to marry women. While

CONCLUSION

Brierly eventually found a more sympathetic psychiatrist, Brown dutifully complied with the advice of his and was forced to hide his sexuality from his wife for over a decade.

Both the armed forces and the prison service began to pursue this curative tack, spurred on by the claims of psychoanalysts. In the late 1940s the prison service began to discuss whether a psychiatrist should be appointed to the service in order to distinguish between 'irredeemables' and those who might be amenable to treatment.[23] These discussions were informed by the Scottish Advisory Council who in 1948 published its recommendations for sexual offenders. The document classified male offenders into three categories; episodic criminals who committed crimes during their adolescence, subjects who might respond to psychotherapeutic treatment, and those in which medical treatment had no chance of success. It was recommended that adolescent offenders be should be treated by a psychiatrist and prosecuted if they refused to submit. Those who it was believed might respond to treatment would be put under prohibition or into prison and treated, depending on the severity of their crime. Men in the third category, 'where treatment would have no reasonable chance of success', should 'either ... be sentenced to a period of preventative detention not exceeding fourteen years or ... be detained in a State Mental Hospital ... on the certificate of two qualified psychiatrists'.[24]

Men who found themselves before a court of law for same-sex offences could often secure more lenient sentences if they agreed to undergo some form of 'curative' treatment.[25] Psychiatric counselling was the most innocuous 'cure' out of a catalogue of treatments which included lobotomies, emetics based on Pavlovian principles, hormone injections and electro-convulsive shock treatment.[26] For the latter, patients were shown pictures of their preferred sex and if they failed to switch off each image in less than eight seconds, they were administered a twelve-volt electric shock.[27]

The press seemed to delight in compounding and exacerbating this climate of fear. The downmarket press in particular produced a plentiful supply of articles and reports which fuelled the hostility towards same-sex desire. The most famous of these was the *Sunday Pictoral's* two-part series published in 1953 titled 'Evil men'. The author of the articles, Douglas Warth, described garrison towns flooded with 'perverts' who picked up soldiers desperate for money and entertainment. 'On Fridays, when they [the soldiers] are paid ... they are more likely to be out with women.'[28] Downmarket papers were not the only ones giving credence to such claims. In 1954, *The Times* compelled the lawmakers to consider setting the age of consent for homosex at twenty-one, thereby protecting the national serviceman 'who is compelled to live for two years in a predominantly male community and faces rather special risks of mixing with homosexuals'. [29]

The presumed explosion of same-sex activity, embodied in a three-fold increase in rates of arrest and prosecution between 1938 and 1952, including a number of high-profile cases, forced the government to consider the application of law in relation to same-sex activity between men.[30] One of the most public prosecutions was that of Lord Edward Montagu, Peter Wildeblood and Michael Pitt-Rivers who, in 1954, were charged with conspiring to incite two members of the RAF to commit 'unnatural offences'.[31] Montagu had contacted the police to report a stolen camera but upon searching his flat for evidence of the theft, the police discovered private correspondence which suggested that Montagu had been engaging in sexual relationships with other men. Montagu was subsequently sentenced to a year's imprisonment for gross indecency while his friends Wildeblood and Pitt-Rivers faced eighteen months. Montagu's dignified pleas for leniency and the subsequent pressure applied by the Church of England and the Hardwicke Society helped to persuade Maxwell-Fyfe that a committee should be established to discuss whether a change in the law was needed. The Church of England was particularly active in calling for change. In 1954 its Moral Welfare Council published *The Problem of Homosexuality: An Interim Report* which argued that although sex between men was a sin, so were adultery and fornication, yet these activities were not punishable by the law. The publication called for a change in the legislation to stop the trend towards police corruption, blackmail and suicides.

The result of this concern was a committee headed by Sir John Wolfenden. Known as the Wolfenden Committee, it was convened for the first time in 1954 and was originally formed to examine the legal status of prostitution, although its remit covered the wider issue of vice. It called together a number of eminent doctors, lawyers and members of the Church and requested information from over two hundred organisations and individuals including the armed forces. By September 1957 the committee had agreed that homosex between adult males in private should no longer be deemed illegal. The justification for this decision was that sex between men was, to quote Wolfenden, 'morally repugnant' but that the law was impractical and should be changed. There was a degree of charitable pity to this argument. Queer men were viewed by the committee as social rejects who could not have wives or children. Therefore they should be granted the freedom to express their desires in private without fear of legal retribution.[32] Staying within the law, however, meant setting the age of consent at twenty-one, a decision which was justified in order to protect the vulnerable young men who were undergoing their national service.[33] In defence of this decision, Wolfenden drew on long-standing concerns about the meagre pay of service personnel.

> We have a good deal of evidence that young men doing their period of National Service are at present very much tempted ... by others. [F]inancial inducements of one kind or another are brought to bear on them and with the point made here of the segregation of large numbers of them into one-sex communities for a long time ... there is more likely to be ... opportunity for them to indulge with them and on them during those ages than perhaps any other time.[34]

Wolfenden's observation tuned into long-held concerns about the paltry pay of the servicemen and, in particular, the sexual and financial transactions that had long occurred between civilians and guardsmen. There was, however, a separate consideration. In the opinion of the Air Ministry the advent of peacetime conscription meant that 'men born with homo-sexual tendencies who would not normally be attracted to service life are now being called up for their National Service'.[35] Even though 'men with 'homo-sexual tendencies' volunteered and were conscripted during the Second World War, the authorities displayed no such anxiety over their entrance into the services. It would seem that the laissez-faire approach which had dominated the earlier 1940s was no longer quite so appropriate. Based on evidence and data submitted by the Admiralty and the War Office, the Wolfenden Committee argued that homosex should not be decriminalised in the armed forces, given that the special nature of service life was threatened by the presence of queer men.[36] This recommendation prompted the services to tighten up their policies on same-sex activity which already, since the end of the war, had become more punitive. The toleration which had dominated the war years was evidently conditional and temporary. Since conscription continued after the war, until 1960, many more men who desired members of the same sex found themselves drafted into the armed services and into a military culture less tolerant than even their predecessors had found in the years of total war. It would take the advent of the new century and a case brought against the Ministry of Defence by the European Court of Human Rights to see any change in the British military's policy.

Notes

1. See Bérubé, *Coming Out under Fire*.
2. This is also the conclusion that is reached by John Howard. See *Men Like That*, p. xviii.
3. Home Office, *Report of the Committee on Homosexual Offences and Prostitution*, p. 53.
4. Houlbrook, *Queer London*, p. 270.
5. Hugh David uses Crisp's quotation as the title for his chapter on post-war Britain. See David, *On Queer Street*, p. 152.
6. Transcript of interview with Dennis Campbell, 3bmtv, *Conduct Unbecoming* (Channel 4 1996), p. 18.
7. Richard Briar, interviewed by Emma Vickers, 9 November 2005.
8. John Booker, interviewed by Emma Vickers, 10 November 2006.
9. Francis Kennedy, interviewed by Emma Vickers, 5 December 2005.
10. Jimmy Jacques, interviewed by Emma Vickers, 21 July 2005.
11. See P. M. Thane, 'Population politics in post-war British Culture', in B. Conekin, F. Mort and C. Waters (eds), *Moments of Modernity: Reconstructing Britain, 1945–1964* (London: Rivers Oram, 1999), pp. 114–134. See also P. M. Thane, 'The debate on the declining birth-rate in Britain: the "menace" of an ageing population, 1920s–1950s', *Continuity and Change*, 4:2 (1990), pp. 238–305, and Weeks, *Sex, Politics and Society*, pp. 232–9.
12. Jivani, *It's Not Unusual*, p. 89.
13. Home Office, *Report of the Committee on Homosexual Offences and Prostitution*, p. 131.
14. Houlbrook, *Queer London*, pp. 34–6.
15. P. Higgins, *Heterosexual Dictatorship: Male Homosexuality in Post-War Britain* (London: Fourth Estate, 1996), p. 266.
16. Higgins, *Heterosexual Dictatorship*, p. 61.
17. Colin Spencer, quoted in David, *On Queer Street*, p. 157.
18. P. Wildeblood, *Against the Law* (Weidenfield and Nicholson, 1955), London. pp 32.
19. D. West, *Homosexuality* (London: Duckworth, 1995: rev. edn, Penguin, 1960), G. Westwood [pseud. of M. Schofield], *Society and the Homosexual* (London: Victor Gollancz, 1952), G. Westwood [pseud. of M. Schofield], *A Minority: A Report on the Life of the Male Homosexual in Great Britain* (London: Longmans, 1960), C. Allen, *Homosexuality: Its Nature, Causation and Treatment* (London: Staples Press, 1958).
20. J. Tudor Rees and H. V. Usill, *They Stand Apart: A Critical Survey of Homosexuality* (London: Heinemann, 1955).
21. David, *On Queer Street*, p. 181. Homosexuality remained on this list of psychiatric disorders until 1993.
22. C. Waters, 'Disorders of the mind, disorders of the body social: Peter Wildeblood and the making of the modern homosexual', in B. Conekin, F. Mort and C. Waters (eds), *Moments of Modernity: Reconstructing Britain, 1945–1964* (London: Rivers Oram, 1999), pp. 141–2.
23. Ahrenfeldt, *Psychiatry in the British Army* p. 139.
24. Scottish Home Department, *Psycho-Therapeutic Treatment of Certain Offenders with Special Reference to the Case of Persons Convicted of Sexual and Unnatural Offences* (Edinburgh: HMSO, 1948), p. 10.

25 Jivani, *It's Not Unusual*, p. 123.
26 See G. De M. Rudolf, 'The experimental effect of sex-hormone therapy upon anxiety in homosexual types', *British Journal of Medical Psychology*, 18:3-4 (1941), pp. 317-22.
27 'Four prisons used in 1950s research; gays in jail subjected to electric shock tests', *Glasgow Herald* (28 November 1997), p. 11, Oram and Turnbull (eds), *The Lesbian History Sourcebook*, p. 125, Jivani, *It's Not Unusual*, pp. 122-8.
28 D. Warth, 'Evil men', *Sunday Pictoral* (1 June 1952).
29 'The problem of homosexuality', *The Times* (26 February 1954), p. 26.
30 Jivani, *It's Not Unusual*, p. 98.
31 For first-hand accounts of the repressive climate in the 1950s see Croft-Cooke, *The Verdict of You All*, Wildeblood, *Against the Law* and J. Kirkup, *A Poet Could Not But Be Gay* (Peter Owen: London, 1991).
32 G. Bedell, 'Coming out of the Dark Ages', *The Observer, Review* supplement (4 June 2007), p. 6.
33 Higgins, *Heterosexual Dictatorship*, p. 63.
34 Sir John Wolfenden, cited in Higgins, *Heterosexual Dictatorship*, p. 63.
35 TNA, AIR 2/10673, RAF and WRAF, homosexual offences and abnormal sexual tendencies, 1950-68, loose minute sheet from B. C. Yarie, Provost Marshal, to DPS(A), 20 November 1951.
36 Home Office, *Report of the Committee on Homosexual Offences and Prostitution*, p. 53.

Epilogue

In 2000, the ban on queer personnel serving in the armed forces was finally lifted. Three servicemen and a former nurse took the Ministry of Defence to the European Court of Human Rights. They had been dismissed for being queer, and alleged that the investigations into their private lives and subsequent dismissal violated their human rights. It was subsequently ruled that the bar on entry into the armed forces was illegal under the European Convention on Human Rights, given that the professional skills required of queer service personnel were no different from those expected of heterosexual servicemen and women.[1] In addition to lifting the ban, the armed forces introduced a new code of conduct, which remains in place today, for all personnel and their relationships, based on the concept of acceptable and unacceptable behaviour. If the conduct of a person undermines 'trust ... cohesion and damage[s] the morale or discipline of a unit', they will be punished.[2]

Despite General Sir Anthony Farrar-Hockley's ominous prediction that the lifting of the ban would 'strike at morale and discipline' and that 'sexual squabbles' would be 'fatally disruptive',[3] there is little evidence to suggest that the voluntary recruitment of queer men and women and their open inclusion in the armed forces has had a detrimental impact on the services as a whole. Indeed, research by Belkin and Evans at the University of California discovered that the lifting of the ban has had a minimal impact on discipline and cohesion.[4] Officially, the MoD has mirrored the findings of Belkin and Evans in acknowledging that the lifting of the ban has barely affected morale.[5] It has also sought to support its queer personnel and encourage other queer men and women to join the services. In February 2005, the Royal Navy became one of Stonewall's Diversity Champions, and in August of the same year the Army and the RAF could be seen recruiting at Manchester's Gay Pride weekend with the latter displaying an oversized cockpit and a banner proudly proclaiming 'RAF rise above the rest'. At the Army recruitment stall, men in uniform were reportedly 'mingl[ing] with eager would-be recruits, one dressed in tight leather shorts and a pink cowboy hat'.[6] Lieutenant Colonel Leanda Pitt, Commander of Regional Recruiting for the North West, was said to be 'delighted' to be taking part. 'As far as the Army is concerned, sexual orientation is a private matter.'[7] Change did not stop there. In June 2007, Wing Commander Phil Sagar, who runs the Armed Forces Joint Equality and Diversity Training Centre and advises on government policy, apologised to queer personnel who had suffered discrimination and the loss of their careers in the decades before the lifting of the ban. It is thought that compensation will soon follow for these men and women, which may cost the Ministry of Defence something in the region of £50 million.[8]

As recently as 2011, the RAF achieved ninety-seventh position on Stonewall's Top 100 employer list and launched the first ever official LGBT peer support network.[9] A year earlier, in response to US senators blocking a debate into queer personnel being able to serve openly in the American military, Colonel Mark Abraham, head of diversity for the British Army, commented that the lifting of the ban on queer personnel serving in the British armed forces had 'no notable change at all' and actually made the armed forces more productive. 'A lot of gay and lesbian soldiers who were in the Army before the ban was lifted, reported that a percentage of their efforts was spent looking over their shoulder and ensuring they weren't going to be caught. That percentage of time can now be devoted to work and their home life, so actually they are more effective than they were before.'[10] Aside from this progress, perhaps the most symbolic display of support was made by the Army. In 2009, an openly queer trooper, James Wharton, appeared on the front cover of the Army's official publication *Soldier*. Clad in his dress uniform and complete with Iraq medal, Wharton appeared next to the headline 'Pride'.[11] Such developments are likely to rankle the old guard, yet they demonstrate that, publicly at least, the armed forces are finally willing to acknowledge the value of difference.

Notes

1 'Gays win military legal battle', *BBC News Online* (27 September 1999), http://news.bbc.co.uk/1/hi/uk/458714.stm, accessed 18 October 2004.
2 The Armed Forces Code of Social Conduct, appendix 2 of the Armed Forces Bill, 8 January 2001, research paper 01/03, www.parliament.uk/commons/lib/research/rp2001/rp01-003.pdf., accessed 1 February 2005.

3   B. Summerskill, 'Save us from the armchair generals', *The Guardian Online* (4 August 2004), www.guardian.co.uk/military/story/0,11816,1275547,00.html, accessed 22 January 2005.
4   A. Belkin and R. L. Evans, *The Effects of Including Gay and Lesbian Soldiers in the British Armed Forces: Appraising the Evidence* (Santa Barbara: Centre for the Study of Sexual Minorities in the Military, 2000), p.60.
5   B. Summerskill, 'It's official: gays do not harm forces', *The Observer* (19 November 2000), accessed 10 September 2006, and AFLaGA (Rank Outsiders) press release www.rank-outsiders.org.uk/info/_press/001119.htm, accessed 29 January 2005.
6   Jonathan Leake and Philip Cazly, 'Army on Parade for gay recruits', *Times Sunday* (28 August 2005), www.thesundaytimes.co.uk/sto/news/uk_news/article146254.ece, accessed 23 November 2005.
7   'Army marches with Pride Parade', *BBC News Online* (27 August 2005), http://news.bbc.co.uk/1/hi/engalnd/manchester/4189634.stm, accessed 23 November 2005.
8   M. Evans, 'We're sorry, MoD tells gay victims of persecution', *The Times Online* (28 June 2007), www.timesonline.co.uk/to/life_and_style/mes/article1996445.ece, accessed 29 June 2007. See also Phil Sagar's interview on 'Cleaning out the camp' (part 2) BBC Radio 4, 28 June 2007, which prompted the press to report the story.
9   P. Lloyd, 'Royal Air Force launch official LGBT support network', *Pink Paper* (13 October 2011).
10 'British Army claims having openly gay soldiers has "increased productivity"' *Pink Paper*, (29 September 2010), www.pinknews.co.uk/2010/09/29/british-army-claims-having-openly-gay-soldiers-hasincreased-productivity, accessed 9 January 2011. At the time of writing *Queen and Country*, the US Senate has voted to overturn its policy of 'don't ask, don't tell'.
11 T. Judd, 'How the forces finally learnt to take pride; nine years after the military lifted its ban on gays, the army has put an openly homosexual soldier on the cover of its magazine', *The Independent* (27 July 2009).

Biographies of Interviewees

Frank Bolton
b. 1924, Blackburn
RAF, acting sergeant and meteorologist

John Booker (pseud.)
b. 1920, Christchurch
Army, Royal Signals, Japanese translator

Richard Briar (pseud.)
b. 1922, Essex
Army, Ordnance Field Park, lance corporal

John Brierly (pseud.)
b. 1922, Sheffield
Army, Royal Signals, telecommunications mechanic

Frank Brown (pseud.)
b. 1920, London
RAF, armament engineer and flight sergeant

Dennis Campbell (pseud.)
b. 1924, Dundee
RAF, flight engineer

Lawrence Harney
b. 1926, Manchester
Royal Navy, ordinary seaman

Jimmy Jacques
b. 1920, St John's Wood
Army, Royal Artillery, gunner and projectionist

Francis Kennedy (pseud.)
b. 1919, Peckham
Army, Corps of Royal Engineers, mechanic

BIOGRAPHIES OF INTERVIEWEES

Albert Robinson
b. 1912, West Kensington
Army, Catering Corps, cook

Stevie Rouse (pseud.)
b. 1921, London
WAAF, telephonist and corporal

Bibliography

Primary sources

Archival sources
BBC People's War Archive
A4452301: Bailey, B.
A6126563: Dibben, S.
A8174018: Humphries, M.
A4984581: Renwick, D.
A2789472: Scott, L.
A3224350: Shaw, A.
A2329116: Waller, L.
Imperial War Museum Department of Documents
87/48/1: Engler, K.
92/30/1: Goossens, L.
85/2/1: Hill, W. A.
89/1/1: Lloyd-Jones, R. H.
01/19/1: McNelie, E.
PP MCR/115: Morgan, G.
91/36/1: Wallace, J.
87/42/1: Waller, L.
87/12/1: Witte, J. H.
London Metropolitan Archives
A/PMC/40: Public Morality Council, Patrolling Officers Reports, 1938-42.
A/PMC/41: Public Morality Council, Patrolling Officers Reports, 1941-45.
A/PMC/42: Public Morality Council, Patrolling Officers Reports, 1942-47, and correspondence with patrolling officer.
A/PMC/72: Morals in the Forces, 1941-44, women and soldiers.
A/PMC/77: File concerning 'On Leave in London', bulletin published by the London Regional Committee for Education, n.d.
A/PMC/80: Homosexuality, 1955-59.
PH/GEN/3/19: Papers of Letitia Fairfield: Homosexuality, 1947-61.
PH/GEN/3/21: Papers of Letitia Fairfield: Women's Services, 1939-43.
PS/TOW/A/01/203-19: Tower Bridge Magistrates' Court Register September 1939 - May 1945.
National RAF Museum
AC 72/17, Box 5: Miscellaneous papers of Dame Katherine Trefusis-Forbes, welfare and discipline, 1939-45.
AC 72/17, Box 8: Miscellaneous papers of Dame Katherine Trefusis-Forbes, welfare and discipline, 1939-45.
Personal acquisitions
Transcripts of 3bmtv, *Conduct Unbecoming* (Channel 4, 1996).

Personal correspondence
E-mail from S. H., to Emma Vickers, 31 August 2005.
E-mail from Heap, C., to Emma Vickers, 11 August 2005.
E-mail from Robertson, Major (ret'd) D., to Emma Vickers, 6 March 2005.
E-mail from Stringer, C., to Emma Vickers, 29 November 2005.
Letter from Blake, D. H., to Emma Vickers, 18 October 2006.
Letter from Clarke, J., to Emma Vickers, 10 October 2005.
Letter from Lane, M., to Emma Vickers, 30 April 2006.
Letter from Maddocks, S., to Emma Vickers, 27 April 2006.
Letter from Mader, S., to Emma Vickers, 6 September 2005.
Letter from R. M., to Emma Vickers, 6 February 2006.
Letter from Tavern, R. G., to Emma Vickers, 29 September 2006.

Royal Naval Museum Archive
350/88 (30*5) 11.4.0: Disciplinary Regulations for the Women's Royal Naval Service, n.d.

The National Archives
ADM 1/9837: Holding of Courts-Martial in Camera, Amendment of BR II – Admiralty Memorandum and Naval Court-Martial Procedure, 1939.
ADM 1/25754: Departmental Committee on Homosexual Offences and Prostitution – Admiralty Evidence, 1954–55.
ADM 105/104: Homosexuality in the Royal Navy: connection with security and blackmail, 1957–69.
ADM 116/4291: Status of the Judge Advocate General and the Judge Advocate of the Fleet, 1939.
ADM 116/5559: Psychology and psychiatry in the services, 1943–45.
ADM 156/193: Attempted gross indecency: W. A. Antin Stoker 1st Class, C. Rice, Stoker 1st Class.
ADM 156/258A: Report of Court Martial, indecent assault, HMS *Jamaica*, 1944.
ADM 178/346: Alleged indecency of Cdr R. B. H. Johnstone: insufficient evidence for court-martial, 1944.
ADM 194/59–84: Returns of Officers tried by court martial and disciplinary court, 1939–45.
ADM 194/277–301: Returns of Petty Officers, Seamen and Marines tried by court martial, 1939–40.
ADM 330/32: Increase in the number of cases of homosexuality in the Royal Navy, 1969–70.
AIR 2/4085: WAAF: Introduction of trousers for working dress, 1939.
AIR 2/4090: WAAF: Status and Discipline, 1939–43.
AIR 2/4892: RAF Provost Branch, August 1942.
AIR 2/6345: Proposal of selection of candidates for aircrew by combined psychiatric and psychological methods, 1941–43.
AIR 2/6402: Markham: medical aspects, 1942.
AIR 2/6486: Review of WAAF disciplinary cases in the light of the Markham Committee Report, 1942–44.

BIBLIOGRAPHY

AIR 2/9485: Discharge of airmen for reasons of misconduct during the war, 1940–50.
AIR 2/10246: Powers of Provost and RAF Police, 1940.
AIR 2/10673: RAF and WRAF, homosexual offences and abnormal sexual tendencies, 1950–1968.
AIR 2/12407: Government Committee on homosexual offences, Air Ministry evidence, record of discussions in the Select Committee, 1954–55.
AIR 2/13859: WRAF, Treatment of immorality, 1945–68.
AIR 2/13907: RAF, Courts Martial, Press Questions and policy, 1926–62.
AIR 2/17160: Homosexual and other unnatural offences, Wolfenden and its application to the RAF, 1957.
AIR 2/18644: Moral Welfare: unnatural friendships (homosexual practices, 1970–73).
AIR 20/9483: Medical Advisory Board, 1924–61.
AIR 20/10864: WRAF moral welfare, 1960–68.
AIR 21/1B: Field General Courts Martial, Abroad, RAF, 1918–49.
AIR 21/2: General Courts Martial, Abroad, RAF, 1918–60.
AIR 21/3: General Courts Martial, Home, RAF, 1918–60.
AIR 21/4B: District Courts Martial, Home and Abroad, RAF, 1938–42.
AIR 21/5: District Courts Martial, Home and Abroad, RAF, 1942–45.
CAB 21/920: Psychological Statistics: Out Patients at EMS Neurosis Centres, 1944.
CAB 21/2548: Validation of psychiatric procedures in the services, August 1943 – January 1945.
CAB 21/2549: Validation of psychiatric procedures in the Services, 1943–45.
CAB 57/16: Code of instructions for civilian medical boards, 1937–38.
CRIM 4/1700: Central Criminal Court, Indictments, 29 June 1943.
CRIM 5/13: Central Criminal Court, Indictments, September 1936 – December 1944.
DEFE 7/392: Report of the Army and Air Force Courts Martial Committee, 1946.
DEFE 70/96: Army Discipline: homosexuality, 1955–68.
FD 1/5493: Selection tests for the forces, 1939–40.
FD 1/5494: Selection tests for the forces, 1940–41.
HO 45/24955: Medical psychologist appointed to the Prison Service, 1932–54.
HO 345/7: Documents submitted to Wolfenden from the Admiralty, 1954.
LAB 6/144: Scheme for eliminating recruits with latent disabilities from being examined by the Medical Boards, 1939–53.
LAB 6/150: Naval and Air Force recruiting preferences, 1940.
LAB 6/153: National Service, prevention of evasion: regulations, 1940.
LAB 16/329: Ministry of Labour and National Service: Circular Notes to Chairmen, 1941–52.
LAB 21/165: Medical Board Statistics relating to Grade IV, 1940–56.
LAB 29/258: Instructions for the guidance of medical boards under National Service Acts, 1948.

BIBLIOGRAPHY

LAB 44/249: Ministry of Labour and National Service, 1941.
MEPO 2/1655: Lectures by Metropolitan Women's Police Force to Women's Auxiliary Air Force Police, 1941-42.
MEPO 2/8859: Activities of homosexuals, soldiers and civilians: co-operation between the Army and the police, 1931-50.
MEPO 2/9066: Study by Cambridge University on sexual offenders: facilities given by police, 1950-53.
MEPO 3/758: Caravan Club, disorderly house, male prostitutes, 1934-41.
MEPO 3/1147: Private Jack Robotka alias Robotkin: alleged epileptic: with brother Samuel conspiring to evade military service or secure discharge on medical grounds, 1940.
MEPO 3/2331: The importance of legal aid in cases likely to cause publicity, 1943.
MH 76/318: Medical Advisory Committee, Rehabilitation, 1940-41.
MH 76/397: Emergency Medical Service. Instruction booklet No. 1 with Supplements Nos. 7-58.
MH 102/187: Wellesley Nautical School: copy of Chief Inspector's report concerning an investigation into indecent behavior among the boys, 1939.
NSC 9/1062: RAF discharges, 1939-45.
NSC 9/1545: Service Personnel discharged before VE Day, Navy, 1945.
PIN 15/3734: Record of disabilities and assessments for the guidance of medical boards in reporting, 1942-69.
PRO 17/147: Ministry of Labour and National Service: general, 1940-51.
WO 22/102: Military personnel discharged on medical grounds during 1942.
WO 32/9789: Army Medical Board Advisory Meetings, 1941-49.
WO 32/9796: Medical Committees, WO Medical Board, 1941-61.
WO 32/9814: Recruiting: General, Introduction of Selection Tests, 1941-47.
WO 32/10072: The Army Act Code 67B: application to Women's Forces, 1941-46.
WO 32/10575: Director of Research, Army Medical Statistics, 1943-47.
WO 32/12436: Consideration by Army Education Advisory Board of Sex Instruction, 1947-50.
WO 32/15225: Press Publicity for Courts Martial, 1940-66.
WO 32/15251: Offences of an indecent or unnatural kind, Army Act, 1953-60.
WO 32/18997: Recommissioning of officers discharged through misconduct or as result of civil court proceedings, 1941-51.
WO 71/1049: Bernard, C. B. A., Offence: indecency, 1940.
WO 71/1062: Latham, H. P., Offence: indecency, 1942.
WO 71/1069: Upton, H. E. P. M. S., Offence: indecency, 1943.
WO 84/53: Judge Advocate General's Office: courts Courts Martial Charge Books, 1 October - 31 December 1939.
WO 84/55: Judge Advocate General's Office: Courts Martial Charge Books, 1 March - 16 April 1940.
WO 84/62: Judge Advocate General's Office: Courts Martial Charge Books, 16 May - 2 August 1941.
WO 86/97: District Courts Martial: Register, Home and Abroad, Army, 1938-40.

WO 86/98: District Courts Martial: Register, Home, Army, 1940-45.
WO 90/8: General Courts Martial: Register, Abroad, Army Officers, 1917-43.
WO 90/9: General Courts Martial: Register, Abroad, Army, 1943-60.
WO 92/4: General Courts Martial: Register, Home, Army, 1917-45.
WO 93/55: Summaries of Courts Martial, Army, 1939-67.
WO 93/58: Army and RAF, homosexual offences, 1952-54.
WO 163/417: Medical Advisory Committee, 1940-41.
WO 163/495: Interdepartmental Committee to consider the recommendations in the Report of the Army and Air Force Courts Martial Committee, 1946.
WO 165/101: Directorate of Selection of Personnel War Diary, June 1941 – July 1945.
WO 213/35-66: Field General Courts Martial (Home and Abroad), Army, 1939-45.
WO 222/8: Notes on the administration of Army Psychiatry for the period September 1939 – May 1943.
WO 222/218: Morale, Discipline and Mental Fitness, circular to Medical Officers from A.M.D.11, no date.
WO 222/1452: Medical Quarterly Report, No. 3 Corps Psychiatrist October-December 1944.
WO 226/8: Administration and Organisation of Military Detention Barracks and Military Prisons, 1943.
WO 277/7: *Second World War, 1939-45 Army: Discipline.*
WO 277/19: Personnel selection, Army, 1939-45.

University of Kent, British Cartoon archive

WH4840: W. K. Haselder, 'Our beautiful women athletes', from *Daily Mirror* (9 June 1926).

University of Sussex, Mass Observation archive

Directive Replies, December 1942, Wartime Sexual Behaviour, roll 14.
Observation Archive File Report Article II, 'The Knowledge of Sex', 3 October 1949.
Topic Collection, Sexual Behaviour 1939-50, box 4, Sexual Behaviour Report on Sex.

Wellcome Library

PP/BOW/C5/2/3, Box 109: Notes on selection and diagnosis in the Army, 1942.
PP/BOW/C5/3/12: Vocational Guidance and Selection, recruitment of officers, 1945.
PP/BOW/C5/3/8: R.T.C., Memos on Officer Selection and on the selection of civil servants, 1944-49.

Women's Library

SA/PVD: National Society for the Prevention of Venereal Disease, correspondence, 1937-45.
3/AMS/4/01, Box FL 314: Records of the Association for Moral and Social Hygiene, Armed Forces – Correspondence and Papers relating to Venereal Disease, Part 5, 1941-44.

3/AMS/4/01, Box FL 314: Records of the Association for Moral and Social Hygiene, Armed Forces – Correspondence and Papers relating to Venereal Disease, Part 6, 1944–46.

Oral interviews
Brighton Our Story Archive: oral interviews
Allen, S. (pseud.), 29 November 1990.
Ashdown, I., 'Bubbles', 22 February 1993.
British Library Sound Archive: oral interviews
C456/003: Alcock, J.
C456/089: Trevor-Roper, P.
C547/11: 'John'.
C1159/58: Plumley, W., 'Before Stonewall'.
Imperial War Museum Sound Archive: oral interviews
16355/5: Amyes, G. A.
17286/5: Arnold, D.
22585/4: Bell, W. H. 'Dinger'
9951/16: Brown, W. P.
18357/5: Carew, T. A.
21107/7: Chandler, R. D.
12411/6: Coup, W. E. 'Ted'
22131/3: Elliott, G. M.
9552/23: Farrer, B.
12715/24: Foulds, R. L.
12315/4: Furzer, G. A.
20303/6: Goddard, A. J.
10702/4: Hallsworth, D. P.
872/4: Hannam, C. L.
9724/4: Hanson, D.
6323/10: Harding, W. A.
20891/4: Inskip, J. H.
22599/10: Knowles, J.
17330/38: Lawson, J. C. A. D.
13251/28: Lovell, K. C.
26621/9: Marler, S.
18200/5: Maxted, D. J.
14986/11: Middleton, D.
20737/7: Millard, W. O.
25270/3: Muller, H.
23817/4: Pallant, C.
14788/15: Parker, A.
21565/16: Partridge, B.
12032/6: Peck, G.
16085/14: Penlington, F.

18201: Simpson, E. R. P.
10230/7: Sinclair, C. E.
16783/3: Tawse, W. B., 'Bill'
12242/17: Thompson, H.
21584/3: Weekes, A.W., 'Ted'
12409/30: Whittaker, E.
20318/15: Workman, C.

Oral interviews personally collected
Bolton, F., interviewed by Emma Vickers, 19 June 2006.
Booker, J. (pseud.), interviewed by Emma Vickers, 10 November 2006.
Briar, R. (pseud.), interviewed by Emma Vickers, 9 November 2005.
Brierly, J. (pseud.), interviewed by Emma Vickers, 28 August 2006.
Brown, F. (pseud.), interviewed by Emma Vickers, 10 November 2006.
Campbell, D. (pseud.), interviewed by Emma Vickers, 22 November 2005.
Harney, L., interviewed by Emma Vickers, 5 October 2006.
Hennegin, M., interviewed by Emma Vickers, 1 September 2005.
Jacques, J., interviewed by Emma Vickers, 21 July 2005.
Kennedy, F. (pseud.), interviewed by Emma Vickers, 5 December 2005.
Robinson, A., interviewed by Emma Vickers, 5 October 2005.
Rouse, S. (pseud.), interviewed by Emma Vickers, 17 June 2006.

Royal Naval Museum: oral interviews
115/1994 (1): Carter, E.
23/1994 (1): Holmes, I.
69/1994 (1*2): Gordon, J.

Second World War Experience Centre: oral interviews
99.141: Banks, A. G.
2003–2170: Lloyd-Jones, R. H.
2844: Newman, E.
519/520: White, P. (pseud.)
2001–864: Williams, J. E.

Books
Air Ministry, *The Women's Auxiliary Air Force* (London: The Air Ministry, 1953).
Allen, C., *Homosexuality: Its Nature, Causation and Treatment* (London: Staples Press, 1958).
Carpenter, E., *The Intermediate Sex* (London: Allen and Unwin, 9th edn, 1952).
Carrington Spencer, J., *Crime and the Services* (London: Routledge and Kegan Paul, 1954).
Cowper, J. M., *The Auxiliary Territorial Service* (London: HMSO, 1949).
Ellis, H., *Studies in the Psychology of Sex Volume One* (London: F. A. Davis and Co, trans. 7th edn, 1892).
Forel, A., *The Sexual Question: A Scientific, Psychological, Hygienic and Sociological Study* (New York: Physicians and Surgeons Book Company, 1924).

Haire, N., *Encyclopaedia of Sexual Knowledge* (London: London Encyclopaedic Press, 1934).
Incorporated Council of Law, *The Law Reports: The Public and General Statutes*, 16 (London: William Clowes and Sons Ltd, 1881).
MacAndrew, R., *Encyclopedia of Sex and Love Technique* (London: Wales Publishing, 1941).
MacAndrew, R., *The Red Light: Intimate Hygiene for Men and Women* (London: Wales Publishing, 1941).
Norwood East, W., and de Hubert, W. H., *Report on the Psychological Treatment of Crime* (London: HMSO, 1939).
Norwood East, W., *Medical Aspects of Crime* (London: J. and A. Churchill, 1936).
Pendlebury, W. J., *A Precis of the King's Regulations and the Manual of Military Law for Officers* (Shrewsbury: HMSO and Wilding and Son, 1941).
Rees, J. R., *The Shaping of Psychiatry by War* (London: Chapman and Hall, 1945).
Russell, G. L., *Sex Problems in Wartime* (London: Christian Movement Press, 1940).
Ryley Scott, G., *Sex Problems and Dangers in War-Time: A Book of Practical Advice for Men and Women on the Fighting and Home Fronts* (London: T. Werner Laurie, 1940).
Stopes, M., *Enduring Passion* (New York: Blue Ribbon, 1931; reprinting London: Hogarth Press, 1923).
Tudor Rees, J., and Usill, H. V., *They Stand Apart: A Critical Survey of Homosexuality* (London: Heinemann, 1955).
Vernon, P. E., and Parry, J. B., *Personnel Selection in the British Forces* (London: University of London Press, 1949).
Walker, K., Strauss, M., and Eric, B., *Sexual Disorders in the Male* (London: Cassell, 1954).
War Office, *Statistics of the Military Effort of the British Empire during the Great War 1914–1920* (London: HMSO, 1922).
War Office, *Manual of Military Law* (London: HMSO, reprinted 1939).
War Office, *The Statistical Health of the Army 1943–45* (London: HMSO, 1948).
War Office, *The Soldier's Welfare – Notes for Officer* (London: HMSO, n.d.).
West, D., *Homosexuality* (London: Duckworth, 1995: rev. edn, Penguin, 1960).
Westwood, G. [pseud. of M. Schofield], *Society and the Homosexual* (London: Victor Gollancz, 1952).
Westwood, G. [pseud. of M. Schofield], *A Minority: A Report on the Life of the Male Homosexual in Great Britain* (London: Longmans, 1960).

Articles

Anderson, C., 'On certain conscious and unconscious homosexual responses to warfare', *British Journal of Medical Psychology*, 20:2 (1944), pp. 161–74.
Anon., 'Mental fitness of U.S. recruits', *The Lancet*, 1941:2, pp. 100–10.
Anon., 'Obituary of Letitia Fairfield, *British Medical Journal* (11 February 1978), pp. 372–3.

BIBLIOGRAPHY

Bennet, E., and Slater, P., 'Some tests for the discrimination of neurotic from normal subjects', *British Journal of Medical Psychology*, 20:3 (1945), pp. 271-82.

Berg, C., 'Clinical notes on the analysis of war neurosis', *British Journal of Medical Psychology*, 19:2 (1942), pp. 155-85.

Burt, C., 'Validating tests for personnel selection', *British Journal of Psychology*, 34:1 (1943), pp. 1-19.

Burt, C., 'Psychology in the forces', *Occupational Psychology*, 21:3 (1947), pp. 141-6.

Curran, D., 'Homosexuality', *The Practitioner*, 141 (1938), pp. 285-7.

De La Garforth, F. I., 'War Office selection boards', *Occupational Psychology* 19:2 (1945), pp. 97-108.

Esher, F. J. S., 'The mental defective in the Army', *British Medical Journal* 2 (1941), pp. 187-90.

Eysenck, H. J., 'Screening Out the Neurotic', *The Lancet*, 1947:1, pp. 530-1.

Fitzpatrick, G., 'War Office selection boards and the role of the psychiatrist in them', *Journal of the Royal Army Medical Corps*, 84 (1943), pp. 75-8.

Harrisson, T., 'The British soldier: changing attitudes and ideas', *British Journal of Psychology*, 35:2 (1945), pp. 34-9.

L'Etang, H. J. C. J., 'A criticism of military psychiatry in the Second World War', parts 1, 2 and 3, *Journal of the Royal Army Medical Corps*, 97 (1951), pp. 192-7, 236-44, 316-27.

Jones, E., 'War and individual psychology', *Sociological Review*, 8:3 (1915), pp. 167-80.

Mercer, E. O., 'Psychological Methods of Personnel Selection in a Women's Service', *Occupational Psychology*, 19:4 (1945), pp. 180-200.

Money-Kyrle, R. E., 'The development of war: a psychological approach', *British Journal of Medical Psychology*, 16:3 (1937), p. 235.

Morris, B. S., 'Officer selection in the British Army 1942-1945', *Occupational Psychology*, 23:4 (1949), pp. 219-34.

Myers, C. S., 'The selection of Army personnel: a short history of the development of the D.S.P.', *Occupational Psychology*, 17:1 (1943), pp. 1-5.

Parry, J. B., 'The selection and classification of RAF air crew', *Occupational Psychology*, 21:4 (1947), pp. 158-69.

Raven, J. C., 'Standardization of progressive matrices', *British Journal of Medical Psychology*, 19:1 (1941), pp. 137-50.

Rees, J., 'Three years of military psychiatry in the United Kingdom', *British Medical Journal* 1:1 (2 January 1943), pp. 1-6.

Rodger, A., 'The work of Admiralty psychologists', *Occupational Psychology*, 19:3 (1943), pp. 134-9.

Rudolf, G. De M., 'The experimental effect of sex-hormone therapy upon anxiety in homosexual types', *British Journal of Medical Psychology*, 18:3-4 (1941), pp. 317-22.

Rudolf, G. De M, 'Sex in the fighting services at an isolated station', *British Journal of Medical Psychology*, 21:2 (1948), pp. 127-34.

Schonberger, S., 'Disorders of the ego in wartime', *British Journal of Medical Psychology*, 21:4 (1948), pp. 248–53.

Tuck, G. N., 'The Army's use of psychology during the war', *Occupational Psychology*, 20:3 (1946), pp. 113–18.

Vernon, P. E., 'The Rorschach inkblot test', parts 1, 2 and 3, *British Journal of Medical Psychology*, 13:2 (1933), pp. 89–118.

Vernon, P. E., 'A study of war attitudes', *British Journal of Medical Psychology*, 19:2 (1941), pp. 271–91.

Vernon, P. E., 'Psychological tests in the Royal Navy Army and ATS', *Occupational Psychology*, 21:2 (1947), pp. 53–74.

Pamphlets

Benjamin, H., *The Sex Problem in the Armed Forces* (New York: The Urologic and Curtaneous Press, 1944).

Winner, A. L., *Homosexuality in Women*, reprinted from *Medical Press*, 217:5652 (September 1947), pp. 3–7.

Government reports

Home Office, *Committee on Homosexual Offences and Prostitution* (London: HMSO, 1957).

Markham Committee, *The Markham Report: Report the Committee on Amenities and Welfare Conditions in the Three Women's Services* (London: HMSO, 1942).

Ministry of Defence, *Report of the Homosexuality Policy Assessment Team* (London: Ministry of Defence 1996).

Scottish Home Department, *Psycho-Therapeutic Treatment of Certain Offenders with Special Reference to the Case of Persons Convicted of Sexual and Unnatural Offences* (Edinburgh: HMSO, 1948).

Southborough Committee, *Report of the War Office Committee of Enquiry into 'Shell Shock'* (London: HMO, 1922).

War Office, *The Second World War 1939–1945, Army: Discipline* (London: War Office, 1950).

Surveys

UK Data Archive, survey SN3434, www.data-archive.ac.uk/findingdata/sn Description.asp?sn=3434&key=Sexual, accessed 3 January 2007.

UK Data Archive, survey SN5223, www.data-archive.ac.uk/findingdata/sn Description.asp?sn=5223&key=Sexual, accessed 3 January 2007.

Hansard Parliamentary Debates

House of Commons, 5 April 1977, vol. 92, col. 1485.
House of Commons, 27 June 1918, vol. 107, cols 1257–72.
House of Commons, 2 December 1941, vol. 376, cols 1027–30.
House of Commons, 4 December 1941, vol. 376, col. 1235.

House of Commons, 10 February 1942, vol. 377, col. 1369.
House of Commons, 19 February 1942, vol. 377, col. 1961.
House of Commons, 9 December 1942, vol. 385, cols 1558–60.
House of Commons, 4 May 1995, vol. 259, col. 458.

Newspaper articles

Anon., 'The problem of the Army', *The Times* (24 February 1903).
Anon., 'The war and after', *The Times* (13 September 1919).
Anon., 'The vulgarity of lesbianism', *New Statesman* (25 August 1928).
Anon., 'Colonel Barker in the dock at the Old Bailey', *Daily Herald* (25 April 1929).
Anon., 'The Caravan Club raid: seventy-six defendants discharged', *The Times* (6 September 1934).
Anon., 'Warn the ATS. girls!', *Sunday Dispatch* (25 February 1940).
Anon., 'MP to be tried by court-martial, Commons informed of his arrest', *The Times* (1 August 1941).
Anon., 'Paul Latham resigns', *The Times* (20 August 1941).
Anon., 'Court-martial of Sir Paul Latham', *The Times* (5 September 1941).
Anon., 'Court-martial of Sir Paul Latham, not guilty on three of 14 charges', *The Times* (6 September 1941).
Anon., 'Sir P. Latham sentenced', *The Times* (24 September 1941).
Anon., 'Mr Bevan's defence of the ATS', *Daily Telegraph* (11 December 1941).
Anon., 'Lord Lauderdale acquitted', *The Times* (24 November 1943).
Anon., 'The problem of homosexuality', *The Times* (26 February 1954).
Anon., '94–49 vote for change in homosexual law', *The Times* (25 May 1965).
Warth, D., 'Evil men', *Sunday Pictorial* (1 June 1952).

Fiction

Aldiss, B., *A Soldier Erect* (London: Corgi, 1971).
Barron, A., *From the City, from the Plough* (London: Pan, 1953).
Garland, R., *The Heart in Exile* (London: W. H. Allen, 1953).
Green, H., *Caught* (London, Vintage, 1943; 2001).
Hall, R. M., *The Well of Loneliness* (London: Jonathan Cape, 1928).
Nichols, P., *Privates on Parade* (London: Faber and Faber, 1977).
Waters, S., *The Nightwatch* (London: Virago, 2006).

Autobiographies and diaries

Beck, P., *Keeping Watch* (Manchester: Goodall, 2004).
Bell, B., *Just Take Your Frock Off* (Brighton: OurStory, 1999).
Benge, R. C., *Confessions of a Lapsed Librarian* (London: Scarecrow Press, 1984).
Behan, B., *Confessions of an Irish Rebel* (London: Arrow, 1991).
Boyd-Carpenter, J., *A Way of Life* (London: Sidgwick and Jackson, 1980).
Buckle, R., *The Most Upsetting Woman* (London: Collins, 1981).
Coates, P., *Of Generals and Gardens* (London: Weidenfeld and Nicolson, 1976).

Crisp, Q., *The Naked Civil Servant* (London: Fontana, 1977).
Croft-Cooke, R., *The Verdict of You All* (London: Secker & Warburg, 1955).
Croft-Cooke, R., *The Licentious Soldiery* (London: W. H. Allen, 1971).
Currier Briggs, N., *Young Men at War* (Norfolk: Gay Men's Press, 1996).
Dady, M., *A Women's War: Life in the ATS* (London: Book Guild, 1986).
De Hegedus, A., *Don't Keep the Vanman Waiting: A Chapter of Autobiography* (London: Nicholson and Watson, 1944).
Green, G. F., *A Skilled Hand: A Collection of Stories and Writing by G. F. Green*, ed. C. Green and A. D. Maclean (London: Macmillan, 1980).
Hildyard, M., *It Is Bliss Here: Letters Home, 1939-1945* (London: Bloomsbury, 2006).
Kirkup, J., *A Poet Could Not but Be Gay* (Peter Owen: London, 1991).
Lehmann, J., *In the Purely Pagan Sense* (London: Gay Modern Classics, 1985).
MacDonald Frazer, G., *Quartered Safe Out Here* (London: Harper Collins, 2000).
Melly, G., *Rum, Bum and Concertina* (London: Weidenfeld and Nicolson, 1989).
Wildeblood, P., *Against the Law* (Weidenfield and Nicolson, 1955).
Winn, G., *The Positive Hour* (London: Michael Joseph, 1970).
Wishart, M., *High Diver* (London: Quarter, 1978).
Witte, S. H., *The One That Didn't Get Away* (Boynor Regis: New Horizon, 1983).
Wyndham, J., *Love Lessons: A Wartime Diary* (London: Heinemann, 1985).
Wyndham, J., *Love is Blue: A Wartime Diary* (London: Heinemann, 1986).

Secondary sources

Books

Abelove, H., Borale, M. A., and Halperin, D. M., (eds), *The Lesbian and Gay Studies Reader* (London: Routledge, 1993).
Ahrenfeldt, R. H., *Psychiatry in the British Army* (London: Routledge and Kegan Paul, 1958).
Aldrich, R., and Wotherspoon, G. (eds), *Who's Who in Contemporary Gay and Lesbian History from WWII to the Present Day* (London: Routledge, 2001).
Arthur, M., *The Royal Navy 1914-1939* (London: Hodder and Stoughton, 1996).
Baikie, L., *Sexuality and Older People* (Leicester: BPS, 1995).
Baker, R., *Drag: A History of Female Impersonation in the Performing Arts* (London: Cassell, 1994).
Bargielowska, Z., *Managing the Body: Beauty, Health and Fitness in Britain, 1880-1939* (Oxford: Oxford University Press, 2010).
Barnett, C., *Britain and Her Army, 1509-1970: A Military, Political and Social Survey* (London: Penguin, 1970).
Barnett, C., *Engage the Enemy More Closely: The Royal Navy in the Second World War* (New York: W. W. Norton and Company, 1991).
Barrow, A., *Quentin and Phillip* (London: Macmillan, 2002).
Bartlett, N., *Who Was That Man?* (London: Serpent's Tail, 1988).

BIBLIOGRAPHY

Baudelaire, C., *The Flowers of Evil*, trans. James McGowan (Oxford: Oxford University Press, 1993).

Bech, H., *When Men Meet: Homosexuality and Modernity* (Chicago: University of Chicago Press, 1997).

Begman, D., *Camp Grounds: Style and Homosexuality* (Amherst: Massachusetts University Press, 1993).

Bell, C. M., *The Royal Navy, Seapower and Strategy between the Wars* (London: Macmillan, 2000).

Bell, D., *Pleasure Zones: Bodies, Cities, Spaces* (Syracuse: Syracuse University Press, 2001).

Bell, D., and Valentine, G. (eds), *Mapping Desire* (London: Routledge, 1995).

Belshaw, P., *A Kind of Private Magic* (London: Carlton, 1994.)

Bérubé, A., *Coming Out under Fire* (New York: Free Press, 1990).

Bet-el, I. R., *Conscripts: Lost Legions of the Great War* (Stroud: Sutton, 1999).

Bingham, A., *Family Newspapers? Sex, Private Life, and the British Popular Press 1918-1978* (Oxford: Oxford University Press, 2009).

Bishop, P., *Fighter Boys: Saving Britain 1940* (London: Harper Perennial, 2003).

Bourke, J., *Dismembering the Male: Men's Bodies, Britain and the Great War* (London: Reaktion Books, 1996).

Bourke, J., *An Intimate History of Killing* (London: Granta, 1999).

Brady, S., *Masculinity and Male Homosexuality in Britain 1861-1913* (London: Palgrave, 2005).

Brighton Ourstory Project, *Daring Hearts: Lesbian and Gay Lives of the 1950s and 60s* (Brighton: QueenSpark Books, 1992).

Bristow, J., *Effeminate England: Homoerotic Writings after 1885* (New York: Columbia University Press, 1995).

Brown, D., *The Royal Navy and the Mediterranean*, vol. 1, *September 1939 – October 1940* (London: Frank Cass, 2001).

Brownmiller, S., *Femininity* (London: Hamish Hamilton, 1984).

Brod, H., and Kaufman, M. (eds), *Theorizing Masculinities* (London: Sage, 1994).

Burg, B. R., *Gay Warriors: A Documentary History from the Ancient World to the Present* (New York: New York University Press, 2002).

Butler, J., *Gender Trouble: Feminism and the Subversion of Identity* (New York: Routledge, 1990).

Calder, A., *The People's War: Britain 1939-45* (London: Jonathan Cape, 1969).

Calder, A., *The Myth of the Blitz* (London: Jonathan Cape, 1991).

Castle, T., *The Apparitional Lesbian: Female Homosexuality and Lesbian Culture* (New York: Columbia University Press, 1993).

Central Statistical Office, *Fighting with Figures* (London: HMSO, 1995).

Chauncey, G., *Gay New York* (New York: Basic Books, 1994).

Cocks, H. G., *Nameless Offences: Homosexual Desire in the Nineteenth Century* (London: T. B. Tauris, 2003).

Cocks, H. G., and Houlbrook, M. (eds), *The Modern History of Sexuality* (London: Palgrave, 2006).

Cohler, D., *Citizen, Invert, Queer: Lesbianism and War in Early Twentieth-Century Britain* (London: Minnesota University Press, 2010).
Connell, R.W., *Masculinities* (Cambridge: Polity, 2nd edn, 2005).
Connelly, M., *We Can Take It: Britain and the Memory of the Second World War* (London: Pearson, 2004).
Constantine, S., *Social Conditions in Britain 1918-1939* (London: Methuen, 1983).
Cook, M., *London and the Culture of Homosexuality, 1885-1914* (Cambridge: Cambridge University Press, 2003).
Cook, M., Mills, R., Trumbuch, R., and Cocks, H. G. (eds), *A Gay History of Britain: Love and Sex between Men since the Middle Ages* (Oxford: Greenwood, 2007).
Cosslett, T., Lury, C., and Summerfield, S. (eds), *Feminism and Autobiography: Tests, Theories, Methods* (New York: Routledge, 2000).
Costello, J., *Love, Sex and War: Changing Values, 1939-1954* (London: Collins, 1985).
Crang, J., *The British Army and the People's War 1939-1945* (Manchester: Manchester University Press, 2000).
Crew, E. A. E. (ed.), *History of the Second World War: The Army Medical Services Administration II* (London: HMSO, 1955).
Davenport-Hines, R. P. T., *Sex, Death and Punishment: Attitudes to Sex and Sexuality in Britain since the Renaissance* (London: Collins, 1990).
David, H., *On Queer Street: A Social History of British Homosexuality 1895-1995* (London: Harper Collins, 1997).
Davidson, R., and Hall, L. (eds), *Sex, Sin and Suffering: Venereal Disease and European Society since 1870* (London: Routledge, 2001).
Dear, I. C. B. (ed.), *The Oxford Companion to the Second World War* (Oxford: Oxford University Press, 1995).
De Courcy, A., *Debs at War: How Wartime Changed Their Lives* (London: Weidenfeld and Nicolson, 2005).
DeGroot, G. J., *Blighty: British Society in the Era of the Great War* (London: Longman, 1996).
Dixon, N. F., *On the Psychology of Military Incompetence* (London: Futura, 1976).
Doan, L., *Fashioning Sapphism: The Origins of a Modern English Lesbian Culture* (New York: Columbia University Press, 2001).
Doan, L., and Bland, L., *Sexology Uncensored* (London: Polity Press, 1998).
Duberman, M., *About Time: Exploring the Gay Past* (London: Penguin, 1991).
Duberman, M., Vicinus, M., and Chauncey, G., *Hidden from History: Reclaiming the Gay and Lesbian Past* (London: Penguin, 1991).
Ellis, J., *World War Two: The Sharp End* (London: Windrow and Greene, 1990).
Ellis, J., *The World War II Databook* (London: BCA, 1993).
Enloe, C., *Does Khaki Become You? The Militarism of Women's Lives* (London: Pandora, 1988).
Epstein, J., and Straub, K., *Body Guards: The Cultural Politics of Gender Ambiguity* (New York: Routledge, 1991).

Escott, B. E., *Women in Air Force Blue* (Welling borough: Patrick Stephens, 1989).
Faderman, L., *Surpassing the Love of Men: Romantic Friendship and Love between Women from the Renaissance to the Present* (London: Junction Books, 1981).
Fletcher, M. H., *The WRNS: A History of the Women's Royal Naval Service* (London: Batsford, 1989).
Forty, G., *The British Army Handbook* (London: Chancellor Press, 2000).
Foucault, M., *History of Sexuality: The Will to Knowledge: vol. 1* (London: Penguin, 1990).
Fraser, D., *And We Shall Shock Them: The British Army in the Second World War* (London: Cassell, 1999).
French, D., *Raising Churchill's Army: The British Army and the War against Germany, 1919-1945* (Oxford: Oxford University Press, 2001).
French, D., *Military Identities: The Regimental System, the British Army and the British People 1870-2000* (Oxford: Oxford University Press, 2005).
Freud, S., *Three Essays on Sexuality* (London: Pelican, 1977).
Fuss, D., *Inside/Out: Lesbian Theories, Gay Theories* (New York: Routledge, 1991).
Fussell, P., *Wartime: Understanding and Behaviour in the Second World War* (Oxford and New York: Oxford University Press, 1989).
Garber, M., *Vested Interests: Cross Dressing and Cultural Anxiety* (New York: Routledge, 1992).
Gardiner, J., *A Class Apart: The Private Pictures of Montague Glover* (London: Serpent's Tail, 1992, repr. 1999).
Gardiner, J., *Who's a Pretty Boy Then?* (London: Serpent's Tail, 1998).
Gardiner, J., *From the Closet to the Screen: Women at the Gateways Club, 1945-85* (London: Pandora, 2003).
Gardiner, J., *Wartime: Britain 1939-1945* (London: Review, 2005).
Garfield, S., *Our Hidden Lives: The Everyday Diaries of Forgotten Britain* (London: Ebury, 2004).
Gibbs, N. H., *History of the Second World War: Grand Strategy*, 1 (London: HMSO, 1976).
Ginsberg, E. K. (ed.), *Passing and the Fictions of Identity* (Durham, NC: Duke University Press, 1996).
Gledhill, C., and G. Swanson (eds), *Nationalising Femininity: Culture, Sexuality and Cinema in World War Two Britain* (Manchester: Manchester University Press, 1996).
Goldstein, J. S., *War and Gender: How Gender Shapes the War System and Vice Versa* (Cambridge: Cambridge University Press, 2001).
Goodman, P., *Women, Sexuality and War* (Basingstoke: Palgrave Macmillan, 2001).
Halberstam, J., *Female Masculinity* (Durham, NC: Duke University Press, 1998).
Haley, B., *The Healthy Body and Victorian Culture* (Cambridge: Harvard University Press, 1978).
Hall-Carpenter Archives and Gay Men's Oral History Group, *Walking after Midnight: Gay Men's Life Stories* (London: Routledge, 1989).

Hall-Carpenter Lesbian Oral History Group (eds), *Inventing Ourselves* (London: Routledge, 1989).

Hall, E., *We Can't Even March Straight: Homosexuality in the British Armed Forces* (London: Vintage, 1995).

Hall, L. A., *Hidden Anxieties: Male Sexuality 1900–1950* (Cambridge: Polity Press, 1991).

Hall, L. A., *Sex, Gender and Social Change in Britain since 1880* (London: Palgrave Macmillan, 2000).

Halsey, A. H. (ed.), *Trends in British Society since 1900* (London: Macmillan, 1972).

Hamer, E., *Britannia's Glory: A History of Twentieth-Century Lesbians* (London: Cassell, 1996).

Hartley, J. (ed.), *Hearts Undefeated* (London: Virago, 1995).

Haste, C., *Rules of Desire* (London: Chatto, 1992).

Hayward, T., and K. Ashton, *The Royal Navy, Rum, Rumour and a Pinch of Salt* (Glasgow: Brown, Son and Ferguson, 1985).

Hamilton, N., *The Full Monty: Montgomery of Alamein, 1887–1942*, 1 (London: Allen Lane, 2001).

Herbert, M. S., *Camouflage Isn't Only for Combat: Gender, Sexuality, and Women in the Military* (London: New York University Press, 1998).

Higate, P., *Military Masculinities: Identity and the State* (Westport: Praeger, 2003.)

Higgins, P., *A Queer Reader* (London: New Press, 1994).

Higgins, P., *Heterosexual Dictatorship: Male Homosexuality in Post-War Britain* (London: Fourth Estate, 1996).

Higgs, D., *Queen Sites* (London: Routledge, 1999).

Higham, R., *Armed Forces in Peacetime: Britain 1918–1940* (London: G. T. Foulis and Co., 1962).

Higonnet, M. R., Jenson, J., Michel, S., and Collins Weitz, M. (eds), *Behind the Lines: Gender and the Two World Wars* (New Haven: Yale University Press, 1989).

Hornsey, R., *The Spiv and the Architect: Unruly Life in Postwar London* (Minneapolis: Minnesota University Press, 2010).

Houlbrook, M., *Queer London: Perils and Pleasures in the Sexual Metropolis, 1918–57* (Chicago and London: University of Chicago Press, 2005).

Howard, J., *Men Like That: A Southern Queer History* (Chicago: Chicago University Press, 1999).

Humphreys, S., *A Secret World of Sex* (London: Sidgwick and Jackson, 1998).

Hyam, R., *Empire and Sexuality: The British Experience* (Manchester: Manchester University Press, 1990).

Hyde, H. M., *The Other Love: A Historical and Contemporary Survey of Homosexuality in Britain* (London: William Heinemann, 1970).

Hynes, S., *A War Imagined: The First World War and English Culture* (London: Pimlico, 1992).

Jackson, P., *One of the Boys* (Montreal and Kingston: McGill–Queen's University Press, 2004).

Jennings, R., *A Lesbian History of Britain: Love and Sex between Women since 1500* (Oxford: Greenwood, 2007).

Jennings, R., *Tomboys and Bachelor Girls: A Lesbian History of Post-War Britain, 1945–71* (Manchester: Manchester University Press, 2007).

Jivani, A., *It's Not Unusual* (London: Michael O'Mara, 1997).

Kaplan, M., *Sodom on the Thames: Sex, Love, and Scandal in Wilde Times* (Cornell: Cornell University Press, 2005).

Kaufman, M. (ed.), *Theorizing Masculinities* (London: Sage, 1994).

Kennedy, P., *The Rise and Fall of British Naval Mastery* (London: Fontana, 3rd edn, 1991).

King, D., and Elkins, R. (eds), *Blending Genders: Social Aspects of Cross-Dressing and Sex-Changing* (London: Routledge, 1996).

Kosofosky Sedgwick, E., *Between Men* (New York: Columbia University Press, 1985).

Lant, A., *Blackout: Reinventing Women for British Wartime Cinema* (London: I. B. Tauris, 1998).

Laughton Mathews, V., *Blue Tapestry* (London, Hollis and Carter, 1948).

Lesbian History Group (ed.), *Not a Passing Phase: Reclaiming Lesbians in History 1840–1985* (London: Women's Press, 1989).

MacIntyre, D., *The Battle for the Mediterranean* (London: Severn, 1964).

Mangan, J. A., *Athleticism in the Victorian and Edwardian Public School* (Cambridge: Cambridge University Press, 1981).

Mason, U., *Britannia's Daughters: The Story of the WRNS* (London: Leo Cooper, 1992).

McIntosh, P. C., *Physical Education in England since 1800* (London: Bell, 1968).

McLaine, I., *Ministry of Morale: Home Front Morale and the Ministry of Information in World War Two* (London: George Allen and Unwin, 1979).

McLaren, A., *The Trial of Masculinity* (Chicago: University of Chicago Press, 1997).

Medurst, A., and Munt, S. (eds), *Lesbian and Gay Studies: A Critical Introduction* (London: Cassell, 1997).

Mellor, W. F. (ed.), *History of the Second World War: United Kingdom Medical Series – Casualties and Medical Statistics* (London: HMSO, 1972).

Miller, N., *Out of the Past* (London: Vintage Books, 1995).

Moran, L. J., *The Homosexual(ity) of Law* (London: Routledge, 1996).

Mosse, G. L., *Nationalism and Sexuality: Middle Class Morality and Sexual Norms in Modern Europe* (New York: Fertig, 1985).

Mosse, G. L., *The Image of Man* (Oxford: Oxford University Press, 1996).

Nardi, P. (ed.), *Gay Masculinities* (London: Thousand Oaks Sage Publications, 2000).

Neild, S., and Pearson, R., *Women Like Us* (London: The Women's Press, 1992).

Noakes, L., *War and the British: Gender, Memory and National Identity* (London: I.B. Tauris, 1998).
Noakes, L., *Women in the British Army: War and the Gentle Sex 1907–1948* (London: Routledge, 2006).
Nye, R. A. (ed.), *Sexuality* (Oxford: Oxford University Press, 1999).
Oram, A., *Her Husband Was a Woman! Women's Gender-Crossing in Modern British Popular Culture* (London: Routledge, 2007).
Oram, A., and Turnbull, A. (eds), *The Lesbian History Sourcebook: Love and Sex between Women in Britain 1780–1970* (London: Routledge, 2001).
Plummer, K., *The Making of the Modern Homosexual* (London: Hutchinson, 1981).
Plummer, K., *Modern Homosexualities: Fragments of Gay and Lesbian Experience* (London: Routledge, 1992).
Porter, R., *The Facts of Life: The Creation of Sexual Knowledge in Britain, 1650–1950* (New Haven: Yale University Press, 1995).
Read, D. (ed.), *Edwardian England* (London: Croom Helm, 1982).
Rexford Welch, S. C., *History of the Second World War, The Royal Air Force Medical Services*, 1, *Administration* (London: HMSO, 1954).
Rich, A., *Compulsory Heterosexuality and the Lesbian Existence* (London: Onlywoman Press, 1981).
Richards, D., *The Royal Air Force 1939–1945* (London: HMSO, 1953).
Richards, J., *Sex, Dissidence and Damnation: Minority Groups in the Middle Ages* (London: Routledge, 1991).
Robb, G., *British Culture and the First World War* (London: Palgrave, 2002).
Robb, G., *Strangers: Homosexuality in the Nineteenth Century* (London: Picador, 2004).
Roberts, R., *The Classic Slum: Salford Life in the First Quarter of the Century* (Harmondsworth: Penguin, 1973).
Roper, M., and Tosh, J. (eds), *Manful Assertions: Masculinities in Britain since 1800* (London: Routledge, 1991).
Rose, S. O., *Which People's War? National Identity and Citizenship in Britain 1939–1945* (Oxford: Oxford University Press, 2003).
Roskill, S., *Naval Policy between the Wars*, 1 (London: Collins, 1968).
Ross, A. E., *Through Eyes of Blue* (Shrewsbury: Airlife, 2002).
Roy, T., *Woman in Khaki: The Story of the British Woman Soldier* (London: Columbus, 1988).
Rubin, G. R., *Murder, Mutiny and the Military: British Court Martial Cases 1940–1966* (London: Francis Buntle, 2005).
Salusbury MacNalty, A., *The Civilian Health and Medical Services*, 1, *The Ministry of Health Services; Other Civilian Health Services and Medical Services* (London: HMSO, 1953).
Salusbury MacNalty, A., and Mellor, W. F. (eds), *Medical Services in War: The Principal Medical Lessons of the Second World War* (London: HMSO, 1968).
Sargant, T., *Bugger's Talk: Social History of British Gay Life 1900–1975* (London: Gay Men's Press, 2002).

BIBLIOGRAPHY

Shephard, B., *A War of Nerves: Soldiers and Psychiatrists 1914–1994* (London: Pimlico, 2002).
Sinfield, A., *The Wilde Century: Effeminacy, Oscar Wilde and the Queer Moment* (London: Cassell, 1994).
Simpson, M., *Male Impersonators: Men Performing Masculinity* (London: Continuum, 1994).
Simpson, M., and Zeeland, S., *The Queen Is Dead: A Tale of Jarheads, Eggheads, Serial Killers & Bad Sex* (London: Arcadia, 2000).
Spencer, C., *Homosexuality, A History* (London: Fourth Estate, 1995).
Stanley, J., and Baker, P., *Hello Sailor! The Hidden History of Gay Life at Sea* (London: Longman, 2003).
Stevenson, J., *British Society 1914–45* (London: Allen Lane, 1984).
Summerfield, P., *Reconstructing Women's Wartime Lives* (Manchester: Manchester University Press, 1996).
Summerfield, P., and Braybon, G., *Out of the Cage: Women's Experiences in Two World War* (London: Pandora Press, 1987).
Swanson, G., *Drunk with the Glitter: Space, Consumption and Sexual Instability in Modern Urban Culture* (London: Routledge, 2007).
Szreter, C., and Fisher, K., *Sex before the Sexual Revolution: Intimate Life in England 1918–1963* (Cambridge: Cambridge University Press, 2010).
Tatchell, P., *We Don't Want to March Straight: Masculinity, Queers and the Military* (London: Continuum International, 1995).
Taylor, E., *The Women Who Went to War* (London: Robert Hale, 1998).
Terkel, S., *'The Good War': An Oral History of World War Two* (London: Hamilton, 1985).
Terry, R., *Women in Khaki: The Story of the British Woman Soldier* (London, 1988).
Tester, K. (ed.), *The Flâneur* (London: Routledge, 1994).
Thomas, D., *An Underground at War: Spivs, Deserters, Racketeers and Civilians in the Second World War* (London: John Murray, 2004).
Turner, M., *Backward Glances: Cruising the Queer Streets of New York and London* (New York: Reaktion, 2003).
Weeks, J., *Coming Out: Homosexual politics in Britain from the nineteenth century to the present* (New York: Quartet, 1977).
Weeks, J, *Sex, Politics and Society: The Regulation of Sexuality since 1800* (London: Longman, 1981).
Weeks, J., *Sexuality and Its Discontents* (London, Routledge, 1985).
Weeks, J., *Sexuality: Key Ideas* (London: Routledge, 2003).
Weeks, J. (ed.), *Sexualities and Society: A Reader* (London: Polity Press, 2002).
Weeks, J., and. Porter, K. (eds), *Between the Acts: The Lives of Homosexual Men 1885–1967* (London: Rivers Oram Press, 1997).
Weight, R., and Beach, A. (eds), *The Right to Belong: Citizenship and National Identity in Britain, 1930–1960* (London: I. B. Tauris, 1998).
Wells, J., *The Royal Navy* (Dover: Allan Sutton, 1994).

Wheelwright, J., *Amazons and Military Maids: Women Who Dressed as Men in the Pursuit of Life Liberty and Happiness* (London: Pandora, 1989).
White, E., *The Flâneur: A Stroll through the Paradoxes of Paris* (London: Bloomsbury, 2001).
Zeeland, S., *Sailors and Sexual Identity: Crossing the Line Between Straight and Gay in the U.S. Navy* (New York: Harrington Park Press, 1995).
Zeeland, S., *Barrack Buddies and Soldier Lovers: Dialogues with Gay Young Men in the U.S. Military* (New York: Harrington Park Press, 1996).
Zeeland, S., *Masculine Marine: Homoeroticism in the U.S. Marine Corps* (New York: Harrington Park Press, 1996).
Zeeland, S., *Military Trade* (New York: Harrington Park Press, 1999).

Chapters in edited collections
Chauncey, G., 'Christian brotherhood or sexual perversion? Homosexual identities and the construction of sexual boundaries in the World War I era', in M. Duberman, M. Vicinus and G. Chauncey (eds), *Hidden from History: Reclaiming the Gay and Lesbian Past* (London: Penguin, 1991), pp. 294–317.
Coleman, P., 'Ageing and life history: the meaning of reminiscence in later life', in S. Dex (ed.), *Life and Work History Analyses: Quantitative Developments* (London: Routledge, 1991).
Crang, J. A., 'The British soldier on the Home Front: Army morale reports, 1940–45', in P. Addison and A. Calder (eds), *Time to Kill: The Soldier's Experience of War in the West 1939-1945* (London: Pimlico, 1997).
Danchev, A., 'The Army and the home front, 1939-1945', in O. Chandler and I. Beckett (eds), *The Oxford History of the British Army* (Oxford: Oxford University Press, 1996).
Davidson, A. I., 'A new style of psychiatric reasoning', in R. A. Nye (ed.), *Sexuality* (Oxford: Oxford University Press, 1999).
D'Este, C., 'The Army and the challenge of war 1939-1945', in D. Chandler and I. Beckett (eds), *The Oxford History of the British Army* (London: Oxford University Press, 1996).
DeGroot, G. J., 'Lipstick on her nipples, cordite in her hair: sex and romance among British servicewomen during the Second World War', in G. J. DeGroot and C. M. Peniston-Bird (eds), *A Soldier and a Woman* (Harlow: Longman, 2000).
Fee, D., '"One of the Guys": instrumentality and intimacy in gay men's friendships with straight men', in P. Nardi (ed.), *Gay Masculinities* (London: Sage, 2000).
Gooch, J., 'The armed services', in S. Constantine, M. W. Kirby and M. B. Rose (eds), *The First World War in British History* (London: Edward Arnold, 1995).
Grele, R. J., 'Movement without aim', in R. Perks and A. Thompson (eds), *The Oral History Reader* (London: Routledge, 1998).

BIBLIOGRAPHY

Griffin, G., 'History with a difference: telling lesbian herstories', in G. Griffin (ed.), *Outwrite* (London and Boulder, Colorado: Pluto Press, 1993).
Harrison, M., 'Sex and the citizen soldier: health, morals and discipline in the British Army during the Second World War', in R. Cooter, M. Harrison and S. Sturdy (eds), *Medicine and Modern Warfare* (Amsterdam: Rodopi, 1999).
Higate, P., 'Concluding thoughts: looking to the future', in P. Higate (ed.), *Military Masculinities: Identity and the State* (London: Praeger, 2003).
Hollister, J., 'A highway rest area as a socially-reproducible site', in W. Leap (ed.), *Public Sex/Gay Space* (New York: Columbia University Press, 1999).
Jolly, M., 'Love letters versus letters carved in stone: gender, memory and the "Forces Sweethearts" exhibition', in M. Evans and K. Lunn (eds), *War and Memory in the Twentieth Century* (Oxford: Berg, 1997).
Kennedy, E. L., and M. Davis, '"There was no one to mess with": the construction of the butch role in the lesbian community of the 1940's and 50's', in J. Nestle (ed.), *The Persistent Desire* (London: Aylson Publications, 1992).
Knopp, L. 'Sexuality and urban space: a framework for analysis', in D. Bell and G.Valentine (eds), *Mapping Desire* (London: Routledge, 1995).
Mort, F., 'The sexual geography of the city', in G. Bridge and F. Watson (eds), *A Companion to the City* (London: Blackwell, 2000).
Munt, S., 'The lesbian flaneur', in D. Bell and G. Valentine, *Mapping Desire* (London: Routledge, 1995).
Nardi, P., '"Anything for a Sis, Mary": an introduction to gay masculinities', in P. Nardi (ed.), *Gay Masculinities* (London: Sage, 2000).
Oram, A., '"Friends", feminists and sexual outlaws: lesbianism and British history', in G. Griffin and S. Andermahr (eds), *Straight Studies Modified: Lesbian Interventions in the Academy* (London: Cassell, 1997).
Rose, S. O., 'Temperate heroes: masculinities in wartime Britain', in S. Dudink, K. Hagemann, and J. Tosh (eds), *Masculinity at War and in Peace* (Manchester: Manchester University Press, 2004).
Rubin, G., 'The traffic in women: notes on the "political economy" of sex', in R. Reiter (ed.), *Toward an Anthropology of Women* (New York: Monthly Review Press, 1975).
Rubini, D., 'Sexuality and Augustan England: sodomy, politics, elite circles and society', in K. Gerard and G. Hekma (eds), *The Pursuit of Sodomy: Male Homosexuality in Renaissance and Enlightenment Europe* (London: Harrington, 1988).
Thane, P. M., 'Population politics in post-war British culture', in B. Conekin, F. Mort and C. Waters (eds), *Moments of Modernity: Reconstructing Britain, 1945-1964* (London: Rivers Oram, 1999).
Thompson, A., 'Anzac memories', in R. Perks and A. Thompson (eds), *The Oral History Reader* (London: Routledge, 1998).
Trumbach, R., 'London's sapphists: from three sexes to four genders in the making of modern culture', in J. Epstein and K. Straub (eds), *Body Guards: The Cultural Politics of Gender Ambiguity* (New York: Routledge, 1991).

Vicinus, M., '"They wonder to which sex I belong": the historical roots of the modern lesbian identity', in H. Abelove, M. A. Borale and D. M. Halperin (eds), *The Lesbian and Gay Studies Reader* (London: Routledge, 1993).

Waters, C., 'Havelock Ellis, Sigmund Freud and the State: discourses of homosexual identity in interwar Britain', in L. Bland and L. Doan (eds), *Sexology in Culture* (Chicago: University of Chicago Press, 1998).

Waters, C., 'Disorders of the mind, disorders of the body social: Peter Wildeblood and the making of the modern homosexual', in B. Conekin, F. Mort and C. Waters (eds), *Moments of Modernity: Reconstructing Britain, 1945–1964* (London: Rivers Oram, 1999).

Waters, C., 'Sexology', in H. G. Cocks and M. Houlbrook (eds), *The Modern History of Sexuality* (London: Palgrave, 2006).

Weeks, J., 'Inverts, perverts and Mary Annes: male prostitutes and the regulation of homosexuality in the nineteenth century and early twentieth century', in M. Duberman, M. Vicinus and G. Chauncey (eds), *Hidden from History: Reclaiming the Gay Past* (London: Penguin, 1991).

Wotherspoon, G., 'Comrades-in-arms: World War II and male homosexuality in Australia', in J. Damousi and M. Lake (eds), *Gender and War: Australians at War in the Twentieth Century* (Cambridge: Cambridge University Press, 1995).

Journal Articles

Arkin, W., and Dobrofsky, L. R., 'Military socialization and masculinity', *Journal of Social Issues*, 34:1 (1978), pp. 151–68.

Bartlett, A., and King, M., 'British psychiatry and homosexuality', *Journal of Psychiatry*, 175 (August 1999), pp. 106–13.

Bartlett A., King, M., and Smith, G., 'Treatments of homosexuality in Britain since the 1950s – an oral history: the experience of patients', *British Medical Journal*, 328 (2004), pp. 427–32.

Beardsley, E. H., 'Allied against sin: American and British responses to venereal disease in World War I', *Medical History*, 20:2 (1976), pp. 189–202.

Bell, A., 'Landscape of fear: wartime London, 1939–1945', *Journal of British Studies*, 43:1 (2009), pp. 153–75.

Bennet, J. M., 'Lesbian like and the social history of lesbianisms', *Journal of History of Sexuality*, 9:1–2 (2000), pp. 1–24.

Bibbings, L., 'Images of manliness: the portrayal of soldiers and conscientious objectors in the Great War', *Social and Legal Studies*, 12:3 (2003), pp. 33–358.

Blanco, R. L., 'The attempted control of venereal disease in the Army of mid-Victorian England', *Journal of the Society for Army Historical Research*, 45 (1967), pp. 234–41.

Boxwell, D. A., 'The follies of war: cross-dressing and popular theatre on the British front lines, 1914–18', *Modernism/Modernity*, 19:1 (January 2002), pp. 1–20.

Boyd, N. A., 'Who is the subject? Queer theory meets oral history', *Journal of the History of Sexuality*, 17:2 (2008), pp. 177–89.

Brooke, S., 'War and the nude: the photography of Bill Brandt in the 1940s', *Journal of British Studies*, 45:1 (2006), pp. 118–38.

Brown, G., 'Listening to queer maps of the city: gay men's narratives of pleasure and danger in London's East End', *Oral History*, 29:1 (2001), pp. 48–61.

Clarke, A., 'Twilight moments', *Journal of the History of Sexuality*, 4 (January/April 2005), pp. 139–60.

Cocks, H. G., 'The growing pains of the history of sexuality', *Journal of Contemporary History*, 39:4 (2004), pp. 657–66.

Cole, S., 'Modernism, male intimacy and the Great War', *English Literary History*, 68:2 (2001), pp. 469–500.

Connelly, M., and Miller, W., 'British courts martial in North Africa, 1940–3', *Twentieth Century British History*, 15:3 (2004), pp. 217–42.

Dalley, I., 'Taking prisoners: Ellis, Freud and the construction of homosexuality 1897–1951', *Social History of Medicine*, 13:3 (2000), pp. 447–66.

Das, S., '"Kiss me, Hardy": intimacy, gender, and gesture in World War I trench literature', *Modernism/Modernity*, 19:1 (January 2002), pp. 51–74.

Doan, L., 'Topsy-turvydom: gender inversion, Sapphism and the Great War', *GLQ, A Journal of Lesbian and Gay Studies*, 12:4 (2006), pp. 517–42.

Field, G., 'Perspectives on the working-class family in wartime Britain, 1939–1945', *International and Working Class History*, 38 (1990), pp. 3–28.

French, D., 'Discipline and the death penalty in the British Army in the war against Germany during the Second World War', *Journal of Contemporary History*, 33:4 (1998), pp. 531–45.

Friend, R., 'Older lesbians and gay people: a theory of successful ageing', *Journal of Homosexuality*, 20:3-4 (1990), pp. 99–118.

Gilbert, A. N., 'Buggery and the British Navy, 1700–1861', *Journal of Social History*, 10:1 (1976), pp. 72–98.

Halladay, L., 'A lovely war: male to female cross-dressing and Canadian military entertainment in World War II', *Journal of Homosexuality*, 46:3-4 (2004), pp. 19–34.

Halperin, D. M., 'Is there a history of sexuality?', *History and Theory*, 28:3 (1989), pp. 257–74.

Halse, C., and Honey, A., 'Unraveling ethics: illuminating the moral dilemmas of research ethics', *Signs*, 30:4 (2005), pp. 2141–62.

Harrison, M., 'The British Army and the problem of venereal disease in France and Egypt during the First World War', *Medical History*, 39:2 (1995), pp. 133–58.

Harvey, A. D., 'Prosecutions for sodomy in England at the beginning of the nineteenth Century', *Historical Journal*, 21:4 (1978), pp. 939–48.

Harvey, A. D., 'Homosexuality and the British Army During the First World War', *Journal of the Society for Army Historical Research*, 79 (2001), pp. 313–19.

Hegarty, P., 'Homosexual signs and heterosexual silences: Rorschach research on male homosexuality from 1921-1969', *Journal of the History of Sexuality*, 12:3 (July 2003), pp. 400-23.

Heggie, V., 'Lies, damn lies, and Manchester's recruiting statistics: degeneration as an "urban legend" in Victorian and Edwardian Britain', *Journal of the History of Medicine and Allied Sciences*, 63 (2008), pp. 178-216.

Herzog, D., 'Sexuality, memory, morality', *History and Memory*, 17:12 (2005), pp. 238-66.

Houlbrook, M., '"Lady Austin's Camp Boys": constituting the queer subject in 1930s London', *Gender and History*, 14:1 (2002), pp. 31-61.

Houlbrook, M., 'Soldier heroes and rent boys: homosex, masculinities and Britishness in the Brigade of Guards: c.1900-1960', *Journal of British Studies*, 42:3 (2003), pp. 351-88.

Jennings, R., 'The Gateways Club and the emergence of a post-Second World War lesbian subculture', *Social History*, 31:2 (2006), pp. 206-25.

Johnson, P., 'Haunting heterosexuality: the homo/het binary and intimate love', *Sexualities*, 7:2 (2004), pp. 183-200.

McCormick, L., '"One Yank and They're Off": interaction between US troops and Northern Irish women, 1942-1945', *Journal of the History of Sexuality*, 15:2 (May 2006), pp. 228-57.

McGhee, D., 'Looking and acting the part: gays in the Armed Forces-a case of passing masculinity', *Feminist Legal Studies*, 6:2 (1998), pp. 205-44.

Mennesson, C., and Clement, J. P., 'Homosociability and homosexuality: the case of soccer played by women', *International Review for the Sociology of Sport*, 38:3 (1 September 2003), pp. 311-30.

Meyer, L. D., 'Creating G.I. Jane: the regulation of sexuality and sexual behaviour in the Women's Army Corps during World War II', *Feminist Studies*, 18:3 (1992), pp. 581-601.

Mort, F., 'Mapping sexual London: The *Wolfenden* Committee on Homosexual Offences and Prostitution, 1954-57', *New Formations*, 37 (1999), pp. 92-113.

Mosse, G. L., 'Nationalism and respectability: normal and abnormal sexuality in the nineteenth century', *Journal of Contemporary History*, 17:2 (1982), pp. 221-46.

Peniston-Bird, C. M., 'Classifying the body in the Second World War: British men in and out of uniform', *Body and Society*, 9 (2003), pp. 31-48.

Pilcher, J., 'School sex education: policy and practice in England 1870 to 2000', *Sex Education*, 5:2 (2005), pp. 153-70.

Rachamimov, A., 'The disruptive comforts of drag: (trans) gender performances among prisoners of war in Russia, 1914-1920', *American Historical Review*, 111:2 (April 2006), pp. 362-82.

Rapp, D., 'The early discovery of Freud by the British general public', *Social History of Medicine*, 3:2 (1990), pp. 217-43.

Rose, S. O., 'Girls and GIs: race, sex and diplomacy in Second World War Britain', *International History Review*, 19:1 (1997), pp. 146-60.

Rose, S. O., 'Sex, citizenship, and the nation in World War II Britain', *American Historical Review*, 103:4 (1998), pp. 1147-76.

Sasson-Levy, O., 'Individual bodies, collective State interests: the case of Israeli combat soldiers', *Men and Masculinities*, 10:3 (2008), pp. 1-26.

Shefer, T., and Mankayi, N., 'The (hetero)sexualization of the military and the militarization of (hetero)sex: discourses on male (hetero)sexual practices among a group of young men in the South African military', *Sexualities*, 10:2 (2007), pp. 189-207.

Shephard, B., '"Pitiless psychology": the role of prevention in British military psychiatry in the Second World War', *History of Psychiatry*, 10:40 (1999), pp. 491-524.

Soloway, R., 'Counting the degenerates: the statistics of race degeneration in Edwardian England', *Journal of Contemporary History*, 17:1 (1982), pp. 137-64.

Stanley, L., 'Romantic friendship? Some issues in researching lesbian history and biography', *Women's History Review*, 1:2 (1992), pp. 193-216.

Stewart-Smith, J., 'Military law: its history, administration and practice', *Law Quarterly Review*, 85 (October 1969), pp. 478-504.

Stone, T., 'Creating a (gendered?) military identity: the Women's Auxiliary in Great Britain in the Second World War', *Women's History Review*, 8:4 (1999), pp. 605-24.

Summerfield, P., and Crockett, N., 'You weren't taught that with the welding: lessons in sexuality in the Second World War', *Women's History Review*, 1:3 (1992), pp. 435-54.

Summerfield, P., and Peniston-Bird, C. M., 'Women in the firing line: the Home Guard and the defence of gender boundaries in Britain and the Second World War', *Women's History Review*, 9:2 (2000), pp. 231-54.

Taithe, B., 'Morality is not a curable disease: probing the history of venereal diseases, morality and prostitution', *Social History of Medicine*, 14:2 (2001), pp. 337-50.

Thane, P. M., 'The debate on the declining birth-rate in Britain: the "menace" of an ageing population, 1920s - 1950s', *Continuity and Change*, 4:2 (1990), pp. 238-305.

Upchurch, C., 'Forgetting the unthinkable: cross dressers and British society in the case of the Queen vs Boulton and others', *Gender and History*, 12:1 (2000), pp. 127-57.

Valentine, G., '(Hetero)sexing space: lesbian perceptions and experiences of everyday spaces', *Society and Space: Environment and Planning D*, 11 (1993), pp. 395-413.

Vernon, J., 'For some queer reason: the trials and tribulations of Colonel Barkers masquerade in interwar Britain', *Signs: The Journal of Women in Culture and Society*, 26:1 (2000), pp. 37-62.

Winter, J. M., 'Military fitness and civilian health in Britain during the First World War', *Journal of Contemporary History*, 15:2 (1980), pp. 211-44.

Wollacott, A., '"Khaki fever' and its control: gender, class, age and sexual morality on the British Homefront in the First World War', *Journal of Contemporary History*, 29:2 (1994), pp. 325-47.

Unpublished theses

Houlbrook, M., '"A Sun Among Cities": space, identities and queer Male practices, London, 1918-57' (unpublished PhD thesis, University of Essex, 2002).

Sheridan, D., 'ATS Women 1939-1945: Challenge and Containments in Women's Lives in the Military during the Second World War' (unpublished M.Litt. thesis, University of Sussex, 1988).

Stone, T., 'The Integration of Women into a Military Service: the Women's Auxiliary Air Force in the Second World War' (unpublished PhD thesis, University of Cambridge, 1999).

Tinkler, P., 'Constructing Girlhood: Messages and Meanings in Girls' magazines 1920-1950' (unpublished PhD thesis, University of Lancaster, 1988).

Reports

ACE Age Concern England, 'Issues facing older lesbians, gay men and bisexuals', *Policy Position Paper* (London: Age Concern, 2002).

Belkin A., and Evans, R. L., *The Effects of Including Gay and Lesbian Soldiers in the British Armed Forces: Appraising the Evidence* (Santa Barbara: Centre for the Study of Sexual Minorities in the Military, 2000).

Newspaper articles

Anon., 'A gay soldier's story', *Pink Paper* (18 August 1995).

Anon., 'Camp followers', *The Guardian* (8 May 1996).

Anon., 'Gay leaders defend Cenotaph ceremony', *BBC News Online* (2 November 1997), http://news.bbc.co.uk/1/hi/uk/20258.stm, accessed 19 August 2007.

Anon., 'Four prisons used in 1950s research; gays in jail subjected to electric shock tests', *Glasgow Herald* (28 November 1997).

Anon., 'Gays win military legal battle', *BBC News Online* (27 September 1999), http://news.bbc.co.uk/1/hi/uk/458714.stm, accessed 18 October 2004.

Anon., 'UK Remembrance Day honour', *BBC News Online* (14 December 1999), http://news.bbc.co.uk/1/hi/uk/519408.stm, accessed 1 May 2006.

Anon., 'Army marches with Pride Parade', *BBC News Online* (27 August 2005), http://news.bbc.co.uk/1/hi/engalnd/manchester/4189634.stm, accessed 23 November 2005.

Anon., 'Army on parade for gay recruits', *The Times Online* (28 August 2005), www.timesonline.co.uk/article/0,,2087-1753905,00.html, accessed 23 November 2005.

Anon., 'British Army claims having openly gay soldiers has "increased productivity"', *Pink Paper* (29 September 2010), www.pinknews.co.uk/2010/

09/29/british-army-claims-having-openly-gay-soldiers-hasincreased-productivity, accessed 9 January 2011.

Bedell, G., 'Coming out of the Dark Ages', *The Observer, Review* supplement (4 June 2007).

Campbell, D., '3.6m people in Britain are gay – official', *The Observer* (11 December 2005).

Evans, M., 'We're sorry, MoD tells gay victims of persecution', *The Times Online* (28 June 2007), www.timesonline.co.uk/tol/life_and_style/men/article1996445.ece, accessed 29 June 2007.

Hall, E., 'Middle England comes out: Colonel Blimp is on the defensive but the rest of Britain doesn't mind gays in the forces', *The Independent* (21 May 1995).

Hall, S., 'Letters show Monty as "repressed gay"', *The Guardian Online* (26 February 2001), www.guardian.co.uk/Archive/Article/0,4273,4142165,00.html, accessed 2 January 2007.

Judd, T., 'How the forces finally learnt to take pride; nine years after the military lifted its ban on gays, the army has put an openly homosexual soldier on the cover of its magazine', *The Independent* (27 July 2009).

Lloyd, P., 'Royal Air Force launch official LGBT support network', *Pink Paper* (13 October 2011).

Parkin, J., 'War and a piece of the action', *Daily Mail*, Weekend Supplement (28 October 2006).

Patrick, G., 'Were you only gay in Army? Heroes slam quiz "insult"', *The Sun* (13 October 2005).

Reynolds, M., 'Your £82,000 bill for "study" of Irish gays', *Daily Express* (28 March 2008).

Scott, E., 'Gay soldiers study sparks war of words', *South Manchester Reporter* (20 October 2005).

Stone, L., 'What Foucault got wrong', *The Times Literary Supplement* (10 March 1995).

Sullivan, D., 'Lesbo honest. This is a waste of time!', *Sunday Sport* (16 October 2005).

Summerskill, B., 'It's official: gays do mot harm forces', *The Observer* (19 November 2000), http://observer.guardian.co.uk/uk_news/story/0,6903,399798,00.html, accessed 10 September 2006.

Summerskill, B., 'Save us from the armchair generals', *The Guardian Online* (4 August 2004), www.guardian.co.uk/military/story/0,11816,1275547,00.html, accessed 22 January 2005.

Tatchell, P., 'When the Army welcomed gays', www.petertatchell.net/military/when_the_array.htm, accessed 18 April 2005.

Travis, A., 'How the Air Force kept secret watch to track down lesbians', *The Guardian* (22 August 2005).

Vans, A., Letter to *The Independent* (3 February 1993).

Whitehead, A., Letter to *The Guardian Weekend* (23 March 1996).

Documentaries
3bmtv, *Conduct Unbecoming*, Channel 4, 1996.
Timewatch, *Sex and War*, BBC 2, 1998.
UKTV History, *Love, Sex and War*, episode 1: 'Sex with strangers', Testimony Films, 2006.
Wall to Wall Productions, *It's Not Unusual*, BBC 2, 1997.

Radio programmes
BBC Radio 4, 'Cleaning out the camp', 21 and 28 June 2007.
BBC Radio 4, *Making History*, 'Gays and lesbians in the British forces during World War Two', 29 November 2005.

Index

Note: 'n.' after a page reference indicates the number of a note on that page.

65th Field Artillery 66
82nd Field Regiment Royal Artillery 51

abuses of authority 3, 92–93
Admiralty 78, 140, 159
Age Concern 8
   Gloucestershire 8
Africa 13
Air Force 40, 75, 83
Air Ministry 106, 118, 139, 144, 159
Alamein 1
Alcock, John 19n.3, 55, 75, 79, 134–135, 143
Alexandria, 126
Allen, Clifford 156
Allen, Sarah 55, 64
Anchor Holmes 8
Anchor News 8
Anderson, Charles 132, 133, 134, 135
Archbishop of Canterbury 155
Army 3, 5, 7, 11, 12, 13, 24, 25, 27, 29, 37, 40, 41, 45, 50, 51, 53, 55, 56, 57, 58, 50, 63, 64, 66, 67, 69, 77, 78, 83, 84, 86, 87, 93, 95, 105, 106, 108, 110, 111, 112, 113, 114, 115, 117, 118, 119, 120, 122, 125, 127, 128, 129, 132, 133, 134, 135, 136, 137, 140, 141, 142, 143, 144, 154
Army Act 17, 105, 106, 119
Army Council 138
Arnold, Thomas 25
At Ease 8
ATS 12, 37, 55, 56, 64, 97, 106, 121, 122, 123, 124, 130, 140, 144
Australia 5

Bargielowska, Z. 25
Barker (Colonel) Leslie Ivor Victor Gauntlett Bligh 36

Bartley, Bert 65, 67
batmen 57, 70, 71, 92, 95, 97
Baxter, Stanley 97
BBC History War and Conflict Forum 8
BBC Radio
   Derby 8
   Manchester 8
Beardmore, John 56, 57, 87
Bech, Henning 80
Beck, Pip 63
Beith (Major General) John Hay 142
Bell, W. H. 88
Benge, Ronald 13, 86, 97, 126
Berg, Charles 43
Bernard (Captain) Charles 128, 141, 142, 143
Bérubé, Alan 5
Bevin Boys 11
Blake, D. H. 62
Blitz 76, 77
Board of Education 25
Boer War 25, 28
   Britain's performance in 25
Bolton, Frank 30, 55, 58, 61, 63, 65, 68, 79, 87, 97, 151, 154
Booker, John 51, 85, 151, 154
Bowlby, John 13, 122, 133
Boyd-Carpenter, John 141
Brann, Private 142
Bravery 87, 91, 151
Briar, Richard 14, 15, 41, 55, 56, 57, 58, 59, 61, 83, 84–85, 120, 124–125, 151, 153, 154
Bribery 39
Brierly, John 50, 52, 63, 154, 157
Brigade of Guards 5
British Army 5, 25, 29, 132, 163
   see also Army
British Picture Corporation 51, 154

INDEX

Brown, Frank 68, 120, 154
Brown, John 157
Brown, William 92
Brownmiller, Susan 89
Buckle, Richard 78, 97
Buddy 52, 53
Burke (Major) Peter 92, 93, 128

C Division 81
Campbell, Dennis 15, 41, 57, 60, 61, 67, 68, 82–83, 97, 97, 123, 151, 154
Canada 5
Canadian military 78
Catterick 50, 52
Cave, Dudley 3, 134
Central Mediterranean Force 97
Chabbot, Charles 39
Church of England 158
    Moral Welfare Council 158
Citizenship
    and national identity 5
    and service 90
civil marriage 36
Clarke, John 9, 10, 11, 104
Cleaning out the camp 8
Cohen (Labour MP), Harry 1
commercial reward 62
Committee of Imperial Defence
    Manpower Sub-Committee 37
conscription 24, 26, 37, 41, 51, 70, 91, 95, 104, 159
convictions 4, 33, 36, 107, 108, 109, 110, 111, 112, 113, 116, 117, 152
    see also prosecutions
Coombes, Jo 8
Corps of Royal Engineers 66
Costello, John 6, 84
court-martial 92, 106, 107, 108, 109, 110, 111, 113, 114, 115, 116, 118, 119, 120, 125, 129, 135, 136, 136, 137, 138
    records 19
court proceedings 16
court transcripts 19

Criminal Law Amendment Act 17, 80, 105
Crisp, Quentin 34, 42–43, 77, 154
Croft-Crooke, Rupert 67
Croft, David 14
cross-dressing 34, 36, 97, 98
Curran, Desmond 140

Dad's Army 14
Daily Mail 33
Das, Santanu 54
David, Hugh 43
Davies, Rhys (MP for Westhoughton) 39
D-Day Landings 87
death 52, 77
Defence Regulations 78
demobilisation 50, 66, 154
Denith, Jo 87, 88
Directorate of Psychiatry 29
disabilities 27, 39
discipline 1, 12, 84, 104–144
Diva 7
Doan, Laura 34
Doyne, Major 142
Drag 95, 98
Duke of Wellington's regiment 65
Duke of York, HMS 54
Dunkirk 90
Dutchess of Richmond 94
Dyer, Crank 92, 95

East, William Norwood 30
education 55
Egypt 13, 64, 66
    Cairo 84, 93
Ellis, Havelock 130
Emergency Medical Service 133
Emergency Powers Acts 78
Entertainments National Service Association 95
European Court of Human Rights 160
Evil Men 157
exclusion 42

INDEX

Fairfield, Letitia 12, 13, 121, 122, 124, 130, 140
Fee, Dwight 86
female impersonator 95, 98
femininity 64, 90, 97
Ferrier, Arthur 30
  Some seafaring gentlemen may be particular 30, 31
Firminger, Company Sergeant Major 138
First World War 26, 27, 28, 36, 38, 39, 44, 52, 54
Fisher, Kate 15
'flip' 56
France 1, 76
Freeman (Minister) Roger 1
French, David 5
Frazer, George MacDonald 53
Freud, Sigmund 29
friendships 52, 53
Fussell, Paul 6

Garber, Marjorie 97, 98
Gardener, Terry 41, 75, 87, 89, 95
Gardiner, J. 75
Gay Talk 8
Gay Times 7, 15
gender
  affinity 86
  boundaries 34
  identity 64
  inversion 90
  performance 94
  roles 98
  subordination 85
George, Ronald 125
Gibraltar 82, 84, 95, 133
Ginsberg, Elaine 17
Glover, Montague 66
Goldstein, J. 90
good fellow 13, 85–91, 92, 94, 124, 125, 128, 152
good-time girls 5
  anti-citizen status 5
Goossens, Lois 97

Gordon, Jean 77
Great War, the 29, 54
Green, George 125

Haire, Norman 33
Hall, Radclyffe 34, 35
Hall, Ralph 65–66
Hamer, Emily 6, 56
Hardwicke Society 158
Haselden, W. K. 30
  Our beautiful women athletes 32
Haste, Cate 6
Hastings (Sir) Patrick 118
Haward, Elfrida 36
health 28–37
Heggie, V. 25
hegemonic masculinity 87, 91
heterosexual 2, 4, 11, 13, 14, 16, 30, 33, 56, 57, 58, 59, 60, 61, 62, 63, 64, 65, 66, 67, 68, 86, 88, 91, 94, 113, 115, 126, 128, 134, 136, 139, 141, 142, 156
Higgins, Patrick 156
Hildyard, Myles 85
Hill, W. A. 63
Holland Park raid 33
Hollister, John 78
Holmes, Richard 5
homophobia 94
homosex 5, 16, 17, 19, 24, 56–63, 81, 99, 104, 121, 122, 125, 128, 134, 136, 141, 142, 143, 152, 158
homosexual
  influence on military discipline 3
  irrelevance of 2
  mentioned in parliament 1
  offences 116
  'practices' 3
Homosexual Policy Assessment Team 91
homosexuality
  attitudes towards 10, 93
  decriminalization 1
  illegality of 9
  visibility 2

INDEX

homosexuals 2, 78, 122, 126, 132, 133, 134, 135, 138, 139,
   expulsion from armed forces 2
homosocial 10, 54, 55
   contact 70, 83
   experimentation 18
   places 81
homosociability 5, 10, 17, 18, 55, 56, 70
Houlbrook, Matt 5, 32, 33, 57, 58, 79, 154, 156
House of Lords 1
Howard, John 16, 17, 56, 81
Hubert, W. H. de B. 30
human rights campaigns 1

immorality 13, 80, 141
Imperial War Museum 63, 92, 128
importuning 78, 79, 116
indecency 4, 92, 105, 106, 107–121, 129, 136, 137, 138, 139, 141, 143
India 13, 14, 127, 133
individualism 51
institutional paper trails 12
Intelligence Corps 67
interwar period 28, 30, 41
Irons, Evelyn 35
It Ain't Half Hot Mum 14
The Independent 2

Jackson, Paul 5
Jacques, Jimmy 24, 40, 41, 45, 51, 70, 77, 82, 83, 127, 151, 154, 155
Jamaica, HMS 112
James, Pat 135
Jennings, Rebecca 76, 131
Jivani, Alkarim 6
Johnson, Paul 94
Jones, Ernest 43
Judge Advocate General 105, 119, 136, 137

Katz, Jonathan Ned 15
Kennedy, Francis 41, 66, 69–70, 151, 154, 155

King's Regulations 95, 99, 104, 105, 106, 107, 129, 137, 143, 153

Land Army 11
Lane, Margaret 130
Latham (Sir) Paul 118, 140
law 105–107
   military law 1, 17, 18, 19, 153
   and same-sex desire 104–144
   manuals 12
   civilian law 1, 17, 105, 106
Lehman, John 76
lesbians 2, 4, 89, 135
   desire 30, 34, 121, 130, 140
   exclusion 37
   identification 9, 37
   identity 36
   public identification of 34, 35
   sociability 76
lesbianism 34, 56, 106, 121, 130, 136
L'Etang (Captain) H. J. C. J. 29
Lewis, Greta 94
Libya, Eastern 92
Lloyd-Jones, R. H. 53
London 24, 75, 76–81, 90, 142, 156
London Metropolitan Archives 12, 13
Long Benton 55
Lovell, K. C. 93, 94

MacAndrew, Rennie 13, 130
McGhee, Derek 91
McLaine, Ian 68
Maddocks, Stan 84
Maitland (Captain) Ian Colin 118, 142
Making History 8, 9
Mankayi, Nyameka 64
Marines 2
martial
   culture 85
   masculinity 89
masculinity 10, 14, 30, 34, 35, 44, 64, 65, 67, 88, 90, 91, 97, 151
Mass Observation 4
masturbation 56, 57, 116, 118, 127, 141
Maxted, Dennis 94

INDEX

Maxwell-Fyfe (Sir) David 156, 158
medical boards 12, 18, 24, 25–28, 36, 45, 151
   civilian 37–40
   queer experiences 40–44
medical inspections 24, 28
mental health 28, 43, 44
Mersey River 140
Metropolitan Police Act 1839 78
Middle East 84
military detention centres 138
Millard, B. 95
Ministry of Defence 2, 3, 91, 159–160
Ministry of Information 68
Ministry of Labour 24
Mississippi 81
Money-Kyrle, R. E. 44
Montagu (Lord) Edward 158
Monte Cassino
   forgotten soldiers 11
   veterans association 9
Montgomery (Field Marshal) Bernard 1
morality 25, 68, 79, 80, 81, 107, 129, 155
morbidity 28
mortality 28
   see also death
Mosse, George 25, 26
Mountford (Group Captain) D. J. 3

national press 2
National Archives 1, 108, 112
National Service (no. 2) Act 37
National Services (Armed Forces) Act 37
National Survey of Sexual Attitudes and Lifestyles 3
Navy 2, 31, 40, 42, 53, 56, 57, 60, 62, 71, 87, 88, 95, 96, 97, 98, 105, 108, 110, 111, 112, 113, 115, 117, 118, 135, 143
Navy News 7
neurosis centres 133
New Zealand Army 7, 80
New York 81

Newman, Edith 56
News of the World 33
Nichols, Peter 97
Niebour, Ronald 38
North Africa 85, 133
North British Hotel 41
Nottinghamshire Yeomanry 85

Offences against the Person Act 105
oppo 53, 57, 70, 71
Oxford and Buckinghamshire Light Infantry 128
oral history recordings 7, 13
Oram, A. 36, 75, 130
Ordnance Field Park 55
Orkney 86
Otherness 5, 69
OurStory
   Brighton 7
   Scotland 7
OutRage! 1, 2, 3, 4 19n.5

Palestine 85, 93
'pansy cases' 33
parks 79–80
Parks Regulation Act 80
passes 81
passing 17, 18, 50–71, 98, 152, 155
Patrick, Nick 8
patronage 78
Pawsey, Chris 9
People's Friend, the 7
Penlington, Frank 92
pensions 27, 28, 29, 44
people's war 6, 10, 11, 68–70, 91
   sacred nature of 11
performance 95–99
Perry, Jimmy 14
Pether, Charles 59, 89, 96, 126
perversion
   codification of 26
Pitt-Rivers, Michael 158
Pink Paper 7
physical relationship 55
playing away 18, 75–99

INDEX

popular press 30
post-war period 5
policy documents 12
Prattley, Dennis 60, 69, 98, 135
pregnancy 37, 64, 141
preoccupation with sexuality 26
press, the 120
Prideaux, Francis 29
Primary Training Units 50–56
prisoners of war 3, 119, 137
   camps 6
prosecution 18, 26, 33, 143, 155, 156, 158
   see also convictions
Proud to Serve 8
Psychiatric Bulletin 7
Public Morality Council 13, 61, 72n.47
punishment 1, 126

Queen Alexandra's Royal Nursing Corps 9
Queen's Own Cameron Highlanders 142
queer 17, 24, 34, 40, 55, 65, 70, 95, 153
   bodies 24, 75
   community, modern day 15
   exclusion of 24, 42, 43
   experience 5, 40–44
   history 12
   identity 4, 14, 16, 30, 33, 44, 59, 69, 82, 104, 121, 122, 127, 142, 143
   involvement in the Second World War 6
   men 3, 10, 11, 13, 16, 30, 39, 40, 60, 62, 63, 67, 75, 78, 80, 81, 83, 85, 87, 88, 89, 90, 90, 91, 94, 96, 97, 123, 126, 134, 155, 159
   portrayal of 15
   military masculinity 91
   personnel 19, 91, 128, 155
   policing in London 76–81
   Queer Remembrance Day 3
   service 3, 4
   sociability 76–81
   spaces 81, 154
   veterans 3, 7, 11, 69

women 3, 9, 37, 39, 40, 55, 56, 75, 76, 85, 89, 121, 123, 134, 155
queerness 68, 88, 93, 132, 134, 135, 143, 154
   acceptance of 7, 69, 93
   national service 44
   people's war 10, 68, 69, 70, 91
   rank 92–95
Question Time 2

radio 4, 8
RAF 7, 37, 39, 41, 53, 55, 57, 59, 60, 63, 65, 66, 68, 69, 82, 83, 84, 92, 94, 97, 108, 110, 111, 113, 115, 117, 118, 120, 123, 124, 126, 143
Ramsbotham (Sir) Herwald 28
Rank Outsiders 1
reappraisal of physical health 25
recognition of same-sex partners 3
Rees, J. R. 38
Regulation of the Forces Act 105
Reid Simpson, Elizabeth 88, 89, 124
rejection 43, 44
relationships 52
Remembrance Day 3
   see also Queer Remembrance Day
Renwick, Douglas 84
Report on the Committee on Amenities and Welfare Conditions in the Three Women's Services 13
Report on the Psychological Treatment of Crime 30
Rich, Adrienne 63
Roberts, Robert 27
Robinson, Albert 40, 65, 85, 151, 154
Robotka, Jack and Samuel 42
Robson, Vick 55
Rose, Sonya 5, 68, 90
Rouse, Stevie 131, 141
Royal Army Medical Corps 79
   journal 7
Royal Army Service Corps 64, 122
   52 Division 128
Royal Artillery 14, 41, 51, 82, 118, 140
Royal British Legion 3

INDEX

Royal Corps of Signals 65, 67
Royal Engineers 41, 66
Royal Signal Corps 50, 52
Royal Navy 62, 94, 105, 108, 111, 143, 162
Rubin, Gerry 106
Russell, G. L. 13, 141

Sacredness of Allied campaign 10
safety 1, 50, 97
Salvation Army 79
same-sex
    activity 4, 6, 7, 12, 14, 17, 18, 24, 61, 62, 64, 69, 78, 80, 85, 106, 113, 115, 126, 129, 139, 143, 156, 158, 159
    acts, illegality of 6
    between women 17, 34, 140
    attraction 44
    communities 97
    desire 4, 5, 6, 9, 10, 11, 12, 13, 14, 15, 16, 17, 18, 25, 26, 28, 29, 30, 33, 34, 36, 37, 40, 43, 55, 70, 85, 90, 98, 104, 131, 132, 133, 139, 142, 144, 151, 152, 153, 155, 157
    and citizenship 5
    and military law 104–144
    between women 36, 141
    identification by medical boards 24
    identity 33, 86
    incompatibility with military masculinity 11
    in military history 14
    official institutional story 13
    post-war construction 14
    public image of 14
    relationship with the armed forces 11
    expression 6, 11, 79, 83, 98, 104
    ignoring of 18
    interaction 43
    intimacy 4, 55, 61
    medical boards 25–28, 37–40
    moral distaste 24

sociability 84
toleration 5, 7, 90, 92, 159
Sandhurst 141
Schlesinger, John 97
Schofield, Michael 156
Scott, George Ryley 13, 61, 141
Scottish Advisory Council 157
Shephard, Ben 39
sexological discourse 5
sexology 26
sexual
    deviancy 36, 90
    desire 94
    harassment 58
    identity 71
    perversion 42–43
    predators 92
Sexual Offences Act 1
sexuality 36, 40
Shaw, A. 129
Shefer, Tamara 64
shell shock 28
Shell Shock Committee 29
    see also Southborough Committee
social history 5
Sod's Operas 96
South East Asia 85
Southborough Committee 28, 29
Spencer, Colin 156
Stars in Battledress 95
Statistical Health of the Army, The 132
stereotypes 14, 30, 63, 151
Stonewall 2
Stopes, Marie 34
Stringer, Charles 96
Sullivan, David 10
summary punishments 121, 129, 136
Sun, The 9, 10
Sunday Pictorial 30, 90, 157
Sunday Sport 10
surveillance 18, 64, 78, 79, 80, 81, 83, 99
Sutcliffe, George 86, 88
Szreter, Simon 15

201

INDEX

Tatchell, Peter 2, 3, 4
Tawse, Bill 140
Thompson, Harold 93
Tilley, Vesta 34
Times, The 25, 117, 118, 158
Tower Bridge magistrates' court 115, 116
'trade' 62, 72n.34.
transgender identity 36
transvestism 95, 98, 134
Trefusis-Forbes, Violet 123, 124, 130, 140
Trevor-Roper, Patrick 80
Troubridge, Una 34, 35
Turnbull, A. 75

Ullsworth 55
uniform 75, 76, 77, 78, 80
United States 5
Union Jack Club 79

venereal disease 59, 61, 64, 65, 128, 141
visibility 14, 26, 30, 35, 75, 79

WAAF 13, 37, 55, 63, 88, 106, 123, 124, 127, 130, 131, 135, 136, 140, 144
Waller, Len 51, 53
War Office 25, 29, 45, 108, 119, 138, 142, 152, 159

Warth, Douglas 157
Waters, Chris 29
Waters, Sarah 75
Weekes, A. W. 86, 88
Wellcome Library 13
Wellington 141
West, D. J. 156
Westwood, Gordon 156
    see also Schofield, Michael
Wharncliffe Neurosis Centre 132, 133, 135
White, Peter 66, 67
Wilde, Oscar 26
Wildeblood, Peter 156, 158
Williams, Kenneth 97
Winger 57, 70, 71
Winner, Albertine
Winter, J. M. 27
Wishart, Michal 78
Witte, J. H. 64
Wolfenden Committee 1, 153, 158
Wolfenden (Sir) John 158, 159
women's services 17, 53, 131, 136
working-class queans 30
World Health Organisation 156
Wotherspoon, Garry 5, 10
WRNS 37, 106, 130, 136
Wyndham, Joan 13, 127

Milton Keynes UK
Ingram Content Group UK Ltd.
UKHW030617131124
451106UK00018B/233

9 781784 991180